CENTRE-PERIPHERY RELATIONS IN RUSSIA

Centre-Periphery Relations in Russia

The case of the Northwestern regions

Edited by

GEIR HØNNELAND
The Fridtjof Nansen Institute

HELGE BLAKKISRUD
The Norwegian Institute of International Affairs

LONDON AND NEW YORK

First published 2001 by Ashgate Publishing

Reissued 2018 by Routledge
2 Park Square, Milton Park, Abingdon, Oxon OX14 4RN
711 Third Avenue, New York, NY 10017, USA

Routledge is an imprint of the Taylor & Francis Group, an informa business

Copyright © Geir Hønneland and Helge Blakkisrud 2001

All rights reserved. No part of this book may be reprinted or reproduced or utilised in any form or by any electronic, mechanical, or other means, now known or hereafter invented, including photocopying and recording, or in any information storage or retrieval system, without permission in writing from the publishers.

Notice:
Product or corporate names may be trademarks or registered trademarks, and are used only for identification and explanation without intent to infringe.

Publisher's Note
The publisher has gone to great lengths to ensure the quality of this reprint but points out that some imperfections in the original copies may be apparent.

Disclaimer
The publisher has made every effort to trace copyright holders and welcomes correspondence from those they have been unable to contact.

A Library of Congress record exists under LC control number: 2001086758

ISBN 13: 978-1-138-63563-0 (hbk)
ISBN 13: 978-1-138-63564-7 (pbk)
ISBN 13: 978-1-315-20421-5 (ebk)

Contents

Contributors *vii*

List of Tables *ix*

List of Maps *ix*

List of Figures *x*

Preface *xiii*

PART I: INTRODUCTION

1 Introduction
  Helge Blakkisrud and Geir Hønneland   3

PART II: GENERAL DEVELOPMENT TRENDS IN LAW, POLITICS AND ECONOMY

2 Relations Between Moscow and the Regions of Northwestern Russia – The Legal Aspect
  Brynjulf Risnes   35

3 The Russian Regionalisation Process: Decentralisation by Design or Disintegration by Default?
  Helge Blakkisrud   61

4 Russian Regions in Transition: Centralisation through Decentralisation?
  Per Botolf Maurseth   91

PART III: SECTORAL STUDIES: RESOURCE MANAGEMENT AND MILITARY PRESENCE

5   Offshore Developments:
    The Compatibility of Federal Decisions and Regional Concerns
    Arild Moe   133

6   Centre-Periphery Tensions in the Management of Northwest
    Russian Fisheries
    Geir Hønneland   165

7   The Military Sector:
    Federal Responsibility – Regional Concern
    Anne-Kristin Jørgensen   187

PART IV: CONCLUSIONS

8   Conclusions
    Helge Blakkisrud and Geir Hønneland   213

Bibliography   *231*

Index   *241*

Contributors

HELGE BLAKKISRUD is a political scientist from the University of Oslo and the Head of the Centre for Russian Studies at the Norwegian Institute of International Affairs, Norway. He has specialised in studies of the development of Russian centre-region relations and the development of Russian federalism, and has published a number of reports and articles on these subjects, including the monograph *Den russiske føderasjonen i støpeskjeen* (The Russian Federation in the Making) (Spartacus, 1997). Correspondence: helge.blakkisrud@nupi.no.

GEIR HØNNELAND is a doctor of political science from the University of Oslo and the Director of the Polar Programme at the Fridtjof Nansen Institute, Norway. He has published widely in academic journals on the management of natural resources and the environment in the European Arctic. He is also the author of *Coercive and Discursive Compliance Mechanisms in the Management of Natural Resources* (Kluwer Academic Publishers, 2000) and co-author of *Integration vs. Autonomy: Civil-Military Relations on the Kola Peninsula* (Ashgate Publishing, 1999). Correspondence: geir.honneland@fni.no.

ANNE-KRISTIN JØRGENSEN is a political scientist from the University of Oslo and a Research Fellow at the Fridtjof Nansen Institute, Norway. She specialises in the management of natural resources and environmental issues in Northwestern Russia and has published a number of reports and journal articles on the subject. She is also the co-author of *Intergration vs. Autonomy: Civil-Military Relations on the Kola Peninsula* (Ashgate Publishing, 1999). Correspondence: anne-k.jorgensen@fni.no.

PER BOTOLF MAURSETH is an economist from the University of Oslo and a Research Fellow at the Section for International Economics at the Norwegian Institute of International Affairs. He has written a number of articles and reports on the transition from planned to market economy and on economic growth and technological change, among them several monographs on economic co-operation between Norway and Russia in the north. Correspondence: perb.maurseth@nupi.no.

ARILD MOE is a political scientist from the University of Oslo and the Deputy Director of the Fridtjof Nansen Institute, Norway. He has specialised in studies of the Russian energy sector, in particular the oil and gas industry, and is the co-author of several books, among them *Gazprom: Internal Structure, Management Principles and Financial Flows* (Royal Institute of International Affairs, 1996) and *The Development of European Gas Markets: Environmental, Economic and Political Perspectives* (John Wiley & Sons, 1995). Correspondence: arild.moe@fni.no.

BRYNJULF RISNES is a lawyer from the University of Oslo and a Research Fellow at the Centre for Russian Studies at Norwegian Institute of International Affairs, Norway. He has studied law at the University of St Petersburg and specialises in Russian law. He has published a number of reports and articles on Russian constitutional law and other issues related to the current legal development in Russia. Correspondence: brynjulf.risnes@nupi.no.

List of Tables

Table 4.1	Regression of change on population and change in income (heteroscedasticity consistent t-values in brackets)	114
Table 4.2	Employment by sector in Murmansk Oblast, 1991 and 1998, per cent	117
Table 4.3	Employment by main firm and population in some Murmansk towns	118
Table 4.A1	Correlation Matrix	127
Table 6.1	Total catches of fish and marine mammals by vessels registered in Murmansk Oblast during the period 1991-97 (in 1,000 tonnes)	172
Table 6.2	The main decision-making bodies of Northwest Russian fisheries and governmental bodies and user groups represented	176

List of Maps

Map 1.1	Northwestern Russia	10
Map 1.2	The Republic of Karelia	13
Map 1.3	Arkhangelsk Oblast and Nenets Autonomous Okrug	18
Map 1.4	Murmansk Oblast	25
Map 6.1	The Barents Sea	167

List of Figures

Figure 2.1	The legal hierarchy for distribution of competence between the federal and regional levels	41
Figure 4.1	Transport, tonne-kilometres, per unit of GDP, 1988	95
Figure 4.2	Real GDP and industrial production 1980-99, 1989 = 100	97
Figure 4.3	Change in CPI from same period the year before	98
Figure 4.4	Correlation between income in 1995 and 1997	102
Figure 4.5	Ranking of regions in 1995 and 1997	103
Figure 4.6	Kernel estimates of the regional distribution of income per capita	105
Figure 4.7	Share of regional support fund in regional budget 1997	109
Figure 4.8	Real transportation costs	112
Figure 4.9	The population of Murmansk and Arkhangelsk Oblasts, 1926-99	116
Figure 4.10	Structure of Murmansk Oblast industrial production, 1997	117
Figure 4.11	Structure of Arkhangelsk Oblast industrial production, 1994	119
Figure 4.12	Industrial production in Murmansk and Arkhangelsk Oblasts	120

Figure 4.13	Output of some industrial products in Murmansk Oblast, 1998	121
Figure 4.14	Output of some industrial products in Arkhangelsk Oblast, 1998	122
Figure 5.1	Interesting hydrocarbon fields and structures in Russian Barents and Kara Seas	136
Figure 7.1	The Kola CATFs	201

Preface

This book is the result of several years of co-operation between the Centre for Russian Studies at the Norwegian Institute of International Affairs (NUPI) and the Polar Programme of the Fridtjof Nansen Institute (FNI). A joint project on centre-periphery relations in the Russian Federation started the formal co-operation in 1997, leading up to an international seminar on the same theme in Oslo in January 1998. The second co-operative project, carried out in 1999 and 2000, narrowed in on the northwestern periphery of the Russian Federation and its relations with the federal centre. It is the results of this project that are presented in this book. Both projects were financed by the Norwegian Research Council through its funds to further co-operation between the various Norwegian research institutes studying international relations. We would like to express our sincere gratitude for this support, without which this book would not have materialised.

The contributions to this volume are partly built on research previously conducted by the individual authors, partly on joint data collection during the project period. All the authors of the book visited Murmansk and Arkhangelsk together in September 1999. We would like to thank Tatyana Barandova, Jon Fredriksen, Lyudmila Ivanova, Vladimir Kozlov, Nataliya Kukarenko, Boris Ostistyy and Galina Sokolvyak for intellectual and practical assistance during the visit. Thanks to Jens Chr. Andvig, Andrew Bond, Anders Fogelklou, Mark Galeotti, Philip Hanson, Jakob Hedenskog, Lyudmila Ivanova, Pål Kolstø and Larisa Ryabova for commenting on various parts of the manuscript. Finally, thanks to Claes L. Ragner of FNI for producing the fine maps presented in the book, to Indra Øverland at NUPI for language assistance, to Jildou Dorenbos at FNI for help in the editing process and to Maryanne Rygg at FNI for producing the camera-ready copy of the text.

Chapter 5 and parts of Chapter 7 are revised versions of an article published in *Post-Soviet Geography and Economy*. Part of the background material in Chapter 6 has previously been published in articles in *Marine Policy* and *Society & Natural Resources*, as well as in another book by the author. Thanks to V.H. Winston & Son, Inc., Elsevier Science Ltd., Taylor

& Francis and Kluwer Academic Publishers for giving the authors permission to use the material also in this book.

In the transcription of Russian words into Latin letters, we have chosen to pay attention to both general practice and consistency. While attempting to give consistency the upper hand, we have occasionally allowed exceptions in order not to depart from what might be considered general practice. While Russian *ë* is generally transcribed as *yo*, we maintain customary English transcriptions such as *Gorbachev*. Russian *e* is written as *ye* at the beginning of words and after vowels. Nevertheless, we skip the *y* in proper names that already have a common spelling in English, e.g. *Karelia*. The Russian hard and soft signs are not transcribed.

Lysaker and Oslo
August 2000

Geir Hønneland
Helge Blakkisrud

PART I
INTRODUCTION

1 Introduction

HELGE BLAKKISRUD AND GEIR HØNNELAND

The relationship between Moscow and the federal subjects has been one of the main issues of contention in Russian politics since the establishment of the Russian Federation in 1991. Whereas traditionally most attention has been paid to the political struggle between what popularly has been labelled 'Democrats' and 'Communists' or 'pro-' and 'anti-reform' groups in Moscow, a no less fierce battle is being fought out between the federal centre and the regions. The days when one could analyse Russian politics in terms of who stood next to whom at the top of the Lenin Mausoleum are long since gone. Today's analysts have to look further, even beyond Moscow's Garden Ring, to understand the dynamics of Russian politics.

The objective of this book is to contribute to this growing literature on centre-region relations in the Russian Federation[1] by focusing on the power balance between Moscow and the Federation's northwestern periphery, here understood as Murmansk and Arkhangelsk Oblasts, the Republic of Karelia and Nenets Autonomous Okrug. Whereas a number of books have been published on transregional relations in the context of the Barents Euro-Arctic Region (BEAR),[2] the position of Northwestern Russia within the new Russian federal structure is still largely unexplored. Among the questions we want to discuss are: Which framework conditions are laid down by the political and legal process of decentralisation? To what extent is the administrative and legal decentralisation followed by economic decentralisation in order for regional actors to achieve real decision-making power? How far has the decentralisation process gone within various sectors of particular importance to Northwestern Russia, such as fisheries, the offshore oil and gas industry and defence? Through a number of case studies we hope to answer these questions in order to reach our main objective: to depict the status and potential of Northwestern Russia within the Russian Federation.

Before we present our case studies, we would like to give a short introduction to the general framework of centre-periphery relations in the Russian Federation; its Soviet legacy and current formulation, as well as its main challenges.

Centre-Periphery Relations in the Russian Federation

The present federation is based on a framework inherited from the Soviet period, a heritage encompassing two diametrically opposite principles. On the one hand, Lenin had supported the principle of national self-determination, granting the plethora of ethnic groups within Soviet Russia administrative autonomy. On the other hand, the Soviet legacy consists of a system permeated by the principle of democratic centralism. When the two principles came into conflict, the latter always prevailed. In spite of the fact that both the Soviet Union and the RSFSR (The Russian Soviet Federative Socialist Republic) formally were built up as federations,[3] the Soviet power structure was strictly hierarchic. Thus, in reality the Soviet Union represented a *pro forma* ethno-federal structure covering up a reality of extreme centralisation.

The RSFSR was by far the largest and administratively most complex of the Soviet republics. It consisted of no less than 16 autonomous republics, five autonomous oblasts, ten autonomous okrugs, six krays, 49 oblasts and two cities with federal status. While the first three of these categories belonged to the ethno-federal hierarchy, the latter three were purely administrative-territorial entities within the union republic. Furthermore, in the 1989 census more than 60 ethnic groups were recorded as having their traditional core area within the borders of RSFSR.[4] The majority of these groups, however, were numerically insignificant: only six minority groups numbered more than one million members.

With the break-up of the Soviet Union, the question of the future organisation of the RSFSR became topical. Due to size, as well as historical precedence, there seems to have been a relatively widespread consensus on the need for retaining some kind of federal arrangement. As regards the number of federal subjects and the level of decentralisation within a new federation, however, there were widely differing views.[5]

In the end, the Russian authorities settled for a slightly modified version of the old Soviet structure. In the new Federal Treaty of March

1992, no territorial units were merged and no borders redrawn.⁶ Furthermore, the division between ethnically and territorially defined units was preserved. The most important formal change compared to the old Soviet structure was an upgrading in status for the former autonomous republics and four of the five autonomous oblasts.⁷ Although Russian authorities thus on the face of it opted for a model which resembled the Soviet structure, the Federal Treaty nevertheless introduced important changes: the Federal Treaty envisaged a federation that was not only federal in form, but also in content. For the first time in Russian history, central authorities accepted a *de facto* devolution of power – to match the former *de jure* asymmetric federal structure.

The federal principle was reconfirmed as the basis for the state structure in the new Russian Constitution adopted in December 1993. This document nevertheless envisages a somewhat different federal model from what had been foreseen in the Federal Treaty. Whereas the Constitution sustains the Federal Treaty's division into various categories of federal subjects, it simultaneously ascertains that all federal subjects are equal with respect to their status vis-à-vis the federal centre. The republics were no longer described as sovereign, and even if the Constitution confirmed the right to national self-determination this was undermined by the emphasis on the inviolability of borders and territorial integrity of the Federation. According to the Constitution, the Federation was thus to assume a more symmetric character.

With the adoption of the Federal Treaty and the Constitution, the general legal-administrative framework of the Russian Federation was in place. This did not, however, imply that the debate on the federal arrangement came to an end. As a result of the inherent inconsistencies and the different visions of the federal structure in the two documents, as well as the lack of basic mechanisms and traditions for devolution of power and regional self-government within the Federation, the discussion on how to fill the framework with a rational and meaningful content continues. The different approaches to Russian federalism can be divided into three main categories: strong regions, strong centre, and strong centre – strong regions.

Strong Regions

First, there are the supporters of strong regions, i.e. a further devolution of power from the federal centre. Even after the dissolution of the Soviet Union, Russia is still the world's largest state with a total area of 17 million km^2. From east to west it spans 11 time zones, and from north to south a spectrum of climatic zones – from tundra and permafrost along the reaches of the Arctic Ocean to the monsoon belt in the Far East and the steps and semi-desert along the southern border. There is also great variation among the federal subjects both with respect to population (which ranges from 20,300 in the Evenk Autonomous Okrug to 8.5 million in Moscow City) and in area (from 7,600 km^2 in Adygeya to 3.1 million km^2 in Sakha). Because of the vast differences in population, size, ethnic composition, wealth, climate, etc., the interests of the federal subjects could, according to this position, best be taken care of through enhanced self-government.

The champions of strong regions usually support the kind of treaty-based federalism that emerged in 1994 when Tatarstan concluded a bilateral agreement with the federal centre. Tatarstan had refused to sign the Federal Treaty in 1992, and to formalise the republic's relationship with Moscow, a treaty on the delimitation of power and responsibilities was negotiated. This, the supporters of strong regions have claimed, changed the Russian Federation from a top-down to a bottom-up type of federation. In their view, power and responsibilities should be understood as delegated from the regions to the centre and not vice versa. So far, 46 federal subjects have concluded this type of bilateral treaties with the federal centre. Not surprisingly, most heads of ethno-federal subjects are to be found within the group of supporters of strong regions (the most prominent being Tatarstan's Mintimer Shaymiyev and Bashkortostan's Murtaza Rakhimov), but also a number of oblast and kray governors have taken up similar positions.

Strong Centre

The second group of arguments can be lumped together under the heading 'strong centre'. Born out of a process of fragmentation, the new state was itself vulnerable to separatism. The advocates of a strong centre wanted to prevent the Russian Federation from sharing the fate of the Soviet Union.

Upon closer examination, however, the 'strong centre' group embraces disparate ideological leanings. First, there are the traditionalists, who argue that Russia has always been a centralised state formation. To them, history has proven that Russia needs a strong centre to be a strong state.

Second, there are Russian nationalists who oppose the asymmetric, ethno-federal basis of the present state. Although more than 80 per cent of the total population are ethnic Russians, more than 50 per cent of the territory is currently subject to some form of ethno-federal autonomy. According to nationalist rhetoric, ethnic Russians have always had to pay for the development and support of the other nationalities within the Russian state. The state has neglected the interests of the Russian people, they claim. The nationalists therefore want the ethnic autonomies to be abolished and the state to be Russianised.

Third, there are reformists who argue that the present structure is too fragmented to form a viable basis for an effective state. A rationalisation and centralisation through a merger of federal subjects is deemed necessary to streamline the federal structure. A number of central Russian politicians (e.g. Yevgeniy Primakov, Yuriy Luzhkov, and Vladimir Zhirinovskiy) have openly supported a re-centralisation through reducing the number of federal subjects from the present 89 to about a dozen. Some reformists also argue in favour of a strengthening of the centre to facilitate the redistributive function of the state.

Strong Centre – Strong Regions

The reformists are in some respects close to the intermediate position taken up in this debate, which covers arguments that can be subsumed under the heading 'strong centre – strong regions'. This group consists of those who claim that without strong regions, Russia as a state cannot return to her former might. In their view, a certain degree of decentralisation is not a threat to, but rather a precondition for the development of a strong, viable Russian state formation. Soviet centralism, although undoubtedly an effective model for large-scale industrialisation in the 1930s, has proven incapable of addressing the problems Russia is currently facing. On the other hand, decentralisation is neither a goal in its own right, nor a process that should continue *ad absurdum*. The purpose of decentralisation must be to facilitate economic recovery at the regional level.

Today, only about a dozen of the federal subjects do not receive transfers from the Federal Fund for Support of the Regions. The federal centre's scarce resources are thus spread thinly over some 75 entities, resulting in the centre not being able to fulfil its economic obligations neither at the federal, nor at the regional level. Without prospering regions, their argument goes, Russia as a whole will not be able to prosper.

'Strong centre – strong regions' was originally a slogan formulated by Soviet President Mikhail Gorbachev, but has resurfaced in the debate in the 1990s. Former presidential advisor on regional affairs Leonid Smirnyagin is one example of a supporter of this position. In many respects, 'strong centre – strong regions' can be seen as a *status quo*-oriented position, an attempt to justify the course Russian centre-region relations have taken over the past decade in the face of harsh criticism of excessive decentralisation.

Almost a decade after the dissolution of the Soviet Union, the Russian federal structure is still a matter of negotiation and re-negotiation. The overall picture is a process characterised more by *ad hoc* solutions than guided by a formal legal framework. The aim of this book is to examine this process through a case study of one region: Northwestern Russia. Before we delve into the discussion, however, we should briefly present the region.

Russia's Northwestern Periphery – An Introduction

This section is devoted to an initial presentation of the northwestern periphery of the Russian Federation. First, the geographical concept 'Northwestern Russia' is discussed and defined for further use in the book. Next, a brief historical background is provided. Finally, some main characteristics of the region are presented. These characteristics will function as points of departure for various hypotheses about the region's relations with the federal authorities.

Northwestern Russia – A Concept Definition

In Russia, there are several 'official' definitions of the country's northwestern part. The Russian *Northwestern economic region*, for instance, is defined as the oblasts of Novgorod, Leningrad and Pskov as well as the city of St Petersburg; whereas Murmansk, Arkhangelsk and Vologda Oblasts, the Republics of Karelia and Komi and Nenets Autonomous Okrug are defined as the *Northern economic region*.[8] The *Northwestern Association*, on its part, was established in early 1993 to facilitate co-ordination of the northern regions' relations with the federal centre and to draw Moscow's attention to its particular problems.[9] It includes the Republics of Karelia and Komi, as well as Arkhangelsk, Vologda, Kaliningrad, Kirov, Leningrad, Murmansk, Novgorod and Pskov Oblasts, Nenets Autonomous Okrug and the city of St Petersburg.

The Russian conceptions of 'Northwestern Russia' are all either significantly broader than – or totally different from – those found in the West, in particular in the Nordic countries. In the West, the term 'Northwestern Russia' is normally used when referring to the Russian part of the Barents Euro-Arctic Region, i.e. Murmansk and Arkhangelsk Oblasts, the Republic of Karelia and Nenets Autonomous Okrug. As already mentioned, this is also the definition used for the purposes of this book. However, there is a tendency at least in Norway to understand the term even more narrowly; people occasionally speak of Northwestern Russia even if they primarily have in mind the Kola Peninsula or Murmansk Oblast. In practice, there is an inclination to pay particular attention to Murmansk Oblast in this book too, which probably reflects the Norwegian background of the authors.[10]

The geographical focus of the different chapters of the book varies somewhat with the particular theme under discussion. The three general chapters – on legal, political, and economic preconditions for regional autonomy – cover the entire geographical area of Northwestern Russia to a larger extent than the three branch chapters focusing on the offshore oil and gas industry, fisheries, and the military.[11] The geographical bias of the three latter chapters will naturally have to reflect 'real world biases'. Hence, the chapter on oil and gas will focus on Murmansk, Arkhangelsk and Nenets since these regions are closest to where the offshore hydrocarbon reserves are found. Similarly, although the northern fishery basin of the Russian Federation is defined as including the fisheries of Murmansk and Arkhangelsk Oblasts, the Republic of Karelia and Nenets Autonomous Okrug, the vast majority of fishing enterprises are located in Murmansk Oblast, and subsequently this federal subject is given most attention in the chapter on fisheries management.[12] Murmansk and Arkhangelsk Oblasts will also be in focus in the chapter on defence-related matters since the military presence is far heavier here than in the other federal subjects under discussion.

Map 1.1 Northwestern Russia

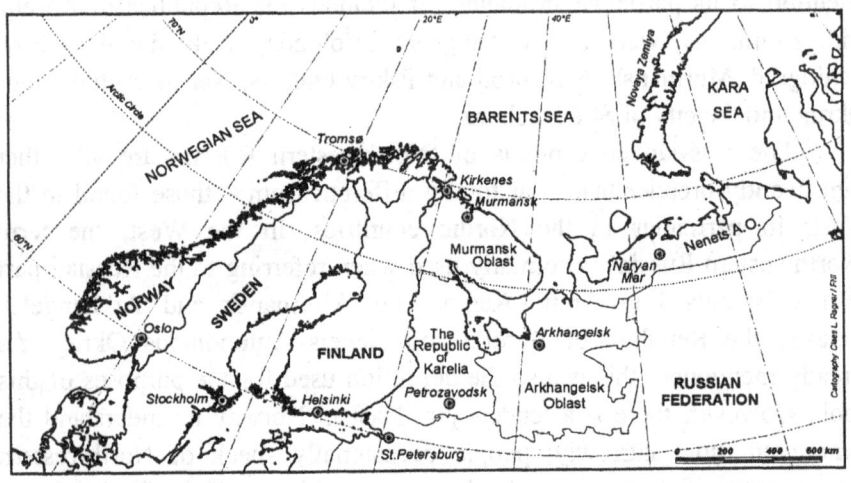

A Brief Historical Background

Northwestern Russia is a micro-cosmos of Soviet and Russian administrative-territorial engineering. The four federal subjects that represent the focus of our study include the three main categories of Russian federal entities: Karelia is a republic, Nenets an autonomous okrug, and Arkhangelsk and Murmansk are oblasts.[13] A brief historical background to these regions, as well as some of the main present day characteristics, are provided in the following. Population figures are from 1998.

The Republic of Karelia Karelia is an ethnically defined federal subject built up around the existence of an autochthonous population – the Karelians. The Karelians traditionally populate the southeastern part of present-day Finland (Northern and Southern Karelia), the southwestern part of Arkhangelsk Oblast (Dvina-Karelia), and the northern part of Leningrad Oblast (the Karelian Isthmus), as well as the territory of the present republic (Ries, 1994, p. 2). The Karelian language, which belongs to the Finno-Ugric language group, is closely related to Finnish.

Since the Middle Ages, the area populated by Karelians has constituted a disputed border region at the intersection between the Nordic and Russian spheres of interest and between Western and Eastern Christianity. The first official partition of Karelia occurred in 1323 as a result of the peace treaty of Nöteborg, which was concluded between the Swedish king and the Republic of Novgorod. With Novogorod's fall in 1478 and the ascent of the Muscovite Principality, eastern Karelia for the first time came under Moscow's influence. Over the next century, Sweden and Russia fought several wars over the Karelian territory (1473-97, 1555-57, 1570-95). During the Livonian war (1570-95), the border was pushed eastwards and Moscow closed off from the Baltic Sea. In 1617, Russia, seriously weakened by internal upheaval (*smutnoye vremya*), had to reconfirm her losses in the peace treaty of Stolbova.

Towards the end of the 17th century, however, Moscow had acquired sufficient strength to challenge Swedish hegemony in the Baltic region. Peter the Great sought an outlet on the Baltic Sea, a 'Window on Europe', and during the Great Nordic War (1700-21), the Swedes were forced back from the southern shores of the Gulf of Finland. As a result of the Swedish defeat, most of Karelia was ceded to the Russian tsar. New concessions were made in 1743, and in 1809 Russia annexed the remaining Swedish possessions in Finland. Hence, for the first time the whole of Karelia was assembled under the jurisdiction of one state. Already in 1812, however, the Karelian Isthmus as well as large territories northwest of Lake Ladoga were transferred to the nominally autonomous Grand Duchy of Finland through an administrative reform, whereas the eastern part of Karelia became part of the Russian *guberniya* Olonets.

After the Russian Revolution in 1917 and Finland's subsequent secession, eastern Karelia remained under Russian control.[14] During the Soviet era, Karelia's status within the hierarchy of ethnically defined entities changed several times. A Karelian Workers' Commune (an equivalent to an autonomous oblast) was established in 1920. Three years later its status was upgraded to that of an autonomous republic (ASSR) within the framework of the RSFSR. In the 1920s, Karelia was politically dominated by Finnish Communists who had fled to the Soviet Union after the Red lost the Finnish Civil War in 1918, and Finnish was introduced as the language of administration and education. Also members of the Finnish *diaspora* communities in Canada and the United States arrived in Karelia to help build socialism. This Leninist experiment in political-cultural autonomy came to an abrupt end with the Stalinist purges of the party and the national elites in the mid-1930s. By 1938, the use of Finnish was banned within the Karelian ASSR, and the Cyrillic script replaced the Latin one.

The Finnish-Soviet Winter War of 1939-40 resulted in new border changes. The Karelian Isthmus and the area northwest of Ladoga were occupied by the Soviet Union and included in Soviet Karelia, which was now proclaimed a union republic – the Karelo-Finnish Soviet Socialist Republic. In an attempt to reverse their losses, the Finns joined Nazi-Germany in her attack on the Soviet Union in 1941, and succeeded in seizing large parts of Eastern Karelia. During the Finnish occupation, Finnish was the official language, and it remained so also after the Soviets recaptured Karelia in 1944, although publications in Finnish were discouraged.

The Karelo-Finnish SSR was clearly seen as a springboard for a potential Soviet annexation of Finland. As a result of the normalisation of Finnish-Soviet relations, the union republic was therefore dissolved in 1956 and anew replaced by a Karelian ASSR. This devaluation of status meant that Karelian and Finnish culture lost the privileges enjoyed by titular nations of union republics. For the remaining part of the Soviet period, the Karelians underwent rapid assimilation, being absorbed by the greater Russian community. Not until 1990-91, when the 'Parade of Sovereignties' swept across the Soviet Union, were attempts made at reviving Karelian identity. The leaders of the republic demanded increased autonomy and in November 1991 the Karelian ASSR was renamed the Republic of Karelia. This new name (and status) was confirmed through the conclusion of the Federal Treaty in March 1991.

The Republic of Karelia covers a territory of 172,400 km^2. The current population is 775,200, of which 74 per cent live in urban settlements. There are 13 cities in the republic, the largest being the capital Petrozavodsk (with approximately 282,400 inhabitants), Kondopoga (36,600), Segezha (34,900), Kostomuksha (32,200) and Sortavala (20,800).

For a long time, ethnic Karelians have constituted a minority in their own republic. Today they make up 10.1 per cent of the total population. The vast majority are ethnic Russians (73.6 per cent), but there are also groups of Belorussians (7 per cent), Ukrainians (3.6 per cent), Finns (2.3

per cent) and Veps (0.8 per cent). The Veps, a Finno-Ugric minority, enjoy a certain level of autonomy within the republic, and in 1994 a Veps National *Volost* (commune) was created within the Prionezhskiy *Rayon* in southern Karelia.

Map 1.2 The Republic of Karelia

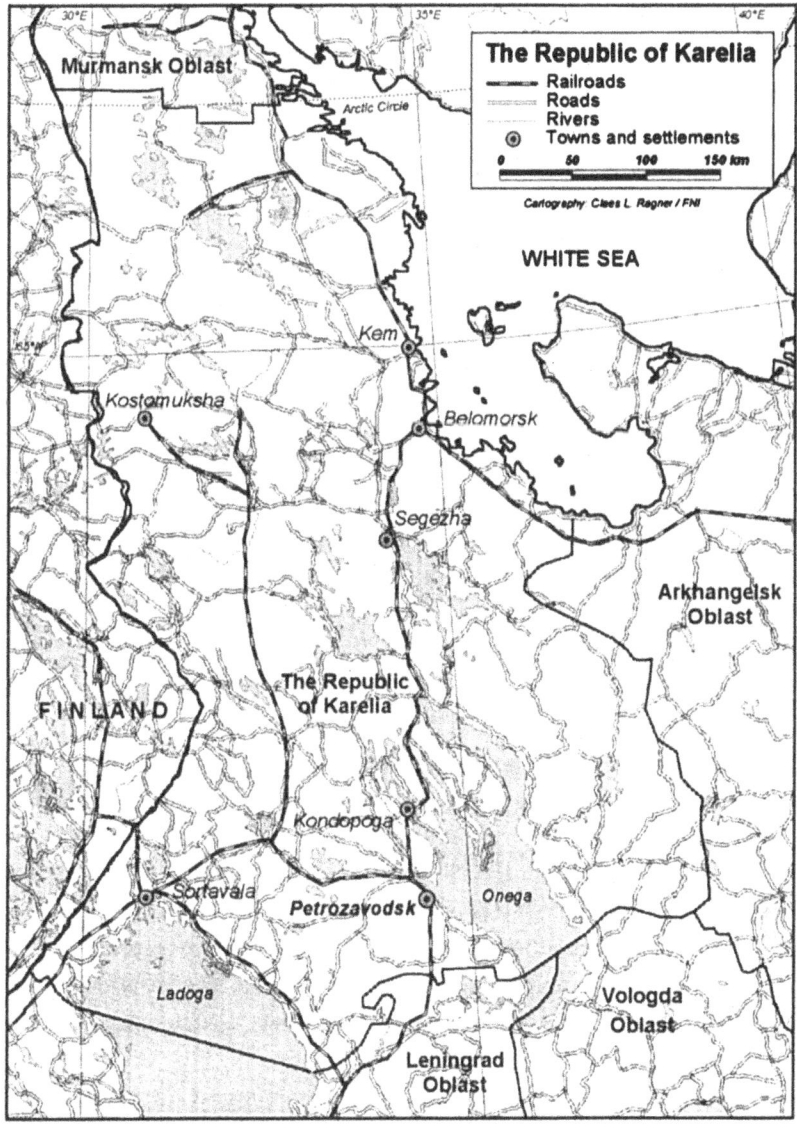

Most ethnic Karelians are bilingual (Karelian and Russian), and only half of them actually declare Karelian as their first language (51.5 per cent in the 1989 census).[15] Also the other Finno-Ugric groups are heavily Russified: three fifths of the Karelian Finns and two thirds of the Veps count Russian as their mother tongue. Karelians write either in Russian or Finnish and only recently steps have been taken to develop a Karelian literary language. This has coincided with new measures to revitalise Karelian national culture in general.

The republic's most important natural resource is undoubtedly timber. More than half the territory is covered with forest (the reserves are estimated to be 849 million m^3 of timber). In addition, there are important deposits of iron ore. The most important industrial activities are also related to forestry: in recent years timber, pulp and paper industry have made up 35-40 per cent of the republic's total industrial production. The agricultural sector is less developed and dominated by milk and meat production. Only 1.2 per cent of the territory is cultivated, out of which 38.2 per cent is arable land.

Karelia's infrastructure is fairly well developed. The White Sea Channel and the St Petersburg-Murmansk railway cross the republic from north to south and there is also a railway connection around Lake Ladoga (the total length of railway track is 2,917 km).

Nenets Autonomous Okrug Just like Karelia, Nenets Autonomous Okrug was set up as a part of the Soviet policy of granting *pro forma* autonomy to ethnic minorities. The titular nation of the okrug is the Nenets, a North-Samoyedic group related to the Enets, Nganasans and Selkups. The Nenets, like the Karelians, occupy a territory much larger than the present okrug. Historically, they have inhabited an area that stretches from the eastern shores of the White Sea in the west to the Yenisey delta in the east. The northern border is formed by the Arctic Ocean (although there have also been Nenets settlements on the Kolguyev and the Novaya Zemlya islands), while the southern border is less well defined.

Up to the 20th century, the Nenets had a subsistence economy based on reindeer herding, fishing, and hunting. Taking into consideration the enormous distances and sparse population, the Nenets are surprisingly homogenous in language and culture. Linguistically, they are usually subdivided into two main groups, the Tundra Nenets and the Forest Nenets, with the former making up more than 95 per cent of the total population. Both groups have been organised in clan structures where pastures, rivers and hunting grounds were the collective property of the clan.

The current territory of Nenets Autonomous Okrug has traditionally been on the fringes of the Russian sphere of influence. The Russian expansion towards the north was spearheaded by the Novgorodians. In Novgorodian chronicles, it is told that the local population was paying taxes to Novgorod as early as at the end of the 10th century. After the fall of Novgorod in 1478, control over the European North was transferred to Moscow. Although the supremacy of the tsar over the inhospitable tundra east of the White Sea was never seriously contested, the severe climate and the inaccessibility clearly limited Russia's ability to rule the region effectively.

There was only a limited influx of Russian settlers in the pre-Soviet period. Russian activity seldom went beyond collecting fur tax (*yasak*) from the local population. The weak influence of the Russian authorities is reflected in the fact that until the middle of the 18th century the Nenets were allowed to decide on the taxation level themselves. Russian commercial interests were more active, however, and Russian merchants brought firearms and other goods, including alcohol, as well as diseases the Nenets had never been exposed to before. Also Russian missionaries were active, and by 1830 almost all Nenets in the European North had been baptised. Traditional shamanism, however, continued to play an important role alongside the official Christendom way into the 20th century.

Despite centuries of contact with Russian settlers, traditional lifestyles prevailed among the Nenets until the October Revolution. Beginning from the 1920s, however, the northern territories were gradually drawn into the project of building a new Soviet state. As early as 1920, the year Soviet power was established in the Arkhangelsk region, a Nenets Executive Committee was formed in the Pechora district. More importantly, an initiative taken by the 9th Nenets Soviet Congress in 1929 led to the establishment of a national okrug for the Nenets in European Russia.[16] Originally, the Nenets National Okrug formed a part of the Northern Kray, which included Arkhangelsk, Vologda, Nyandoma and Severodvinsk Okrugs and Komi Autonomous Oblast. In 1936, Komi was separated from the kray, and the following year the remaining territory was divided into two oblasts, Nenets becoming part of Arkhangelsk Oblast. For the rest of the Soviet period, Nenets National Okrug (from 1977 redefined as an autonomous okrug) remained a constituent part of Arkhangelsk Oblast.

In the economic sphere, the onset of Soviet power brought an end to the tradition of Russian non-interference in the nomadic lifestyle of the Nenets. Socialist construction meant the abolition of private property and the forced collectivisation of the reindeer herds. In many places, the attempt to confiscate reindeer was met with bitter resistance, and herders killed off their animals rather than allow them to fall into the hands of the state.[17] However, by the end of 1934 around 30 per cent of the nomad households in Nenets were collectivised. Still, nomadic life to a great extent remained more or less unchanged until the 1960s, when a campaign was launched to settle the Nenets and the other nomadic peoples of the North. This reform finally put an end to traditional life on the tundra.

Soviet policies also led to the eradication of the traditional cultural and political elite of the Nenets. With the swing away from the relative political liberalism of the early 1920s, the key figures of the indigenous population, the wealthy reindeer owners and the shamans, were branded as *kulaks* and enemies of the people, persecuted and killed, respectively. The partly native-language education of the 1920s and 1930s was replaced by Russification, with children being punished for speaking their native tongue at the boarding schools.

The Soviet period was also marked by a great influx of ethnic Russians. Integrating the Far North into Soviet society meant a demand for new skills. Various kinds of specialists and skilled labourers were sent to the Far North to implement the industrialisation and modernisation programmes. As a result of their higher level of education, the immigrants came to dominate the okrug politically, administratively and economically. The Nenets and their pastoral economy were correspondingly marginalised.

Since March 1992, Nenets Autonomous Okrug, although still formally a part of Arkhangelsk Oblast, has been a federal subject in its own right. The okrug covers a territory of 176,700 km^2. With a total of 45,700 inhabitants, this gives a population density of only 0.26 persons pr. km^2. More than 60 per cent of the population live in what is characterised as urban-type settlements. In reality, there is only one city in the okrug, the capital Naryan Mar, which has 19,200 inhabitants. Naryan Mar, meaning 'the red town' in Nenets, was founded by the Soviet authorities in 1935 to serve as the administrative centre of the new okrug. Over the past decade, the population of the okrug has dropped by 9,100 people or 17 per cent, mainly due to a negative migration balance. The majority of those who have left are ethnic Russians.

Ever since the influx of Soviet experts and administrators began in the 1930s, ethnic Nenets have constituted a minority in their own okrug. Today, the Nenets make up 11.4 per cent of the population. Ethnic Russians constitute an absolute majority with 65.6 per cent, but there are also sizeable groups of Komi (9.5 per cent), Ukrainians (6.9 per cent), and Belorussians (2.0 per cent). Naryan Mar and the larger villages (Iskateley and Amderma) are predominantly Russian, while the majority of Nenets live in the tundra.

The majority of the Nenets are bilingual, and use both Nenets and Russian. As a result of inadequate schooling in the Nenets language, the proportion of Nenets speakers plunged during the Soviet period. In 1989, less than half of the ethnic Nenets (44.8 per cent) declared Nenets their first language.[18] Although some steps have been taken to revive Nenets culture in the 1990s, the language is still threatened with extinction.

Nenets Autonomous Okrug possesses substantial, but largely untapped, oil and gas resources. Although the volume extracted on an annual basis is still modest, oil already dominates the industrial sector, and made up 94.8 per cent of the income generated in the industrial sector in 1998. Among the ethnic Nenets, reindeer herding is still the most important source of income. Due to the harsh climatic conditions, other types of agricultural production are almost non-existent. Just 0.2 per cent of the territory is cultivated, and only 0.8 per cent of this is arable land (the primary crops being potatoes and turnips).

The transport infrastructure of the okrug is poorly developed: there are no railways or roads connecting the okrug with the outside world. All freight has to be done either on water during the short summer season or by air.

Arkhangelsk Oblast The two oblasts of the Northwest Russian periphery, Arkhangelsk and Murmansk, represent old and new Russia, respectively. Whereas Arkhangelsk is a centre of traditional Russian cultural heritage, Murmansk is a prime example of the Soviet industrial and military adventure.

Map 1.3 Arkhangelsk Oblast and Nenets Autonomous Okrug

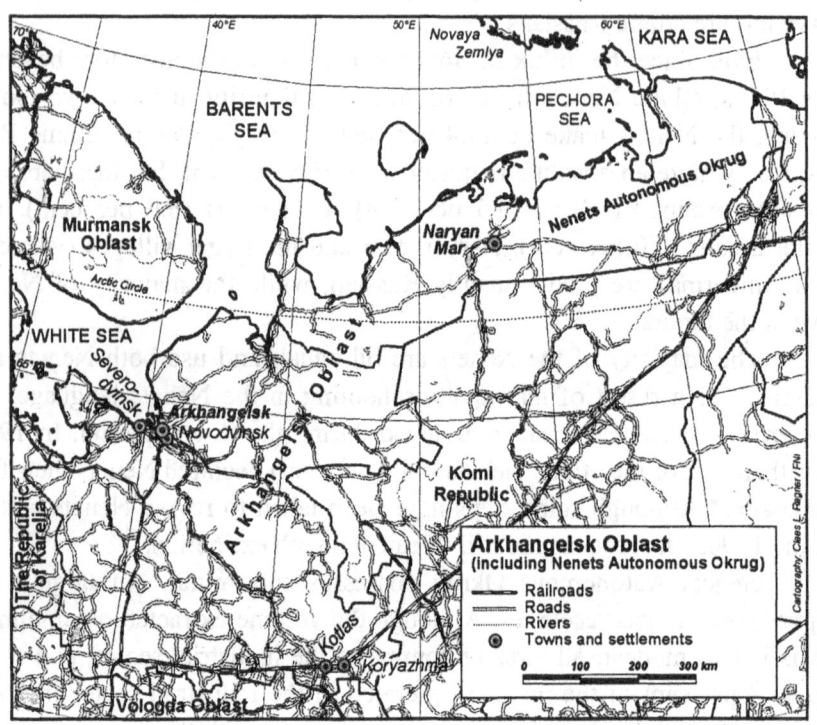

Zavolochya, which is the old name of the region where Arkhangelsk Oblast is now situated, was colonised by the Novgorodians in the Middle Ages. With the fall of Novgorod, the territories along the shores of the White Sea came under Moscow's control. The population was sparse, and settlement spearheaded by hermits and monks. At the site where Arkhangelsk City is located, the Monastery of Michael the Archangel was founded in 1136, and there were also a number of other important monasteries in the region, e.g. on the Solovets Islands.

The original administrative centre of the region was the city of Kholmogory, which in the late 16th century, at the time Arkhangelsk City was founded, had some 1,000 inhabitants. The immediate reason for the founding of Arkhangelsk was Russia's loss of the Baltic port of Narva in 1581, which cut Moscow's access to the Baltic Sea. Some thirty years earlier, the English seaman Richard Chancellor, in a failed attempt to find a northeast passage to China, had landed in the White Sea. Chancellor was received in Moscow by Tsar Ivan IV, who granted England favourable conditions for trade with Russia over the White Sea. Commerce developed rapidly, and after the loss of Narva, Ivan the Terrible in 1584 decided to develop a new port to facilitate this trade at the shore of Northern Dvina, i.e. Arkhangelsk.

The new city soon became an important harbour for trade in grain, furs, leather, lard and wax. In 1693, the first state-run shipyard in Russia was established in Arkhangelsk – what has later been commemorated as the founding of the Russian navy. After Peter the Great opened his 'Window on Europe', St Petersburg, in 1703, however, exorbitant duties were introduced to redirect trade to this new town, and Arkhangelsk lost some of its importance.

In 1708, Arkhangelsk Guberniya was founded. The guberniya was considerably larger than the present oblast, covering the Russian European North from the Danish-Norwegian border to the Urals. Although trade dwindled, Arkhangelsk remained by far the largest city in the Russian north. Moreover, the building of a railway from Moscow to Arkhangelsk in 1898 spurred industrial growth in the region.

In the Civil War that followed the October Revolution of 1917, Arkhangelsk became a centre of resistance against the Bolsheviks and the headquarter of the White Army under General Miller's command. In August 1918, British troops landed in the city, and although they were withdrawn in 1919, Arkhangelsk did not fall into Soviet hands until the following year.

The Soviet development of the Far North led to new growth in Arkhangelsk. While the population of Arkhangelsk City had been 45,000 at the end of the Civil War, it quadrupled over the next decade and peaked at over 425,000 at the end of the Soviet period. Soviet focus on industrialisation and urbanisation led not only to an increased share of urban population (from 39.6 per cent in 1939 to 73.4 per cent in 1989) but also to a fall in rural population in absolute numbers (from 641,800 in 1939 to 417,800 in 1989). Overall, the population of the oblast increased from 1,062,600 in 1939 to 1,515,800 in 1989.

In 1929, Soviet authorities established the Northern Kray, the administrative centre of which was Arkhangelsk City. In 1937, the kray was dissolved and replaced by two oblasts, Arkhangelsk and Vologda. As mentioned under the presentation of Nenets Autonomous Okrug above, Nenets remained a constituent part of the oblast throughout the Soviet period. Today, Arkhangelsk Oblast – including the archipelagos of Novaya Zemlya and Franz Josef Land as well as Nenets Autonomous Okrug – covers a territory of 587,400 km^2. Even if the okrug is excluded on the basis of constituting a separate federal entity, Arkhangelsk, with a territory of 410,700 km^2, remains one of the larger federal subjects.

The present population of the oblast (again excluding the okrug) is 1,491,900 people. 74.1 per cent of the population live in urban settlements. There are 14 cities, the largest being Arkhangelsk City with 368,900 inhabitants. Other important cities are Severodvinsk (239,000 inhabitants), Kotlas (66,800), Novodvinsk (48,700) and Koryazhma (44,500). As a matter of fact, these cities make up two clusters of urban settlements: Severodvinsk, which is a centre for the military-industrial complex and the ship-building industry, and Novodvinsk with its wood-processing industry are satellites of Arkhangelsk, whereas Koryazhma is a satellite of Kotlas, the centre of the southern, agricultural region. On the other hand, Novaya Zemlya and Franz Josef Land as well as the northern parts of the mainland are more or less uninhabited.

Arkhangelsk is a thoroughly Russian oblast: 92.1 per cent of the population is ethnic Russian. The largest minority groups are made up by Ukrainians (3.4 per cent), Belorussians (1.3 per cent), and Komi (0.5 per cent). Local Russians were traditionally known as Pomors, a subgroup of the Russian ethnos. The Pomors distinguished themselves through their occupation (fishing), traditions, culture and distinct dialect. With the influx of newcomers to the region in the Soviet period, however, the Pomor culture has all but disappeared. The aboriginal population (ancient tribes such as the Chuds and Biarms, as well as the present day Nenets and Saami) have either been assimilated or pushed aside throughout the centuries of Russian domination and no longer compose distinct elements (altogether some 750 Nenets live in the oblast).

Topographically and climatically, the oblast varies from tundra and permafrost at Franz Josef Land to an agriculturally more favourable zone in the south. The most important topographical traits of the oblast, however, are the vast forest areas, the taiga, and long rivers (e.g. Onega, Northern Dvina and Mezen).

Historically, forestry has been the most important industry in the Arkhangelsk region. Until the 1970s, when it was surpassed by Irkutsk Oblast, Arkhangelsk was the leading producer of timber in the Soviet Union. Up to two fifths of the industrial production is still related to forestry (saw-timber, furniture, paper, pulp etc). Also shipbuilding has deep roots in Arkhangelsk. The Sevmash and Zvyozdochka shipyards in Severodvinsk serve the military sector (Sevmash builds and Zvyozdochka repairs and modifies nuclear submarines). The traditional fish-processing industry has experienced a serious decline over the last decade as a result of lack of raw materials, the local industry not being able to compete neither in price, nor in location in relation to fishing grounds and markets. A new potential industry is diamond mining, although this is still in its initial phase.

As for agriculture, only the southern part of the oblast is suited for cultivation. A total of 1.4 per cent of the oblast's territory is cultivated, out of which 39.8 per cent is arable land. During the 19th century, local breeders developed the Kholmogory cattle, and milk production is still the most important branch within the agricultural sector.

From the first settlers arrived until the present, the rivers have formed the backbone of the transportation infrastructure. Over the last century, this has been supplemented by the development of the railway network. Today, there are more than 18,000 km of railroad in the oblast. In general, however, the infrastructure of Arkhangelsk has suffered from a poorly developed road system.

Murmansk Oblast The history of Murmansk – both the administrative entity and the city itself – is a relatively short one. In the autumn of 1997, the inhabitants of Murmansk City celebrated the 80th anniversary of its founding. At the same time, those so inclined could celebrate the 80th anniversary of the Bolshevik Revolution, underscoring the relatively brief political and economic history of the region.

Until World War I, the vast territory of the Kola Peninsula was inhabited by only a few thousand people and was of practically no significance, military or otherwise, to the Russian empire. The Terskiy Coast (the eastern part of the peninsula) came under the control of the Republic of Novgorod in the 13th century, but there are no records of permanent Novgorodian settlement on the peninsula until the first half of the 15th century. Following the collapse of the Novgorodian state in 1487, the area became a relatively neglected northern outpost of the Muscovite Principality. Almost a century later, permanent settlements were established along the northern coast at Kola and Pechenga, the first centred around a new fortification, the latter around a monastery.

In 1708, Kola Uyezd (district) was included in the new Arkhangelsk Guberniya. In 1883, however, the uyezd was re-established within the guberniya and subsequently renamed Aleksandrovsk Uyezd in 1899 after the newly established town of Aleksandrovsk (the present closed military town of Polyarnyy). Although the strategic potential of the ice-free Murman Coast had been recognised at least a half-century earlier, the Russian authorities did not move to develop this potential until they were forced to act by the demands of World War I. The lack of ice-free ports in European Russia, except for those in the Black and Baltic Seas where the Russian fleets could easily be cut off at narrow straits, prompted the construction of the Murman railway, which reached the Kola Fjord in 1916. The same year the supply port Romanov-na-Murmane was founded at the end-stop of the railway. In 1917, its name was changed to Murmansk.

During the Civil War 1918-20, Murmansk was a base for British, French and American expeditionary forces against the Bolsheviks, and Soviet power was established only in 1920. The following year, Murmansk became the administrative centre of the newly formed Murmansk Guberniya. From 1927 through 1937, the region was administered as an okrug within Leningrad Oblast. As a result of the region's growing population and economic and political significance, Murmansk attained oblast status in 1938.[19]

During World War II, the strategic importance of Murmansk and the Kola Peninsula was proved again – both as a vital corridor for supplies during the siege of Leningrad and as the home base for the Northern Fleet, which had been founded in 1933. During the subsequent Cold War, Murmansk Oblast was one of the two regions within the Soviet Union that bordered directly with a NATO member and was thus given high priority. The peninsula was heavily militarised, and by 1970 the Northern Fleet had become the largest and most important of the Soviet naval fleets. The military complex employed a significant part of the population and developed into a state within the state, endowed with its own infrastructure, generally superior to the civilian one.

The civilian sector of the post-war economy in the oblast came to be dominated by heavy industry. Entire towns and cities were built from scratch around enormous mining, metallurgical, and chemical enterprises (e.g. Nikel, Monchegorsk, Apatity and Kirovsk). Many of these industrial centres were constructed along the Murman Railway,[20] which still constitutes the infrastructural backbone of the Kola Peninsula. In coastal settlements, and especially in Murmansk City, the fisheries and fish processing industry also played a significant role. The fish processing industry in Murmansk gradually came to supply the USSR as a whole.

Murmansk is a typical Russian northern region in the sense that major population growth post-dated the Bolshevik Revolution and was based on the construction of a relatively small number of massive industrial enterprises and military complexes. The industrialisation policies of the 1920s ushered in a period of mass immigration to the Kola Peninsula, a trend that except for a temporary slump during World War II continued until 1991. The immigrants were attracted by a number of advantages granted to the inhabitants of the Soviet North, such as higher wages, a lower retirement age, and subsidised holidays at resorts at the Black Sea.

Although the standard of living in Murmansk Oblast thus was well above the Soviet average, many of its inhabitants still regarded it as a temporary place of residence rather than as their permanent home. Most workers returned to their former areas of residence upon retirement, if not before, to live on their generous pensions and the savings that the northern system of compensation had allowed them to accumulate. Those working in the military and fisheries sectors, where personnel turnover is generally high, had an even weaker sense of attachment to the region. The region's demographic profile has reflected this situation; the average age of the population was low, and young males were over-represented.

Murmansk Oblast encompasses the geographic area of the Kola Peninsula, covering a land area of 144,900 km^2. Almost all the territory is situated north of the Polar Circle and the oblast covers two climatic zones – tundra and taiga.

During the 1990s, immigration to the oblast slumped and Murmansk, like most other Russian northern regions, experienced a population decline (12.6 per cent over the past decade). At present, the population is 1,034,500. In spite of the recent fall in population, this still makes Murmansk one of the most densely populated areas in the entire Circumpolar

North (7.1 people per km^2). The overwhelming majority of the population (92 per cent) is concentrated in the region's widely scattered urban settlements. There are 16 cities in the oblast, the largest being Murmansk with 387,400 inhabitants (down from more than 468,000 at the end of the Soviet period), Apatity (70,600), Monchegorsk (59,800), Severomorsk (57,100) and Kandalaksha (46,900).

Although immigration to Murmansk came from all over the Soviet Union, the oblast is predominantly Russian, with ethnic Russians making up 83.8 per cent of the total population. Other ethnic groups living in Murmansk are Ukrainians (8.3 per cent), Belorussians (3.5 per cent), Tatars (1 per cent), Mordvins (0.4 per cent) and Chuvash (0.2 per cent). The aboriginal population, the Saami, today number approximately 1,600 (0.15 per cent of the total population), and are concentrated to the Lovozero Rayon.

As already mentioned, mining is one of the principal industries on the Kola Peninsula. The oblast has rich mineral resources, the most important being iron ore, nickel, apatite, and nepheline. If opencast mining of nickel soon will come to a halt, as many experts seem to presuppose, there might come to substantial labour cuts in the mining sector. Underground mining is considered as an option for prolonging mining activities, but is by many seen as too expensive. In the two other main sectors of employment, the military complex and the fisheries, there have already been substantial cutbacks and lay-offs (some 30,000 within the fishing sector alone). For instance, the fish-processing plant in Murmansk City, which used to be one of the largest in Europe, has operated at a fraction of its full potential since the mid-1990s.

Only about 20 per cent of the oblast's territory is covered by forest (taiga). Although the Gulf Stream influences the climate (e.g. during winter the sea does not freeze along the northern shore of the peninsula), this is hardly enough to make the agricultural sector flourish. Only 28,600 hectare or 0.2 per cent of the territory is cultivated. Milk and meat production – including reindeer herding – are the main sectors.

As regards infrastructure, the vital importance of the Murman Railway has already been pointed out. The ice-free port of Murmansk City is another important asset. As Russia has lost control over commercial ports further south as a result of the break-up of the Soviet Union, Murmansk hopes to increase its volume of transit trade.

Map 1.4 Murmansk Oblast

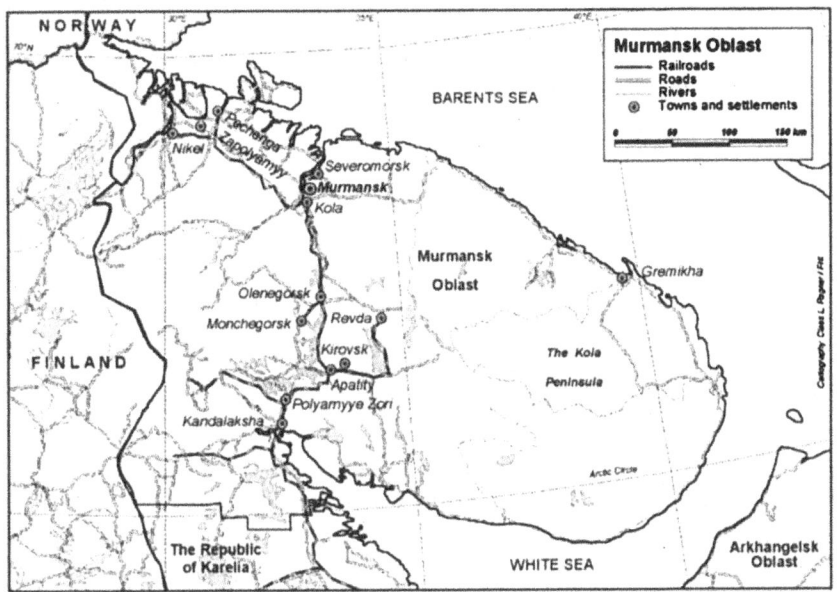

Some Characteristics of Russia's Northwestern Periphery

As follows from the brief presentations above, there are both striking similarities and dissimilarities among the federal subjects of the Northwest Russian periphery. One major contrast is between the old Russian, rural areas of Arkhangelsk and Karelia on the one hand, and the Soviet-type, highly industrialised and urbanised territory of Murmansk Oblast on the other. Nevertheless, the area here defined as Northwestern Russia shares some common traits. First, it is to a large extent dependent on extraction of various natural resources. Second, at least Murmansk and Arkhangelsk have a relatively noticeable military presence on their territory. Third, the federal subjects of Northwestern Russia share some common features typical of peripheral regions. Fourth, located in the periphery of the Federation, they are also so-called *gateway regions* enjoying geographical proximity to foreign countries. These features will be briefly described in the following, emphasising their relevance for the main object of study in this book, namely the process of division of power and responsibilities between the federal and regional levels and its consequences for Northwestern Russia. A few initial assumptions or hypotheses for the study will also be outlined.

Dependence on natural resources The importance of various natural resources for the regional economy is indeed striking for the entire Northwest Russian periphery. On the Kola Peninsula, entire towns and cities are built around the peninsula's mining and metallurgical complex. Likewise, the fishing fleet – earlier heavily engaged in distant water fishing, but now mainly operating in the neighbouring Barents Sea – constitutes a mainstay in the economy of Murmansk Oblast. In Arkhangelsk and Karelia, forests have represented a valuable resource for centuries. Oil and gas are already extracted in Nenets and will potentially be of much greater importance in future.

The multitude and wealth of natural resources in Northwestern Russia is extraordinary. The Barents Sea is one of the most productive ocean areas in the world in terms of living marine resources, and its fisheries among the most successfully managed. The concentration of minerals and hydrocarbon resources within a rather limited geographical area is also remarkable. From the point of view of our discussion, it is interesting how the existence of such abundant resources affects the relationship and power balance between the federal centre and the regional authorities in the federal subjects where the resources are extracted. In particular, three main questions will be addressed: first, to what extent are regional authorities allowed to influence decision making in the public management of resource extraction? Second, to what extent do revenues from the extraction remain in the regions, and to what extent are they channelled into the federal budget? Third, does the existence of valuable natural resources influence relations with the political centre in more general terms?

A heavy military presence The Kola Peninsula is one of the most heavily militarised areas in the world. The Northern Fleet, which is the largest and strategically most important of the four fleets of the Russian Navy, has its main base and administrative centre in the city of Severomorsk on the Kola Fjord. More than half of Russia's strategic nuclear submarines are stationed at the various Kola naval bases. Moreover, about one third of the inhabitants of Murmansk Oblast are probably directly dependent on the military sector, and at least half of these are civilians. Murmansk Oblast being the main base of the Northern Fleet, it is also the federal subject in Russia with the highest concentration of so-called *closed towns*. These are separate administrative units with their own civilian authorities, but are directly subordinate to federal rather than regional authorities. There are six such closed towns in Murmansk and one in Arkhangelsk.

Furthermore, there are significant military-industrial enterprises located in Russia's northwestern periphery. Most important are the large shipyards in Severodvinsk in Arkhangelsk, but also the Kola Peninsula has several shipyards that are crucial for the economic and social infrastructure of the region. An interesting question in this context is how the rather heavy military presence in the region affects the relationship with Moscow. Is it an obstacle to decentralisation? Or are the federal authorities keener to transfer responsibility to the heavily militarised regions now that the extensive problems of Russia's armed forces have rendered the military a burden rather than an asset?

General peripheral traits It can be argued that the entire Northwestern Russia carries several peripheral features of a more general nature. For instance, although there are differences between the four federal subjects, the whole region has a relatively poorly developed infrastructure. This is most apparent in Nenets, which is without rail and road connections, but also typical of Arkhangelsk, where the development of seasonal river transport of goods took place at the expense of the construction of roads. As late as the early 1990s, more than half of the rayon centres of the oblast lacked road connections with the regional centre, Arkhangelsk City (Bjorvatn and Castberg, 1994). The situation is better in Murmansk and Karelia, but even there both roads and railways are in a poor condition. Moreover, cross-regional connections between Arkhangelsk on the one hand and Murmansk and Karelia on the other are inadequate. In general, the harsh climate and partly unfavourable topography have hampered infrastructural development throughout the region.

All federal subjects of Russia's northwestern periphery have experienced a decline in population over the last decade. As often happens in peripheral regions in times of crisis, the most resourceful people tend to leave for more central areas, whereas the old and uneducated remain. The main question for discussion related to these phenomena will be how the location of this region in a typical periphery setting influences its relations with the federal centre. A hypothesis would be that these regions favour close connections and friendly relations with the centre for fear of losing indispensable financial support.

Gateway regions A common theme in the economic development literature on the former Soviet republics – and the Russian Federation in particular – has been that regions located at the borders of the former Soviet Union (so-called gateway regions) may be better positioned for sustainable economic growth during the early post-Soviet period than regions located in the interior. A key assumption underpinning this argument has been that a waning central governmental authority will allow regions more leeway to establish transborder economic ties with neighbouring states that are more developed, have abundant investment capital, or otherwise possess complementary economies to those of Russia's border regions.[21]

The northwestern periphery would appear to possess a number of advantages that might warrant the establishment and deepening of such transborder ties. These include: (1) a rich natural resource base both on land and immediately offshore (fish stocks and hydrocarbon resources); (2) a strategic location affording access to Northwestern Russia by sea; (3) ice-free ports serving as the home base for fishing and commercial fleets as well as important shipyards; and (4) democratic, economically advanced, and generally friendly neighbouring countries (Norway, Sweden and Finland). The federal subjects of Northwestern Russia are involved in several co-operative ventures with the neighbouring Nordic countries. The most important of these to date is the Barents Euro-Arctic Region initiative, formally established in January 1993.[22] One hypothesis would be that the proximity to Western countries seeking to strengthen ties with Russia would render Northwestern Russia in a favourable position for Western investments and influence in general.

As follows from the short description of characteristic traits of Northwestern Russia in this section, various factors may pull in different directions, also when one and the same federal subject is concerned. For instance, Murmansk Oblast is at one and the same time a gateway region enjoying keen interest from neighbouring Norway and Finland, and a heavily militarised region which one would expect the federal authorities to keep in a firm grip. Similarly, Nenets is on the one hand a periphery region with underdeveloped infrastructure but on the other hand contains interesting objects of foreign direct investment, in particular hydrocarbon resources. The rich natural resources of the region can, however, also be a mixed blessing: on the one hand, they represent potential income and bargaining power, on the other, reasons for federal authorities to restrict (or abstain from extending) their autonomy. Likewise, the close connections with the Nordic states may on the one hand represent a valuable source of investments and other types of economic, political, social or moral support. On the other hand, these connections may have the opposite effect: Moscow may conceive of the Nordic countries as a convenient source of revenue for the northwestern regions and turn down their proposals for prerogatives with the argument that their situation is already quite favourable.

Outline of the Book

Some of the characteristics of the Northwest Russian periphery described in the preceding section are dealt with in individual chapters whereas others are in focus in several of them. In particular, the relevance of general peripheral traits and the function of the Northwest Russian federal subjects as a gateway region is directly or indirectly raised by several authors and re-addressed by the editors in the concluding chapter. The military presence is addressed in a separate chapter, whereas the importance of the deposits of natural resources in the region is discussed both in separate chapters on fisheries and offshore hydrocarbon resources and is also raised in several of the other chapters.

Chapters 2-4 attempt to outline general development traits in Russian centre-region relations and their effect on the northwestern periphery. In Chapter 2, Brynjulf Risnes provides an overview of the legal aspects of centre-region relations in the Russian Federation. He recounts how the regions have utilised the weakening of federal legislative power after the disintegration of the Soviet Union, and how the federal centre has responded to the evolving regional legislation. A major theme in Risnes' contribution is the problem of frequent contradictions between federal and regional legislation. Helge Blakkisrud follows up this discussion in Chapter 3 with an account of how centre-region relations have evolved at the level of practical politics. In both these chapters, the Northwest Russian periphery constitutes an interesting empirical setting since it contains all three main categories of federal subjects. In Chapter 4, Per Botolf Maurseth follows up the preceding chapters with a discussion of the degree to which the centre-region relations drawn up by legislation and political agreements are reflected by economic decentralisation. What has the development of fiscal federalism meant for Russia's northwestern periphery?

We then move on to the case studies of various regionally important sectors. In Chapter 5, Arild Moe discusses the importance of the region's offshore oil and gas reserves in a centre-periphery context. The main issue in this debate is the extent to which regional actors are allowed to take part in the exploitation and management of these resources. The same goes for Chapter 6, where Geir Hønneland addresses the participation of regional authorities in the management of Northwest Russian fisheries. Hønneland gives an account of how the regional authorities in Murmansk have attempted to increase their influence on fisheries management since 1993. At issue here is also the power struggle between remnants of Soviet industrial complexes and the new, democratically elected bodies of governance. The relevance of the military presence in the region in a centre-periphery context is raised by Anne-Kristin Jørgensen in Chapter 7. She gives an overview of the most important military units, closed towns and military-industrial enterprises in the area and discusses how their existence influences relations between Moscow and authorities in the regions where they are located. In Chapter 8, the editors provide a conclusion of the entire book, summing up the major empirical findings of its chapters.

Notes

[1] For a discussion of the new centre-region relations in the Russian Federation, see for instance Shlapentokh *et al.* (1997), M. McAuley (1997), Blakkisrud (1997), Stavrakis *et al.* (1997) or Alexseev (1999).
[2] See, for instance, Dellenbrant and Olsson (1994), Stokke and Tunander (1994), Dahlström *et al.* (1995), Dellenbrant and Wiberg (1997) and Flikke (1998).
[3] Whether the Soviet Union and the RSFSR were truly federations is disputed. Since unity was upheld through the centre's use of coercive means, some researchers have described the two as pseudo-federations (Duchacek, 1987).
[4] The number of ethnic groups in the RSFSR fluctuated according to political trends, on the basis of which groups were merged, split, or even banned.

5   For a discussion of the various positions within the debate on the future structure of the Russian Federation, see Sakwa (1993, pp. 126-31) or Blakkisrud (1997).
6   Later, however, Checheno-Ingushetia was divided along ethnic lines. Ingushetia had broken away from Chechnya in the spring of 1991, but was recognised as an independent federal subject by the Supreme Soviet only in June 1992. The border between the republics is still not demarcated.
7   The Jewish Autonomous Oblast was not granted status as republic. Still, it was recognised as an independent federal subject separate from Khabarovsk, the kray it used to be subordinate to during the Soviet period.
8   These terms are mainly used for statistical purposes.
9   All of Russia's 89 federal subjects except for Chechnya belong to one of eight inter-regional economic associations set up between 1992 and 1994, and based on Soviet era economic-administrative divisions (i.e. planning regions). The ambitions and work practices differ somewhat among the associations, but their common goal is to co-ordinate internal co-operation as well as their relations with the political centre. The Siberian Accord is often referred to as the most ambitious, extensive and successful of the inter-regional associations.
10 The geographical scope of the book is determined partly by practical concerns. In Nordic research on the northwestern parts of the Russian Federation, there has been a certain division of labour based on geographical proximity and traditional contacts between individual Nordic countries and various parts of Northwestern Russia. In particular, research on the Republic of Karelia has been dominated by Finnish research circles due to the close cultural bonds between this Russian republic and Finnish Karelia. In Norway, contacts have been closer with Murmansk and Arkhangelsk Oblasts. The latter has primarily been in the focus of Norwegian historians (especially at the University of Tromsø in Northern Norway) occupied with the *Pomor* trade between this region and Northern Norway. For the authors of the present book, all having an affiliation with various international relations research institutes in Oslo, the Murmansk area has played a more central role. This reflects the fact that Murmansk Oblast traditionally has been, and still is, the federal subject in Northwestern Russia that is considered most important in a Norwegian foreign policy context.
11 However, there might be a certain bias towards Murmansk and Arkhangelsk also here since data gathering for the project leading up to this book has been oriented towards these two federal subjects; cf. Preface. With the exception of Chapters 2 and 3, the Republic of Karelia is treated rather superficially.
12 For the sake of language variation, the geographical terms are sometimes used without indication of federal subject category (oblast, republic or okrug). This might serve to confuse the two oblasts of the region with the cities of similar names. However, the cities are always referred to specifically, e.g. as Murmansk City or the city of Arkhangelsk.
13 The presentation of the history of Karelia is largely based on Blakkisrud (1997); of Nenets on Blakkisrud (forthcoming); of Arkhangelsk partly on Bjorvatn and Castberg (1994), and of Murmansk on Castberg (1992) and Hønneland and Jørgensen (1999a). Statistical material is from Makfol and Petrov (1998) and *Regiony Rossii* (1998).
14 Between World Wars I and II, Finland included part of present-day Karelia, namely the northwestern shore of Lake Ladoga, as well as the Karelian Isthmus (now a part of Leningrad Oblast).

[15] This shows a considerably higher level of Russification in Karelia than in the other republics within the Russian Federation.
[16] The Nenets National Okrug set a precedent for the development of territorial autonomy among the small and less developed nations of the Russian Far North. On the basis of experiences drawn from Nenets, eight additional national okrugs were established in the Far North in 1930.
[17] As late as in 1990, it was claimed that the total number of reindeer had still not returned to the pre-collectivisation level (Vitebsky, 1996, p. 96).
[18] The situation is slightly better in the two other Nenets-populated okrugs, Yamal-Nenets and Dolgan-Nenets (Taymyr). Of a total of 34,190 ethnic Nenets in the Russian Federation, 26,553 declared Nenets as their first language in 1989.
[19] The new oblast consisted of the territory of the former Murmansk Okrug, as well as Kandalaksha Rayon, which was transferred from Karelia. In 1945, the former Finnish territory of Petsamo (now Pechenga) and the port of Liinakhamari were transferred to the oblast.
[20] During most of the Soviet period known as the Kirov Railway.
[21] Some of these arguments and general discussion regarding the characteristics of gateway regions are presented in greater detail in Moltz (1992, 1996), Kirkow and Hanson (1994), and Kirkow (1997a).
[22] It was initially to include the three northernmost counties of Norway, Norrbotten from Sweden, and Lapland from Finland, as well as Murmansk and Arkhangelsk Oblasts in Russia. At the initiative of Finland and Russia, the plans were amended to encompass the Republic of Karelia. Subsequently, in 1997 Nenets Autonomous Okrug became a member of BEAR in its own right. The counties of Västerbotten and Oulu (Sweden and Finland, respectively) were included in January 1998. Cf. note 2 for references.

PART II
GENERAL DEVELOPMENT TRENDS IN LAW, POLITICS AND ECONOMY

PART II

2 Relations Between Moscow and the Regions of Northwestern Russia – The Legal Aspect

BRYNJULF RISNES

The complexity of Northwestern Russia is striking in at least three respects, all relevant to a study of legal relations with the federal centre. Firstly, Northwestern Russia reflects the diversity of the legal-administrative composition of the Russian federal structure. Of the six categories of federal subjects, three are found in Northwestern Russia: republic (Karelia), oblast (Murmansk and Arkhangelsk), and autonomous okrug (Nenets). In addition to relations with the federal centre, the Northwest also includes an intraregional legal relation, since Nenets Autonomous Okrug formally is a part of Arkhangelsk Oblast.

Secondly, several of the regions have some form of special status due to geographical or other reasons. Although this was legally more significant during the Soviet period, factors such as bordering on foreign states (Murmansk and Karelia) or housing important military bases (especially Murmansk and Arkhangelsk) are still important (see Chapter 7 by Anne-Kristin Jørgensen).

Thirdly, the current economic strength and future economic potential – a factor often thought to be the driving force in centre-region relations – varies greatly within Northwestern Russia (see Chapter 4 by Per Botolf Maurseth).

Thus, this part of Russia offers extensive material relevant to the objective of this chapter, which is to describe the development of the legal framework for relations between the regions and the federal centre. The legal material will be used both in order to highlight general trends in the legal development and to point to particularities of the legal development in Northwestern Russia.

The legal relation at issue is that between a federal subject and the federal level as defined in the Russian Constitution. In this context, when referring to interrelations between the two federal levels, the Constitution consequently uses the terms 'subject of the federation' and 'the Russian Federation'. However, in the following the terms 'region' and 'centre'/'federal centre' are used synonymously with respectively 'subject of the federation' and 'the Russian Federation'.[1]

The Emergence of a Legal Framework of Russian Federalism

The series of Soviet constitutions had given rise to a complex federal system with a multi-level hierarchy of constituent parts of the union. At the top were the 15 union republics which had their own constitutions, among them the Russian Soviet Federative Socialist Republic (RSFSR). Furthermore, several of the republics were federations in themselves in the sense that they comprised ethno-federal sub-entities. The most complex republic was the RSFSR, which consisted of all the six types of subjects that are found in the Russian Federation today.

The Soviet federal system was in some ways paradoxical. Even though both the Soviet Union and the RSFSR were *de jure* federations, with constitutions granting the regions a certain degree of self-determination, state power was *de facto* concentrated in Moscow. Both the court system and law enforcement agencies were highly centralised and under the strict control of the federal authorities. And superimposed on this was the powerful Communist Party apparatus, being the real institutional binder of the union. The division of state authority between the regions and the federal centre seemed to exist only on paper, i.e. in the Constitution.[2] In reality the Soviet system, at least from the period of Stalin onwards, was increasingly centralised and, as a result, regional self-determination was a legal fiction.[3]

In the late 1980s and early 1990s, the centralised Soviet system was significantly weakened, a situation many regions took advantage of in order to achieve a higher degree of *de facto* independence from Moscow. Not only did the weakening of the centralised structures lead to full independence for the 15 union republics of the Soviet Union, but regions within the former RSFSR also put forward claims for higher degrees of self-determination.[4]

The signing of the Federal Treaty in March 1992 represented a significant step towards legalising federal relations between Moscow and the federal subjects, especially since it was the first time the regions had been invited to negotiate the basis of the federal system. It did not, however, turn Russia instantaneously into a democratic federation where relations between the regions and the federal centre were based on a fully-fledged legal system. The Federal Treaty was still merely a piece of paper and the emerging federation still lacked the comprehensive legal structure and institutions that are required in order to support any federal system based on democratic principles.

After the signing of the Federal Treaty, centre-region relations were overshadowed by a fierce struggle for power in the federal centre. Only after the adoption of a new Constitution in 1993 did the development of federal principles again reach the top of the political agenda. During the years that have passed since the adoption of the 1993 Constitution, centre-region relations have for the first time become the focus of political and legal reform discussions in Russia (see Chapter 3 by Helge Blakkisrud).

A Constitutional Federation

The federal aspect of the Russian Federation is declared already in the first Article of the Constitution: 'The Russian Federation – Russia shall be a democratic federal rule-of-law state with a republican form of government'.[5] This Article, which may seem to state the obvious, has two implications that are important here. Firstly, not only is Russia a federation, but the reference to a rule-of-law state must be taken to imply that relations between the regions and the federal centre are to be regulated by law. Thus, it presupposes the existence of a legal framework regulating relations between Moscow and the regions, which is to be the basis of bilateral relations between a region and the federal centre.

Furthermore, the reference to the rule of law also implies that the relations between each region and the federal centre are to be of a legal character. The reference to the rule of law must at a minimum mean that both the federal centre and the regions have an obligation to comply with the enacted legal framework, and that alleged non-compliance can be challenged in an independent court of law.

The inclusion of the main principles of Russian federalism in the Constitution serves as a safeguard against future changes to the system. Firstly, the adoption of constitutional amendments requires a qualified majority vote in both chambers of the Federal Parliament; two-thirds majority in the State Duma and three-fourths majority in the Federation Council. This provision gives the regions a high degree of control over all constitutional amendments as regions, regardless of their size of population, are evenly represented in the Federation Council.

Secondly, the Constitution grants even a minority of the regions a veto against constitutional amendments. For a constitutional amendment to become valid, Article 136 requires the amendment to be approved by two-thirds of the regional legislatures. This implies that 30 of the 89 subjects of the Russian Federation can effectively block any attempt to amend the Constitution. It is hard to imagine how the federal principle that guarantees regional approval of changes in the state system could be formulated in a more explicit way. In reality, the combination of the two provisions mentioned above give the regions total control over constitutional amendments.

Thirdly, the Constitution provides that the most fundamental sections of the Constitution – sections 1, 2 and 9 – cannot be amended under any circumstances. These sections contain the provisions which the constitutional draftsmen considered the core of the system. They cover basic human rights and provisions of the political and constitutional system, including the main provisions on the federal structure of the state. An attempt to significantly alter the balance of power in favour of the centre would therefore require the adoption of a new constitution.

These three points clearly demonstrate that the Russian Constitution grants the federal subjects control over possible changes to the system. The idea of Russia as a federation composed of autonomous units seems to have permeated the work of the constitutional draftsmen.[6] Perhaps more than any other constitution, it reflects the idea of a federation as a group of sovereign territorial units joined together by common interests, while simultaneously not wanting to commit themselves any further than these common interests imply.

An Asymmetric Federation

The complex composition of Northwestern Russia was inherited from the Soviet system. Thus, after the collapse of the Soviet Union the northwestern regions had varying interests in the process of drafting a new federal treaty that would lay down the main principles for a new federal structure. Karelia, the only republic in the region, would befit from the continuation of the system under the old Constitution, which granted a particularly high degree of autonomy to the republics. However, the other federal subjects were pressing for equal rights for all subjects.

The non-republics were the more successful in the negotiations leading up to the Federal Treaty. Although the republics signed a separate treaty with the federal centre containing formulations reflecting their traditional special status, in substance the treaty did not differ much from the treaty signed by the other subjects of the federation. In reality, the Federal Treaty meant a significant step towards full equality between all subjects of the federation. The republics were in fact left with mainly symbolic formulations underlining their former special status.

The introduction of a new constitution in 1993 signified a further step away from the idea of an asymmetric federation by explicitly stating the principle of all subjects being equal in relation to the federal centre (Article 5, Paragraph 4).[7] Furthermore, the removal of the word 'sovereign' in the description of a republic (cf. Article 5, Paragraph 2) represented a further downgrading of the republics' special status. In fact, the republics were left with only three symbols of special status in the Constitution:

- the use of the word 'state' (*gosudarstvo*) in parenthesis in the description of the republics in Article 5, Paragraph 2;
- the right to call their principle legal document 'constitution' whilst other subjects are left with a 'charter';[8]
- the right to have a second official language in addition to Russian (Article 68, Paragraph 2).

The Constitution leaves little room for arguing that Russia formally is an asymmetric federation. Nevertheless, the rudimentary legal framework laid out in the Constitution does not rule out the possibility of asymmetrical relations between the federal centre and regions based on other legal documents. Thus, indications of individual solutions can be found in regional constitutions, charters and other legislation. A comparison of the Constitution of Karelia and the Charters of Arkhangelsk and Murmansk illustrates this:

The Karelian Constitution repeatedly underlines the fact that the source of state power and sovereignty is in the republic. According to Article 1 of the Constitution, federal authorities only have competence in the areas where state power is delegated to the federal level (*peredany federalnym vlastyam*).[9] On the other hand, the Charters of Arkhangelsk (Article 7) and Murmansk (Article 25) emphasise their formal subordination to the federal level. On the issue of common jurisdiction between the federal and regional levels, both charters explicitly state that regional legislation must comply with federal legislation.[10]

The fact that the official Karelian view is that the republic is the source of state authority is also reflected in the complexity of its constitutional document. Whereas the Charter of Arkhangelsk refers to the Constitution of the Russian Federation regarding the main principles of legal relations between the federal and the regional level, the Constitution of Karelia explicitly regulates all aspects of legal relations with the federal centre. Although the Constitution of Karelia acknowledges the supremacy of the federal Constitution as such, it creates a potential for interpretations of its relation to the federal Constitution.

The regional constitutional documents in Northwestern Russia seem to confirm the overall impression of the federal Constitution in the sense that there is no substantial legal differentiation between the various types of subjects of the federation. Nevertheless, as the comparison of the constitutional documents of Karelia and Arkhangelsk shows, the differing approaches to the principles of federalism in different regions creates a potential for contradictions with federal law in some regions. In Northwestern Russia, the risk of legal conflict arising from regional legislation is most pervasive in the Republic of Karelia.

Distribution of State Power – The Constitution

As the highest source of law on the territory of the Russian Federation, all other legal documents must comply with the federal Constitution.

Legal Aspects of Regionalisation 41

Concerning the distribution of jurisdiction between federal and regional authorities, the federal Constitution lays down a threefold framework.

Firstly, Article 71 lists all issues where federal authorities have exclusive competence. This covers a wide range of legislation and includes foreign and security policy. Secondly, Article 72 defines a comprehensive list of political and juridical issues over which federal and regional authorities have joint jurisdiction. The total list of jurisdictions in Articles 71 and 72 are included in the appendix to this chapter. Finally, Article 73 underlines the federal character of the legal framework by stating that, except for the areas of jurisdiction mentioned in Articles 71 and 72, 'the subjects of the Russian Federation exercise the entire spectrum of state power.' Article 73 provides yet more evidence of the federal idea in the Constitution. It reminds that regions are the ultimate source of public authority within the Federation. Jurisdiction not explicitly designated to the federal level remains in the regions.

In order to reach a comprehensive conclusion concerning the legal framework on the basis of these three articles, one needs finally to consult Article 76, Paragraph 4. This provision completes the picture by stating that on issues of joint jurisdiction 'laws and other regulatory legal acts of the subjects of the Russian Federation may not contravene federal laws'. Hence, federal legislation prevails in this area. In summary, the Constitution provides the legal hierarchy for distribution of competence between the federal and regional levels demonstrated in Figure 2.1.

Figure 2.1 The legal hierarchy for distribution of competence between the federal and regional levels

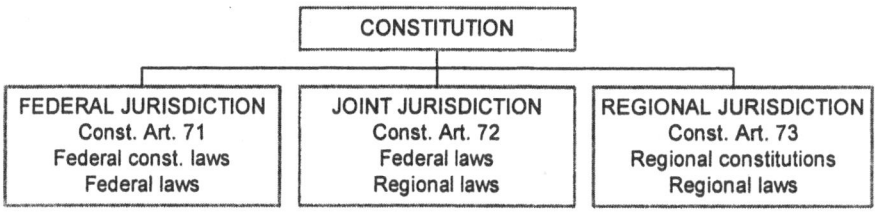

The Achilles Heel – Joint Jurisdiction

In the federal context, Article 72 is the most significant, as it is the only legal hierarchy involving both federal and regional legislation. The impact of Article 72 is further enhanced by the fact that it covers legislation in a number of important areas. The Constitution encompasses a list of 14 different areas in which federal and regional authorities share jurisdiction, including legislation on land, natural resources, environmental protection, and tax law.

As is seen from Figure 2.1, Article 72 of the Constitution grants federal legislation priority over regional legislation in areas of joint jurisdiction. This implies that regional legislation cannot contradict federal legislation, and that the freedom of regional legislators is limited when federal legislation is passed. On the other hand, the scope of regional legislation is not limited by federal legislation and does not have to follow the same scheme or cover the same legal issues. Thus, there can be an almost unlimited number of different regulatory approaches to an area of law.

The federal legislature has so far failed to pass legislation on several important issues under Article 72, leaving room for regional legislators to freely draft regulations. In the absence of federal legislation, many regions have embraced this possibility to regulate important areas of law without having to consult with the federal level. Thus, Article 72 of the Constitution has in reality allowed for regions to gain regulatory competence at the cost of the federal level and thus shifted the balance of power in favour of the regions.

A striking example of regional legislative activity under Article 72 is the regulation of ownership of land. Acknowledging the importance of this issue as a key factor in the transition of the Russian economy, the federal authorities have been working on drafts of a federal land code for a number of years. Unfortunately, the process has stalled due to disagreements between the President and the State Duma on whether to allow the free sale of land. The government has advocated a code allowing for the selling off of state-owned land to individuals and imposing few restrictions on the future trade of land. The early governmental drafts were strongly opposed by a majority of the deputies in the Duma, resulting in repeated redrafting by different Duma fractions and committees.

Meanwhile, more than 50 regions have adopted their own land codes, many of them with few restrictions on the sale of land. As long as the land code is an 'Article 72-law', one can easily imagine the legal battles that may erupt if the federal legislature passes a law that significantly restricts the sale of land. As the implementation of liberal land codes progresses in the regions, the enactment of a federal land code based on significantly different principles may be practically impossible.

As the case of the land code shows, legislation under Article 72 might constitute a serious problem for the future development of the federal system. The current legal development in the area of common jurisdiction, with an accelerating rate of adoption of new laws at the regional level and a continuing legal vacuum at the federal level, is becoming an undetonated bomb under the current legal system. The longer this development is allowed to continue the more conflicts are bound to surface due to the inconsistency between regional and federal laws when federal laws eventually are promulgated.

The composition of the State Duma after the elections in December 1999 gave rise to some hope for the possibility of reaching an agreement on some of the legislative bills that had been rejected by its predecessors. Thus, acting President Vladimir Putin called on the new Duma to end the period under which 'the country is living according to laws written under a different system of government' and asked the parliamentarians to approve proposed codes on land, labour, and civil and criminal proceedings.[11] Nonetheless, reports from negotiations in the new Duma seem to indicate that there is still no sign of an agreement on the land code.[12]

The question of land ownership has so far not been a cause of legal tensions between Moscow and the northwestern federal subjects, as none of these regions have so far passed a land code. Still, the issue of joint jurisdiction is not an unproblematic one. A study of legislation in the region leaves a rather diverse impression of the regulation of the issue of joint jurisdiction.

Most federal subjects in the region merely point to the regulation of joint jurisdiction in the federal Constitution. A typical example is the Charter of Arkhangelsk, Article 7, Paragraph 2, which refers to the federal Constitution as the principal source of law regarding joint jurisdiction. Furthermore, the article states that on issues of joint jurisdiction regional legislation might be enacted, but only on 'the basis of enacted federal laws'. The article, thus, is in full compliance with the legal hierarchy in the federal Constitution.

On the other hand, the Constitution of Karelia has its own approach to the question of joint jurisdiction. First of all, it does not explicitly recognise the superiority of federal laws on issues of joint jurisdiction. The Karelian formulation (Article 41) is that 'on issues of joint jurisdiction the Republic of Karelia enacts laws and other normative legal documents (*akty*) in accordance with the principles of the legislation of the Russian Federation'. The reader is left guessing whether Article 41 means that it is up to the Karelian legislature to consider whether or not a federal regulation on issues of joint jurisdiction amounts to a 'principle' or not. Although the general Karelian recognition of the Russian Constitution should rule out a direct challenge to the principle of joint jurisdiction, the Karelian approach remains ambiguous.

Furthermore, when the Karelian Constitution in the following article goes on to list the areas of joint jurisdiction, it fails to match the corresponding list in Article 72 of the Russian Constitution as the issue of land ownership is missing.[13] An isolated reading of the Karelian Constitution might therefore lead one to draw the conclusion that the question of ownership to land is under the competence of the Republic of Karelia.

There is, however, no reason to draw dramatic conclusions on the basis of such isolated findings. It is not likely that this formal contradiction of the federal Constitution is meant as a political challenge to federal authorities. The case shows, though, that the tendency towards independence in the process of drafting laws in some regions, especially the republics, is an obstacle to the process of creating a unified legal framework for the Russian federal system.

Negotiated Law – Bilateral Agreements on the Distribution of Competence

The break-up of the Soviet Union was the final blow to the centralised administrative regime of the Soviet period. Moscow's answer to the resulting vacuum was an attempt to vitalise the legal framework for centre-region relations. In the sphere of federalism, this attempt was concentrated around two important documents; the Federal Treaty of March 1992 and the new Russian Constitution of December 1993.

The attempted transformation of centre-region relations from a centralised hierarchical system to a legal one turned out to be very difficult. Two of the federal subjects – Tatarstan and Chechnya – even failed to produce a formal recognition of the new federal structure and did not sign the Federal Treaty. As the federal authorities were unable to obtain any concessions from Chechnya, efforts were concentrated on Tatarstan.

The situation became urgent when Tatarstan *de facto* boycotted the referendum on the new Constitution and elections to the Federal Parliament in December 1993. Negotiations were intensified and ended successfully with the signing of an agreement on the distribution of competence on 15 February 1994. The bilateral agreement confirmed Tatarstan's status as a subject of the Russian Federation, and by-elections for the Federal Parliament were organised.

The federal authorities negotiated the agreement with Tatarstan in order to preserve the integrity of the Federation without a protracted confrontation. However, in spite of the particular circumstances surrounding Tatarstan's agreement, it was soon followed by demands from other regions for bilateral negotiations. The federal centre was reluctant to engage in a process of negotiating such agreements with all 89 regions, but could hardly grant this right only to Tatarstan. Consequently, the right to negotiate bilateral agreements was granted only to regions which had particular issues or questions that could not be covered in general legislation. This approach was highlighted when agreements were negotiated with regions such as Kaliningrad Oblast (geopolitical reasons), Krasnodar Kray (traditional centre for federal holiday facilities and sanatoriums) and the Republic of Buryatia (preservation of the Baikal Sea).[14]

Nevertheless, developments over the last years have shown that it is difficult to stick to any criteria for limiting the number of bilateral agreements. With over half of the subjects of the federation having reached agreements with the federal centre, it is no longer possible to outline criteria for the right to negotiate such agreements with Moscow. On the contrary, the constitutional principle that all subjects are equal in relation to the federal centre (Article 5, Paragraph 4) supports the argument that any subject can negotiate a bilateral agreement with the federal centre (see also Chapter 3 by Helge Blakkisrud).

In Northwestern Russia, Murmansk signed an agreement on 30 October 1997, while Arkhangelsk has been negotiating an agreement with Moscow. The Arkhangelsk authorities have pointed to the signing of a bilateral agreement as a top priority in their relations with Moscow.[15] This corresponds to the impression one gets in most Russian regions. Between 1994 and 1998, altogether 46 regions signed bilateral agreements on the division of competence with the federal centre (Ross, 1999).

Why is it then that the drive towards bilateral agreements has been so strong in most regions? As Tatarstan was an emergency case in order to preserve the integrity of the Federation, there should be little need to negotiate agreements with other regions. With all regions except Chechnya having accepted the Federation, one might expect a shift in centre-region relations away from bilateral agreements towards the drafting of comprehensive federal legislation for the federal structure. Nevertheless, in the course of the past six years the bilateral agreement developed into the most dynamic tool in the formation of Russian federal law. There are at least three explanations for this:

The first is related to the slow development of federal legislation. The 1993 Constitution merely introduces the main principles for the division of competence between the federal centre and the regions. As the land code, discussed above, exemplifies well, the drafting of federal legislation has been slow and marred by disagreement. Federal legislation, thus, leaves a considerable legal vacuum. As long as a comprehensive federal framework is not in sight, the number of bilateral agreements is likely to increase.

The second reason is connected to the formal status of bilateral agreements prescribed by the federal Constitution. Article 11, Paragraph 3 of the Constitution states that the division of competence between the federal level and regions is regulated by the Constitution and 'agreements on the division of competence'. Thus, the federal Constitution itself suggests the possibility of negotiating agreements and grants the agreement status equivalent to the status of legislation. In reality, this means that the agreements, when ratified by legislatures on both levels, will be binding for both legislatures in the future.[16] Although it is obvious that the constitutional draftsmen did not foresee the current inflationary development in bilateral agreements, the constitutional provision has clearly supported this development.

Thirdly, the bilateral agreements have shown to be an effective way for regions to reach agreements with Moscow in matters decisive for the future of the regions. In addition to the declaratory provisions on status and co-operation, the agreements are followed by the signing of a number of sub-agreements regulating more practical questions. These agreements are usually signed by the regional administration and the federal government as addenda to the main agreement. Thus, the agreement reached between Murmansk and Moscow in 1997 has 22 different sub-agreements attached to it, each regulating issues of interaction between regional and federal authorities including budgetary issues, the exploitation of natural resources, communications, ecology and state property.

Regional Influence in Moscow – Legislative Initiative

In addition to drafting laws on issues within their competence, regions are also given direct influence in the legislative process at the federal level. First of all, regional leaders have the possibility of controlling federal legislation through their participation in the work of the upper chamber of the Federal Parliament, the Federation Council. The Federation Council, which is composed by the heads of administration and heads of the legislative assemblies of all subjects of the federation, confirms all law bills passed by the State Duma.[17] The Federation Council, thus, gives regional leaders the opportunity to survey and possibly reject any federal law bill.

Although the review of law bills by the Federation Council grants regions considerable influence over federal legislation, it is merely a control mechanism, and the Federation Council is seldom directly involved in the drafting process.[18] Article 104 of the Constitution grants the Federation Council the right to legislative initiative, but the State Duma, in which the regions have no direct representation, is still the main arena for the drafting of new laws in the Federal Parliament. Thus, regions will also be interested in influencing federal legislation through the right to legislative initiative in the State Duma on the hand of regional legislative assemblies, according to the federal Constitution Article 104, Paragraph 1. This is a procedure which is used quite frequently, and which has been utilised by the legislatures in Northwestern Russia.

A bill presented at the federal level by a regional legislature is subject to a lengthy review process in the State Duma. Thus, it is hard to assess the actual degree of regional influence in the Duma. The Murmansk legislative assembly has stipulated that approximately 10-15 per cent of their initiatives towards the State Duma have resulted in the adoption of a law in accordance with the original initiative.[19]

Regional leaders will take a special interest in federal legislation on issues that are subject to joint jurisdiction, as these federal laws will be superior to any regional law on the same issue. As a response to this, regions are granted a third instrument of influence over the drafting of laws on issues of joint jurisdiction. In addition to the general right to legislative initiative and review in the Federation Council, a new law grants regions direct access to the drafting process in the State Duma. The 'Law on Principles on and Procedures for the Division of Competence between Organs of State Power of the Russian Federation and the Organs of State Power of the Subjects of the Russian Federation' of 4 June 1999 introduces a totally new mechanism for regional participation in the drafting process in the State Duma whereby the regions are drawn into the process of drafting of laws on issues subject to joint jurisdiction.[20]

The main component of this new procedure is the introduction of a one month pause after the first reading of a law in the State Duma, in which regional authorities are allowed to submit their comments on the draft. In addition, the law includes procedural safeguards securing a serious consideration of regional concerns, including direct regional participation in the work of Duma committees on draft laws on joint jurisdiction issues.

There is as yet no material that allows for an evaluation of the effect of the new procedure. The hope is that it will be instrumental in facilitating an increased effort from regions in the drafting of federal laws on issues of joint jurisdiction.

Federal Influence in the Regions – Federal Administration

The dissolution of the Soviet Union did not lead to the immediate disappearance of the centralised administrative structure. Although the new Russian leaders did not return to the old command style administration, the centralised bureaucratic system remained intact. The administrative structures responsible for governmental policies and services in almost all spheres of society were still exclusively federal. The federal administration was accomplished through the operation of a fine-meshed administrative system in all regions.

The federal administrative structure is still present in the regions. Compared to the significant changes in post-Soviet federal law, the bureaucracy has changed surprisingly little. The different ministries (*ministerstva*), state committees (*gosudarstvennye komitety*), committees (*komitety*), services (*sluzhby*), and supervisory organs (*nadzory*) still have branches in most regions. The number of federal organs with offices in Murmansk Oblast is approximately 40, while the corresponding number in Arkhangelsk Oblast is 54.[21]

The redistribution of formal competence in favour of the regions has resulted in a need for co-operation between regional administrations and regional branches of the federal administration. Co-operation efforts are often co-ordinated by the presidential representative in the regions, who, despite the fact that he/she represents federal authorities, has the co-ordination of regional and federal authorities as a special task. However, despite the efforts to co-ordinate activities, the federal administrative structure still appears to contradict the constitutional development towards autonomy for the regions. The federal administration, thus, constitutes a buffer against the effective transferral of state power to the regions.

The slow pace of reform of the federal administration structures in the regions is by many considered to be one of the main obstacles to development in the regions. In an economic survey of the Russian Federation, released on 8 March 2000, the Organisation for Economic Co-operation and Development (OECD) concluded that the administrative system prevents economic growth. The organisation noted that the system appears highly centralised, with regional officials having 'very little explicit autonomy in determining their tax policies'. On the other hand, the survey suggests that the system that exists on paper does not work in reality, and regional officials enjoy a 'significant degree of *de facto* autonomy' and function according to 'distorted incentives'.[22]

The OECD survey confirms an argument that has been highlighted by the federal authorities; that regional authorities in reality have enjoyed considerable influence over federal administration in the regions. Reintroducing effective federal control over federal administration in the regions was therefore one of the main purposes of the reform of the federal administration introduced by President Putin in May 2000. The reforms seek to introduce firm federal control over administration in the regions and a restructuring of the federal administration including the creation of seven new federal districts for managing the work of federal agencies in the regions (see also Chapter 3 by Helge Blakkisrud).

Handling Conflicts of Jurisdiction

The most effective way to avoid conflicts between the two levels of state power in a federation is clearly to agree on a legal framework for the division of power between them. The provisions included in Chapter 3 of the Russian Constitution, as discussed above, provide authorities at both levels with guidelines regarding the limits of their respective jurisdiction. In addition, instruments have been introduced to regulate centre-region relations, the most important being the bilateral agreements.

A comprehensive and clear legal framework cannot entirely remove the potential for conflict within a federal system. Legal regulations will contain ambiguities and contradictory provisions from which legal controversies might arise. Furthermore, the risk of legal conflicts is especially high in relation to regulations that try to counterbalance conflicting interests. This is characteristic of the constitutional provisions on the division of jurisdiction between the regional and federal levels.

The idea of constitutional review by the judiciary has been an integral part of Russian legal reforms during the 1990s. A Committee for Constitutional Control was introduced in the Soviet Union in 1990, paving the way for the first Russian Constitutional Court in 1991. The idea of a separate judicial body to rule on legal issues arising from the interpretation of the Constitution was included in the Russian Constitution of 1993.

According to the current Russian Constitution, the federal Constitutional Court has an especially broad authority on questions related to the federal system. Firstly, the Constitutional Court has the ultimate authority on all questions regarding the interpretation of the federal Constitution. Secondly, Article 125, Paragraph 3 extends the court's authority in federal matters by granting it the power to 'resolve disputes over jurisdiction [...] between state bodies of the Russian Federation and state bodies of the subjects of the Russian Federation', as well as conflicts between different subjects. Thus, on issues related to the federal system, the Constitutional Court's authority is not limited to conflicts regarding the interpretation of the Constitution; the Court can resolve any legal conflict relating to the federal system.

During the 1990s, the presidential administration often challenged legislation that contradicted the federal Constitution, and rulings of the Constitutional Court quite frequently struck out provisions in regional legislation for non-compliance with the federal Constitution. There is, nevertheless, no basis for arguing that the Constitutional Court has sided with federal authorities in cases of conflict over jurisdiction with regional authorities. The current Constitutional Court, under the leadership of Vladimir Tumanov and, later, Marat Baglay, has repeatedly demonstrated an ability to concentrate on the principal legal issues involved in each case. Even though several of the federal requests to review regional legislation have been successful, many have not. Statistics from the court rulings do not weaken the Constitutional Court's reputation as an independent interpreter of the Constitution.[23]

A crucial condition for the Constitutional Court to succeed in its efforts to establish constitutionalism, especially in the area of federalism, is that the Court is able to define itself as a separate state organ exercising independent judicial review both of the legislative and the executive branch of power. An important reason for the failure of the former Constitutional Court in 1992-93 (i.e. the Constitutional Court that existed up to the adoption of the current Constitution) was that it failed to distance itself from the ongoing struggle between the President and the Supreme Soviet. In its attempts to decide the details of any question put before it, the Court found itself directly involved in the political battle being fought between the President and Parliament.

The current Constitutional Court has adopted a significantly different approach regarding its own position in the process of developing the legal system and is more reluctant to fill gaps in the legal system by interpreting the Constitution. In several decisions, the Court has refused to review questions as to whether normative acts comply with provisions in the Constitution on the grounds that the issue should be regulated in legislation or bilateral agreements. In effect, it seems that the Court will not hear cases on the understanding of a provision in the Constitution when the Constitution itself presupposes that legislators can further regulate the issue.

A majority of the 215 cases decided by the Constitutional Court since it began its proceedings in 1992 until the end of 1999 have been about the interpretation of the Constitution in relation to legislative documents passed at the federal level. Only 38 of the 215 cases have involved questions of regional legislation and their compliance with the federal Constitution. Most of these cases have been about regional constitutions, charters and legislation that are accused of contradicting the federal Constitution.

The reading of the list of cases decided by the Constitutional Court confirms the impression that legislation of the regions of Northwestern Russia does not often challenge the supremacy of the federal Constitution. Thus, there is not much material at hand regarding judicial review of legislation in this part of Russia.

Intraregional Conflicts – Nenets Autonomous Okrug vs. Arkhangelsk Oblast

An even more complex situation arises in cases where one federal subject formally forms a part of another subject, as is the case with Nenets Autonomous Okrug in relation to Arkhangelsk Oblast. Although the Constitution recognises all subjects of the federation as equal in relation to the federal centre (Article 5), it upholds the system of autonomous okrugs forming a part of an oblast or kray. However, the Constitution does not regulate the legal consequences of the fact that an autonomous okrug is a part of another federal subject. Article 66, Paragraph 4 merely states that legal relations between the autonomous okrug and the oblast or kray it is a part of, can be regulated either in a federal law, or in an agreement between the okrug and the oblast/kray.

Since no law has been passed on this issue at the federal level, the question has been left to be decided at the regional level. In the case of Nenets Autonomous Okrug, this led to a legal conflict between the okrug and the oblast. Both parties based their positions on constitutional arguments. The okrug focused on Article 5, Paragraph 4 declaring the equal status of all subjects, while the oblast put the focus on the expression 'form a part of' (*vkhodit v sostav*) in Article 66, Paragraph 4.

A related case, the case of Tyumen Oblast vs. Khanty-Mansi Autonomous Okrug and Yamal-Nenets Autonomous Okrug, was put before the Constitutional Court in 1997.[24] The background for the request was disagreement regarding Tyumen Oblast's authority to control the two autonomous okrugs, Khanty-Mansi and Yamal-Nenets, economically and administratively. In this case, the Court clearly took the system approach described in the previous section. It refused to engage in a discussion about the meaning of the phrase 'form a part of' in Article 66, 4. Instead, the Court referred to the possibility of regulating the issue in federal law and by bilateral agreements as prescribed by the constitutional provision itself. The Court then concluded that the question at hand should be regulated through legislation and political agreement and not by way of constitutional interpretation.[25]

With no clarification of the issue in sight neither in the federal legislature nor the Constitutional Court, Nenets Autonomous Okrug and Arkhangelsk Oblast have tried to resolve the constitutional deadlock through negotiations. Firstly, through a preliminary agreement in 1994 and later in an expanded agreement of 1996 the two parties have agreed on the main formal principles of their interrelations. Although the current agreement does not solve all questions of formal relations between the two parties, it has contributed to improving the working relations.[26]

Conclusion – Combating Regional Legal Separatism

In December 1997, the then Minister of Justice, Sergey Stepashin, told reporters that after an analysis of 9,000 regional laws his ministry found that one third of them contradicted either the federal Constitution or federal legislation.[27] Around the same time, the then Attorney General, Yuriy Skuratov, concluded that the Constitutional Court had already found about 2,000 regional laws to be in contradiction with the federal Constitution, but added that federal authorities were not able to follow up the regions' compliance with the rulings of the Constitutional Court (Shpak, 1998).

More than two years later, acting president Vladimir Putin repeated the concern over the inconsistencies that exist between regional and federal laws, claiming that 20 per cent of regional laws contradict Russian laws and restrict human rights. He added that the contradictions apparent in these laws 'may reach a critical point capable of blasting the common constitutional space', and warned that 'it might be necessary to declare war on the "legal chaos" in the regions.'[28]

The statements above reflect the fact that the federal leaders are fully aware of the increasing regional legal separatism and its dangers, but that they have so far not been capable of doing anything about it. The new law, mentioned above, on the principles of distribution of competence between regions and the federal level gave the regions one year – until 30 July 2000 – to bring their laws into compliance with federal laws (Article 32). Although there is still no conclusive evidence indicating that the regions will bring all legislation into compliance with federal legislation, several statements from the president and other leading governmental figures indicate that federal pressure will be increased in order to force regions to comply with federal legislation.[29]

Nothing in the development of Northwestern Russia indicates that the federal subjects there are ready to abandon their efforts to create a comprehensive legal framework in order to enhance the conformity of the Russian legal system as a whole. The regions are eager to solve problems connected with the insufficiencies in the legislative framework and are not likely to wait for the federal authorities to reach a national solution. The fact that the northwestern regions have adopted their own legislative solutions is of concern in view of the fact that these regions have tended to be less confrontational towards the federal centre than Russian regions as a whole.

Although regional legal separatism must be viewed as the most significant trend in the development of legal ties between the regions and the federal centre, it is also possible to point to developments in the direction of creating a common legal space in the Russian Federation. Most important is the full legal recognition of the federal Constitution as the supreme source of law of the country. The Constitution creates a basis upon which a comprehensive legal framework of centre-regional relations can be built.

Furthermore, the work of the Constitutional Court in promoting a systematic approach to the legal aspects of Russian federalism should not be underestimated. In my opinion, the conclusion reached by the Constitutional Court in the above-mentioned case of Tyumen vs. Khanty-Mansi and Yamal-Nenets represents the only viable approach towards the development of the legal foundations of relations between the federal centre and the regions. The Constitution merely lays down the fundamental principles of law and leaves it to the federal legislators to develop a comprehensive legal framework.

However, federal law on issues important to centre-region relations is developing slowly. In the resultant vacuum, the overall legal trend is towards bilateral agreements between the federal centre and each region. The bilateral agreements have the paradoxical effect that, although they are instrumental in strengthening the legal basis of centre-region relations, they simultaneously increase the diversity and inconsistencies in the legal system as a whole. The possibility of preserving a single legal space throughout the Russian Federation, thus, is highly dependent on the ability of the federal authorities to introduce federal legislation on important issues and secure their implementation in the regions.

Appendix

The main provisions of the Constitution of the Russian Federation regulating the division of jurisdiction between the Federation and the authorities of the subjects of the Federation are:

Article 71

The jurisdiction of the Russian Federation shall include:

a) the adoption and amendment of the Constitution of the Russian Federation and federal laws and supervision over compliance with them;
b) the federal structure and territory of the Russian Federation;
c) regulation and protection of the rights and liberties of human being and citizen; citizenship of the Russian Federation; regulation and protection of the rights of national minorities;
d) establishment of the system of federal bodies of legislative, executive and judiciary power, procedure for the organisation and activities thereof; formation of federal bodies of state power;
e) federal and state property and management thereof;
f) determining the basic principles of federal policy and federal programmes in the field of state structure, the economy, the environment, and the social, cultural and national development of the Russian Federation;
g) establishment of the legal framework for a single market; financial, monetary, credit and customs regulation; emission of money and guidelines for price policy; federal economic services, including federal banks;

h) the federal budget; federal taxes and levies; federal funds for regional development;
i) federal power grids, nuclear energy, fissionable materials; federal transport, railways, information and communications; space activities;
j) foreign policy and international relations of the Russian Federation, international treaties of the Russian Federation, questions of war and peace;
k) foreign trade relations of the Russian Federation;
l) defence and security; defence production; determining procedures for the sale and purchase of arms, ammunition, military hardware and other equipment; production of fissionable materials, toxic substances, narcotics and procedure for the use thereof;
m) defining the status and protection of the state border, territorial waters, the air space, the exclusive economic zone and the continental shelf of the Russian Federation;
n) law courts; the Prosecutor's Office; criminal, criminal-procedural and criminal-executive legislation; amnesty and pardon; civil, civil-procedural and arbitration-procedural legislation; legal regulation of intellectual property;
o) federal conflict of laws;
p) meteorological service; standards, models, the metric system, and time measurement; geodesy and cartography; names of geographical objects; official statistics and accounting;
q) state decorations and honorary titles of the Russian Federation;
r) federal state service.

Article 72

1. The joint jurisdiction of the Russian Federation and the subjects of the Russian Federation shall include:

a) ensuring compliance of the constitutions and laws of the republics, charters, laws, and other regulatory legal acts of the krays, oblasts, federal cities, the autonomous oblast and autonomous okrugs with the Constitution of the Russian Federation and the federal laws;

b) protection of the rights and freedoms of man and citizen, protection of the rights of ethnic minorities; ensuring legality, law and order, and public safety; the border zone regime;
c) issues of the possession, use and management of the land, mineral resources, water and other natural resources;
d) delimitation of state property;
e) management of natural resources, protection of the environment and ecological safety; specially protected natural reserves; protection of historical and cultural monuments;
f) general questions of upbringing, education, science, culture, physical culture and sports;
g) the co-ordination of health issues, protection of family, motherhood, fatherhood and childhood; social protection including social security;
h) implementing measures to combat catastrophes, natural disasters, epidemics and eliminating consequences thereof;
i) establishment of the general guidelines for taxation and levies in the Russian Federation;
j) administrative, administrative-procedural, labour, family, housing, land, water and forestry legislation; legislation on the sub-surface and environmental protection;
k) cadres of judiciary and law-enforcement agencies; the bar, notary;
l) protection of the original environment and traditional way of life of small ethnic communities;
m) establishment of general guidelines for the organisation of the system of bodies of state power and local self-government;
n) co-ordination of the international and external economic relations of the subjects of the Russian Federation, compliance with the international treaties of the Russian Federation.

2. The provisions of this Article shall equally apply to the republics, krays, oblasts, federal cities, the autonomous oblast and autonomous okrugs.

Article 73

Outside of the jurisdiction of the Russian Federation and the powers of the Russian Federation on issues within the joint jurisdiction of the Russian

Federation and the subjects of the Russian Federation, the subjects of the Russian Federation shall exercise the entire spectrum of state power.

Article 76

1. On issues within the jurisdiction of the Russian Federation federal constitutional laws and federal laws shall be adopted having direct effect throughout the territory of the Russian Federation.
2. On matters within the joint jurisdiction of the Russian Federation and the subjects of the Russian Federation federal laws shall be issued and in accordance with them laws and other regulatory legal acts of the subjects of the Russian Federation shall be adopted.
3. Federal laws may not contravene federal constitutional laws.
4. Outside of the jurisdiction of the Russian Federation and the joint jurisdiction of the Russian Federation and the subjects of the Russian Federation republics, krays, oblasts, federal cities, autonomous oblast and autonomous okrugs shall effect their own legal regulation, including the adoption of laws and other regulatory legal acts.
5. Laws and other regulatory legal acts of the subjects of the Russian Federation may not contravene federal laws adopted in accordance with parts 1 and 2 of this Article. In the event of a contradiction between a federal law and any other act issued in the Russian Federation, the federal law shall apply.
6. In the event of a contradiction between federal law and a regulatory legal act of a subject of the Russian Federation issued in accordance with part 4 of this Article, the regulatory legal act of the subject of the Russian Federation shall apply.

Notes

[1] In some instances, even the term 'Moscow' is used in the meaning of the federal level, i.e. 'the Russian Federation'.
[2] Article 78 of the RSFSR Constitution of 1978 gave the autonomous republics the right to 'independently decide any question outside the prerogatives of SSSR and RSFSR' (*Konstitutsiya (osnovnoy zakon) Rossiyskoy Sovetskoy Federativnoy Sotsialisticheskoy Respubliki ot 12 aprelya 1978*). Given the wide authorities of the two upper levels, it is

Legal Aspects of Regionalisation 59

somewhat difficult to assess the authority of the republics. Close study of the 1978 Constitution shows that the RSFSR hardly qualifies as a federation at all.

[3] A summary of the development of Soviet federalism is given in Blakkisrud (1997, pp. 12-18).

[4] During 1990-91, most of the autonomous republics within the RSFSR adopted declarations on sovereignty.

[5] *Konstitutsiya Rossiyskoy Federatsii.*

[6] A study of the different constitutional drafts in the period from 1990 to 1993 indicates that ideas of changing the territorial division of the country or limiting regional influence in favour of federal were dropped at an early stage in the constitutional process (Blakkisrud, 1997).

[7] The principle that all subjects of the federation are equal in their relation to the federal level is also highlighted in the 1999 law on the principles of distribution of competence, discussed below.

[8] These two differences are both reflected in Article 5, 2: 'A republic (state) shall have its own constitution and legislation. A kray, oblast, federal city, autonomous oblast and autonomous okrug shall have its own charter and legislation.'

[9] The constitution of Karelia (Article 1) states that Karelia enjoys 'all state power on its territory, except that which is transferred to federal organs' (*Konstitutsiya (Osnovnoy zakon) Respubliki Kareliya*).

[10] *Ustav Arkhangelskoy Oblasti*, 23 May 1995, and *Ustav (Osnovnoy zakon) Murmanskoy Oblasti*, 26 November 1997.

[11] *RFE/RL Newsline*, 2 February 2000.

[12] The signs of a continuing deadlock in the parliamentary work on the Land Code prompted acting president Putin to suggest that one should consider a national referendum on the issue (*RFE/RL Newsline*, 10 February 2000).

[13] The article missing from the list of issues of joint jurisdiction is Article 72, Paragraph 1, Point c) of the federal Constitution: 'issues of the possession, use and management of the land, mineral resources, water and other natural resources.'

[14] One of the most authoritative commentaries on the Constitution promotes the view that special circumstances should be the criteria for bilateral agreements (Kundryatsev, 1996).

[15] Author's interview with the presidential representative in Arkhangelsk, Marina Belogubova, Arkhangelsk, 8 September 1999. See Chapter 3 by Helge Blakkisrud for a more pessimistic view on the prospects of Arkhangelsk Oblast achieving a power-sharing agreement with federal authorities.

[16] This is explicitly stated in the agreement between Murmansk and the federal authorities, Article 7.

[17] On the changes in the procedures for the formation of the Federation Council introduced in the summer 2000, see Chapter 3 by Helge Blakkisrud.

[18] According to the Constitution, Article 105, Paragraph 4, the Federation Council either confirms (*odobrit*) or rejects (*otklonit*) a bill. In the latter case, the Federation Council can be involved in the further drafting process through the work in a special commission (*soglasitelnaya komissiya*) aimed at reaching a compromise between the two chambers.

[19] Author's interview with Deputy Chair of Murmansk Oblast Duma, Igor Lebedev, Murmansk, 6 September 1999.

[20] *http://black.inforis.nnov.su/infobase/*.

21 Author's interview with Deputy Governor Igor Chernychenko, Murmansk, 6 September 1999, and the presidential representative in Arkhangelsk, Marina Belogubova, Arkhangelsk, 8 September 1999.
22 *RFE/RL Newsline*, 9 March 2000.
23 The legal dispute between the presidential administration and Tambov Oblast over the Charter (*Ustav*) of the oblast might serve as an interesting example. After a long process prior to court proceedings, the presidential administration finally challenged ten provisions in the Charter. In a ruling of 10 December 1997, the Court struck down five and upheld five. The Constitutional Court ruling was published in *Rossiyskaya gazeta* on 24 December 1997.
24 The Constitutional Court's ruling of 14 July 1997 is published in *Rossiyskaya gazeta* 22 July 1997. For two conflicting commentaries on the Court's ruling, see Krylov (1997) and Piskotin (1997).
25 This 'system approach' on the part of the Constitutional Court is also reflected in other cases. In the so-called Chechnya case from 1995, the Court was asked whether the presidential decree ordering troops to move into Chechnya in reality was the same as calling a state of emergency which – according to the Constitution – would have to be approved by Parliament. The Court's answer was that the Constitution calls for a federal law concerning state of emergency. Again, according to the Court, what was needed was not constitutional interpretation, but the adoption of legislation.
26 The conflict between Nenets and Arkhangelsk is discussed at length in Blakkisrud (forthcoming). See also Chapter 3 by Helge Blakkisrud.
27 *RFE/RL Newsline*, 20 January 1998.
28 *RFE/RL Newsline*, 1 and 10 February 2000.
29 One initiative, a presidential decree of 11 May 2000, is discussed in *RFE/RL Newsline*, 17 May 2000.

3 The Russian Regionalisation Process: Decentralisation by Design or Disintegration by Default?

HELGE BLAKKISRUD

Over the past decade, the Russian Federation has gone through a regionalisation process unparalleled in Russian history. Emerging from the rubble of the Soviet collapse in 1991, the Russian Federation began a process of devolving power to its constituent parts. The aim of this chapter is to analyse the dynamics of this regionalisation process as observed in the relationship between the federal centre and the federal subjects of Northwestern Russia.

Regionalisation is here understood as various political and economic activities geared towards realising greater regional autonomy within a given state.[1] According to such an understanding of regionalisation, the relationship between the centre and the regions is usually seen as competitive, although not necessarily as a zero-sum game (see Chapter 1 by Helge Blakkisrud and Geir Hønneland). A regionalisation process will always be influenced by the specific features of the state in question. Historical experiences often have powerful explicit – as well as implicit – bearings on attitudes to regionalisation. Other important factors that affect a state's propensity to devolve power to the regional level are space (the size of the country, as well as the topographic and climatic differences between substate entities), the political system (the unity of the centre, the degree of pluralism and marketisation of the economy), and cultural traits (the intensity of local patriotism, degree of cultural heterogeneity, etc) (Shlapentokh et al., 1997, p. 7). As pointed out in Chapter 1, Northwestern Russia represents a kind of microcosmos of Russia's regions,[2] comprising both ethno-federal and purely administrative, territorially defined entities, and should thus give ample opportunity to assess both the ethno-cultural, political and economic aspects of the regionalisation process (a more in-depth analysis of the economic factor is undertaken by Per Botolf Maurseth in Chapter 4).

What activated the Russian regionalisation process, and how did it gather momentum? Has the process been one of decentralisation by design, that is, has the devolution of power been guided by principles laid down by the federal centre? Have the legal foundations of the new federation outlined in the previous chapter been followed up by administrative reform, i.e. has the federal centre sought to institutionalise a more decentralised administrative structure? Or has the regionalisation process rather been characterised by disintegration by default? Has it been a process not of designed, but *ad hoc* decentralisation due to the federal centre's increasing difficulties fulfilling its obligations towards the regions as the state coffer has emptied? Or perhaps due to negligence, as other, more acute problems demanded the full attention of federal authorities?

As the regionalisation process is a dynamic process involving both the central and the regional level, the analysis cannot be limited to the actions (or the lack thereof) at the federal centre alone. The study will also have to consider the extent to which the regions themselves, and more specifically, the federal subjects of Northwestern Russia, initiated and substantiated the regionalisation process. What was the motivation of regional leaders for calling for the further devolution of power? Were some of the above-mentioned factors (i.e. history, space, political system and/or cultural traits) used as basis for formulating demands for decentralisation of powers and responsibilities? And did demands from the regions trigger concessions from the centre, indicating a bottom-up oriented process, or was it the centre opening up for the devolution of power within a set framework, that is, a more top-down oriented or designed process? To try to answer these questions, we have to go back to the late 1980s, when the question of increased regional autonomy first appeared on the official agenda in the Soviet Union and the RSFSR.

1990-92: The Initial Euphoria – 'Take as Much Sovereignty as You Can Swallow'

In the late 1980s, a tidal wave of demands for increased autonomy swept across the Soviet Union. Not only the union republics, but also the lesser autonomies (the autonomous republics, autonomous oblasts and autonomous okrugs) joined in what became known as the 'Parade of Sovereignties'. 'The Parade' soon developed a momentum of its own whereby more and more units sought to enhance local control over political and economic development. While Gorbachev tried to halt this process by calling for a renegotiated federal treaty,[3] several leaders at the intermediate level openly supported local demands. Thus in August 1990, the newly elected Chairman of the Supreme Soviet of the RSFSR, Boris Yeltsin, declared before an enthusiastic audience in Tatarstan's capital Kazan that the autonomous areas should 'take as much sovereignty as you can swallow'.

Within the RSFSR, the 'Parade of Sovereignties' was spearheaded by the Karelian ASSR. On 9 August 1990, Karelia, following the example of the union republics, became one of the first autonomous republics to declare sovereignty.[4] The declaration boldly proclaimed Karelia a sovereign state and introduces Karelian citizenship as well as the primacy of the Karelian constitution and laws over those of the RSFSR and the Soviet Union. Karelia was, however, to remain a part of the RSFSR, and some of the republic's state powers were voluntarily delegated to the RSFSR and the Soviet Union.[5] In a further step to distance itself from its Soviet *pro forma* autonomy, Karelia in November 1991 dropped 'Soviet Socialist' from its official name and declared itself a republic. Interestingly, this time around Karelia was the last of the autonomous republics to do so (Ries, 1994).

Before the tidal wave of sovereignty claims subsided, it also reached the northern fringes of the RSFSR where the majority of the autonomous okrugs are located. These okrugs had originally been set up as the titular territories of the so-called 'lesser northern peoples' (*severnye malochislennye narody*), but came to enjoy only very limited self-rule as they were administratively subordinate to oblasts or krays. Eyeing a possibility for more meaningful autonomy, the slumbering okrugs now jumped on the bandwagon, demanding status as autonomous republics or even union republics.[6]

On 27 September 1990, the Nenets Okrug Soviet declared the okrug's territory and natural resources to be the property of the local population.[7] The next step following the logic of 'the Parade' was to declare sovereignty. In Nenets, this came about on 12 November 1990, when the Nenets Okrug Soviet in an extraordinary session declared the okrug to be an autonomous republic within the framework of the RSFSR. The declaration, however, included a self-imposed moratorium: if the Congress of People's Deputies of the RSFSR would grant the okrug status as a federal subject, the okrug would withdraw the demand for republican status.[8]

While the Soviet leaders became increasingly bogged down in the problems of reforming the union structure, the regional elite seized the opportunity to take Yeltsin literally and 'swallow' as much sovereignty as they could. It is difficult to say why Karelia, which was not characterised by a particularly strong reformist leadership, was in the forefront of champions of greater autonomy within the RSFSR. One explanation might be that Karelia had already enjoyed the status of union republic before being demoted in 1956. Earlier historical experiences may also have been of significance (e.g. the traditional ties to Finnish Karelia). Another explanatory factor could be the geographic proximity to the Baltic republics, where 'the Parade' originated, and the pro-reform bastion of Leningrad. In any case, Karelia belonged to the most ardent supporters of increased republican autonomy in the early 1990s.

Although 'the Parade' started up primarily as a centre-periphery conflict, such a process of upgrading status not only in relation to the centre, but also vis-à-vis other federal subjects would in the long run inevitably cause intra-peripheral conflicts. The chairman of the Nenets Okrug Soviet, Leonid Sablin, explained the Nenets declaration of sovereignty not in terms of secessionism, but as establishing 'normal business-like relations' with Arkhangelsk.[9] Nevertheless, the move was not well received in Arkhangelsk, to which the okrug formally was subordinate.[10] In their attempt to 'swallow' sovereignty, some regional leaders had a tendency to overeat, and 'the Parade' consequently stirred up a row of conflicts.

The Ethnic Factor

During 'the Parade', demands for the devolution of power were made on the basis of the Soviet *pro forma* acceptance of ethnic autonomy.[11] Lenin had supported the right of minorities to national self-determination (Lenin, [1914] 1975), and while in principle opposed to federalism, he had been flexible enough to accept it as a compromise in Russia after the October Revolution (Connor, 1984). Now leaders of republics and autonomous areas sought to exploit the inherent potential for ethno-federalism in the Soviet state structure.

The demands for ethnic autonomy were usually followed up by attempts at ethno-cultural revival. In Northwestern Russia, however, the conditions for such a revival were far from optimal. Although Karelia played a leading role in the process of sovereignisation, it was the autonomous republic with by far the smallest share of titular population. In both of the two ethnically defined federal subjects in Northwestern Russia, the titular nation had for decades made up only about ten per cent of the total population.

Nevertheless, titular-nation based pressure groups and grass roots initiatives sprang up both in Karelia and Nenets in the late *perestroika* years. A Karelian Culture Society was set up in 1989 (later renamed the Union of the Karelian People) and the same year, the Nenets founded the Association of the Nenets People – Yasavey. Especially in Karelia, the national revivalist movement soon underwent radicalisation. In 1992, Karelian nationalists organised the National Congress of the Karelian, Finnish and Veps Peoples, and put forward demands for the separate representation of the Finno-Ugric minorities in the Karelian Supreme Soviet and a strengthening of the position of their languages (Ries, 1994). The question of a potential Karelian union with Finland was also raised at the congress, although no resolution was adopted on this issue (*ibid.*).

In spite of the ethno-federal rhetoric, political organisations championing the rights of the titular nations remained a marginal phenomenon both in Karelia and Nenets. Rather than becoming mouthpieces for the titular nations, these organisations soon turned into useful tools for the regional executives in their attempts at wresting additional concessions from the federal centre.

The Economic Factor

Although the ethnic factor was used to rationalise demands put forward during 'the Parade of Sovereignties', the motivation behind 'the Parade' is probably nevertheless better expressed in economic rather than ethnic terms. An integral part of the sovereignisation process was to seek control over natural resources located on the territories of the republics and okrugs. When a republic such as Karelia turned out to be just as staunch a supporter of the devolution of power as for instance Tatarstan (the titular republic of the largest single ethnic minority in the Russian Federation), it seems clear that this behaviour was determined by formal judicial status rather than ethnic composition (Sakwa, 1993).

Karelian authorities pushed more for control over revenues collected in the republic than for support for cultural revival. During the Soviet period, the republic had sent 60 per cent of the revenues to Moscow. After lobbying the new administration, Karelia in 1991 won the right to keep 90 per cent of this sum locally (that is, 90 per cent of the 60 per cent). According to a presidential decree, this money was to be used to establish a special development fund for the promotion of various projects, such as extracting raw materials and increasing export potential (Nemkovic *et al.*, 1994). The decree also made the republic a target area for joint ventures, introducing various tax brakes.

As already mentioned, Nenets had included local ownership of natural resources in its declaration of sovereignty. Regarding the two other federal subjects in question, Murmansk and Arkhangelsk, the 'Parade of Sovereignties' being a mainly ethno-regional current, did less to affect their relationship with the federal centre. Still, calls for special treatment in the economic sphere were heard even there. The Murmansk authorities did for example successfully press for the right to retain 40 per cent of the oblast currency revenues from export trade.

Institutionalisation of Diversity: The Federal Treaty

In the initial phase of the regionalisation process, it was the regions that set the agenda. The Yeltsin administration was too preoccupied with the internal struggle with Gorbachev and the Soviet superstructure, and subsequently, after the break-up of the Soviet Union in the autumn of 1991, with dividing the spoils of power in the federal centre, to devote much attention to regional developments. Realising that they had lost the initiative to the regions, the central authorities focused on preventing a withering away of the RSFSR along the lines of the former Soviet Union.

To achieve this, they set out to strike an accord with the regional executives.

Negotiations for a Federal Treaty to regulate centre-region relations had commenced already before the disintegration of the Soviet Union (Slider, 1994). Nevertheless, it was only after the abortive August Coup that the process gained momentum. The negotiations were complicated by the asymmetric ethno-federal structure inherited from the Soviet period. Furthermore, 'the Parade' had widened the republics' expectations with respect to the degree of autonomy they might enjoy both in relation to the federal centre and vis-à-vis other federal subjects. Having tasted statehood, the republics were not willing to give it up without a fight (Sakwa, 1993). As a consequence, the problem was not only to agree on a model for the vertical devolution of power: even more, it was a question of finding an acceptable formula for the mutual ranking of the federal subjects.

In March 1992, a compromise was hammered out between the centralists and the proponents of the further devolution of power, and on 31 March all federal subjects except Chechnya and Tatarstan signed the new Federal Treaty. The treaty consisted of three separate parts delineating the rights and responsibilities of the main types of administrative units inherited from the Soviet Union: (1) republics, (2) oblasts, krays and federal cities and (3) autonomous oblasts and autonomous okrugs. On the face of it, the new federal structure thus resembled the old Soviet federal model, cementing the asymmetric hierarchy of autonomy. Nevertheless, the conclusion of the Federal Treaty signified that for the first time in Russian history, the centre was willing to bargain with the regions over the devolution of power and the design of the state structure.

The republics successfully insisted on special concessions and the status of 'sovereign republics within the Russian Federation'.[12] According to the treaty, Karelia as a republic now possessed full state powers (legislative, executive and judicial) on her territory unless these powers were transferred to the federal level.[13] Karelia was therefore entitled to acquire a number of attributes normally associated with independent statehood, such as her own constitution and supreme court, and, if she so wished, her own presidency. In spite of this, the Karelian leadership was still not satisfied and insisted on further concessions. Karelia (together with Bashkortostan and Sakha) thus only signed the Federal Treaty after having insisted on separate negotiations that resulted in bilateral addenda that gave rights beyond those provided by the Federal Treaty (Slider, 1994).

The Federal Treaty clearly bears the imprint of being a hurried compromise. It was supposed to outline the rights of the various administrative entities, but more than serving as a guideline on how to develop centre-region relations, it fixated the *status quo*. The most important aspect of the Federal Treaty was therefore probably that it reconfirmed the borders that the 'Parade of Sovereignties' ultimately had challenged: through the Federal Treaty the republics accepted being part of the Russian Federation.

The federal authorities had tried to satisfy the demands of both the ethno-federal and the territorially defined entities; the result was that no side was satisfied with the new treaty. The ethnic republics had sought even wider autonomy, while the oblast and kray leaders were furious about the privileges of ethnic republics compared to their own, particularly with regard to taxes, revenues and subsidies. As a result, the territorially defined entities began demanding greater equality.

In general, the first year of independence was marked by the decline of central power. The Soviet structure was abolished, and the ensuing power vacuum initiated a spontaneous, *ad hoc* decentralisation. Partly as a result of the federal subjects' desire for the devolution of power, partly because the central authorities were unable to fulfil their obligations towards the regions, the federal subjects took on more and more responsibilities. By late 1992, Moscow's control over the regions had weakened dramatically.

1993-94: The Centre Strikes Back

During the first years of independence, the federal centre was ambivalent and indecisive in its relations with the regions. One of the reasons for this was the fact that the Kremlin was pursuing two opposite goals. On the one hand, it wanted to regain control over the unruly regions. On the other hand, Yeltsin sought to enlist the support of the regional leaders in the power struggle with the People's Congress and the Supreme Soviet.[14] As this latter conflict peaked in 1993, however, it brought about a redistribution of power that allowed the federal centre to recapture some of the initiative.

The Bargaining over a New Constitution

Yeltsin's conflict with the Supreme Soviet centred on the question of the future distribution of power in the Russian Federation: Was Russia to be a parliamentary or presidential republic? The conflict was fought out with the new Constitution as the main battleground. The process of drawing up a new federal constitution had commenced already at the end of the *perestroika* period, when in the spring of 1990 the newly elected People's Congress established a Constitutional Commission. In November 1990, the Commission presented its first draft. Due to massive opposition from the Communists, however, the project was more or less put on ice until August 1991. After independence, Yeltsin's growing dissatisfaction with the direction in which the constitutional project had developed led him to draw up his own proposal. As the conflict deepened, both the President and the Supreme Soviet tried to recruit the support of the federal subjects, in particular the support of the republican leaders.

Inspired by their new role as potential power brokers, the republican leaders launched an offensive for increased autonomy. They were not going to back the president for free. In return for their support, the republican leaders demanded the centre's confirmation of 'their state sovereignty', the recognition that they 'voluntarily joined Russia', their 'right of self-determination', and their 'right to secede the Russian Federation without any constraint' (Shlapentokh *et al.*, 1997, p. 106).

As the struggle intensified in early 1993, the Kremlin appeared to be willing to compromise in the vertical power struggle in order to enlist support in the horizontal one. Yeltsin incorporated the Federal Treaty into his constitutional draft and thereby gave a constitutional acknowledgement of the republics' status as sovereign entities. He also floated the idea of reserving half of the seats in the Federation Council, the proposed upper chamber of the new parliament, for the republics. In addition, the Yeltsin administration actively courted the republican leaders, convening them for 'consultations' in Moscow. Among the regional bosses singled out by Moscow for special attention, was the Chairman of the Karelian Supreme Soviet, Viktor Stepanov. Due to Karelia's reputation as a frontrunner in the 'Parade of Sovereignties', the Kremlin saw it as important to win the support of this republic. Nevertheless, in the opinion of some observers, Stepanov 'behaved more and more impertinently towards Moscow'

(Shlapentokh et al., 1997, p. 99). In spite of the concessions and promises made by Yeltsin, Stepanov, as most republican leaders, in the end came out clearly on the side of the Supreme Soviet.

The president's appeasement policy, bestowing increased autonomy on the republics in return for their loyalty, enraged the oblast and kray leaders and led to an upsurge in demands for increased autonomy. A number of territorially defined entities declared themselves republics, insisting on the same rights as the ethnic autonomies. During the hot political summer of 1993, 'republics' mushroomed all over Russia. In Northwestern Russia, an initiative was taken to set up a 'Pomor Republic' in Arkhangelsk,[15] although this, as in most other cases, was never followed up at a political level.[16] All the same, it seems clear that until the final showdown in the autumn of 1993, also the majority of the oblasts and krays sided with the Supreme Soviet. The picture was nevertheless not clear-cut. In Arkhangelsk and Murmansk, as in many other places, loyalties were divided between a pro-Yeltsin governor and a pro-Supreme Soviet legislature.

As the stalemate between the President and the Supreme Soviet seemingly brought the country to the brink of civil war, Yeltsin decided to make a pre-emptive strike. On 21 September 1993, he dissolved the Supreme Soviet and called for early elections. Two weeks later, on 4 October, the opposition's protests were silenced by tanks and their leaders arrested. With the Supreme Soviet out of the way, Yeltsin moved quickly against the regional forces that had sided with the opposition. The republics were punished by having several of their privileges modified or simply withdrawn. The Federal Treaty disappeared from the constitutional draft and the reference to the republics' sovereignty likewise. The final version of the Constitution, which was put forward in a referendum on 12 December 1993, thus represented an attempt at equalising the status of ethnically and territorially defined entities by de-emphasising the hierarchic structure.[17]

Not surprisingly, the republics were dissatisfied with the outcome of the constitutional debate, as was clearly reflected in the referendum, where the voters in more than half of them rejected the draft.[18] In Karelia, however, a clear majority of the voters (69.9 per cent) endorsed it despite the republican leadership's continued opposition to Yeltsin's political dictate. Also the other Northwest Russian federal subjects voted in favour of the new Constitution (69.8 per cent in Murmansk, 71.6 per cent in Arkhangelsk and 72.2 per cent in Nenets). All four federal subjects thus displayed support for the Constitution well above the national average, which according to the official results was 58.4 per cent.

The new Russian Constitution refined rather than reformed the new federal structure. The Constitution, as the Federal Treaty, was unable to harmonise the relationship between the centre and the federal subjects. Compared with Federal Treaty, the Constitution returned some of the initiative to the federal centre. Where the Federal Treaty had attempted to reign in the republics and introduce at least a judicial restraint on secessionism, the new Constitution aimed at rolling back some of what the centre perceived as excessive particularism among the federal subjects.

Yeltsin also declared war on the regional soviets that had opposed him during the previous power struggle. On 9 October Yeltsin, in defiance of all established principles and norms, issued a decree whereby he dissolved all oblast, kray and okrug soviets on the grounds that they represented remnants of the old Communist system. In Northwestern Russia, the local governors dutifully dissolved the soviets in Murmansk and Nenets. In Arkhangelsk, the soviet was not formally disbanded, but nevertheless had to transfer all its executive powers to the oblast administration (Yuffe, 1999). All power was thus concentrated in the executive branch, which was directly subordinate to Yeltsin. As for the republics, Yeltsin did not demand that they dissolve their soviets, but limited himself to recommending that they take into account his decree in reforming their local government (Shlapentokh *et al.*, 1997). In Karelia, a defiant Supreme Soviet refused to step down, but nevertheless agreed to call for early elections in June 1994.

The Kremlin's Control over the Regional Executive

In addition to dissolving the soviets, Yeltsin attempted to strengthen the centre's control by postponing popular elections for the regional executive. In a demonstration of strength, Yeltsin thus chose to ignore the generally accepted principle of popular control over the executive.

Yeltsin had introduced the new executive structure at the regional level as part of institutional *perestroika* on the eve of the dissolution of the Soviet Union. Although the governors were supposed to be popularly elected, after the August Coup Yeltsin won the Supreme Soviet's approval of temporarily appointing them, as a safeguard against a conservative backlash in the regions. The president's control over the regional executive constituted a potentially useful instrument in the power struggle with the Supreme Soviet (as was seen by the aforementioned support for Yeltsin in October 1993) and the Supreme Soviet therefore repeatedly tried to wrest this prerogative out of Yeltsin's hands. Overruling a presidential veto, the Supreme Soviet in the spring of 1992 adopted a law that allowed popular election of governors.[19]

Because of the protracted opposition from the Supreme Soviet, Yeltsin had not been able to fully control the governors until late autumn 1993. With the Supreme Soviet, as well as most of the regional soviets out of the way, however, no popularly elected organ could prevent Yeltsin from taking control over the executive branch. In October 1993, Yeltsin by presidential decree reintroduced central control over appointments and dismissals of governors. Popular elections were postponed and, following a decree adopted in 1994, only to take place after Moscow's explicit approval.

In Northwestern Russia, the governors in Murmansk, Arkhangelsk and Nenets were all Yeltsin appointees. Shlapentokh *et al* (1997, p. 148) have characterised governor Yevgeniy Komarov in Murmansk as a 'conformist-survivor', referring to his lack of active participation in nationwide politics, preferring the *status quo* to any reforms.[20] This description could probably also be extended to Pavel Balakshin in Arkhangelsk and Yuriy Komarovskiy in Nenets. Like Komarov, they were 'survivors' in the sense of being recruited from the old party nomenklatura. And although the population in Northwestern Russia has been considered pro-reform, the political leadership (including in Karelia) was relatively conservative. The governors realised their precarious position and chose not to stick their necks out.

Even the docile leaders of Northwestern Russia were not safe from Yeltsin's cadre reshuffles, however. After October 1993, Yeltsin did not hesitate to use the power temporarily vested in the presidency to discipline the governors, and a number of them were removed. These actions were not limited to those governors who had openly opposed Yeltsin, they were also directed against governors that did not live up to the presidential administration's expectations. The latter was the case in Northwestern Russia, when the pro-Yeltsin Pavel Balakshin in Arkhangelsk and Yuriy Komarovskiy in Nenets were sacked, ostensibly for economic mismanagement. Balakshin was officially removed because of gross abuse of federal credits while Komarovskiy had to step down 'voluntarily' after a number of complaints about economic malpractice.[21] Although the Federation Council hesitated to accept the removal of Balakshin, in the end Balakshin's former colleagues had to back down.[22] The presidential administration thus once again reaffirmed its control over the regional executive.

As an additional safeguard against overly independent-minded governors, Yeltsin wrote the formerly *ad hoc* structure of presidential representatives into the new Constitution.[23] Because of the old nomenklatura's strong position in the regions, the decision to transfer executive power to the governors had not in itself guaranteed the implementation of federal policy at the regional level. In August 1991, the presidential administration had therefore as a temporary measure decided to send plenipotentiary representatives to the regions to be the president's eyes and ears as well as to oversee the uniform implementation of federal policies.[24] The Supreme Soviet was strongly against this measure and had made several recommendations to the president on abolishing the institution. In March 1993, it even passed a resolution demanding that the presidential representatives were dismissed, but President Yeltsin chose to ignore this (Slider, 1994). After the dissolution of the Supreme Soviet, Yeltsin seized the opportunity to institutionalise this control mechanism.[25]

Even though President Yeltsin thus tightened his grip around the regional executive, it is important to underline that the centre's approach was not uniform. Despite the constitutional reference to the federal subjects as equal, the Kremlin continued to differentiate between republics and other federal subjects. In general, republican leaders were elected, not appointed, and usually they also escaped the interference of a presidential representative.[26] This is why Karelia's Viktor Stepanov, at the time unaffected by the Kremlin's cadre reshuffles, could follow a relatively independent course, while the governors of the other Northwest Russian federal subjects had to take heed of the directives of the presidential administration.

The new division of power that emerged after the 1993 crisis developed along what has been called the 'executive vertical'. This vertical replaced the Communist Party as the 'transmission belt' in Russian centre-region politics, while the legislatures at federal as well as regional level were relegated to secondary positions. At the federal level, the subordinate role of the legislature was a result of the previous power struggle, and this imbalance was replicated at the regional level, where the governors and presidents were instrumental in drawing up the new institutional design.

The various governors opted for slightly different institutional arrangements. The new Murmansk Oblast Duma was to consist of 25 representatives elected from triple, double and single mandate constituencies. In Arkhangelsk, the 41 member *Sobraniye* – which included one representative from Nenets – was elected on the basis of single mandate constituencies, and in Nenets, the ten member *Sobraniye* likewise. In Karelia, the republican leadership opted for a bicameral parliament consisting of the Chamber of the Republic (25 permanent representatives) and the Chamber of Representatives (36 regional representatives to meet twice a year). The new legislatures were in some cases co-operative towards the regional administration (as in Arkhangelsk and Karelia), in other more hostile (as in Murmansk and Nenets). Nevertheless, they all shared the common trait of being largely irrelevant to the formulation of regional policies. In Murmansk, Arkhangelsk and Nenets, Yeltsin's appointees set the agenda, and in Karelia the Parliament was overshadowed by a powerful Prime Minister elected by popular vote (Taagepera, 1999).[27]

The Kremlin's Fiscal Lever

Besides the strengthening of the executive vertical, the Kremlin also possessed fiscal levers that could be used to discipline the regions. Increased economic autonomy had been a central issue in the 'Parade of Sovereignties'. The decentralisation that followed the break-up of the old, centralised Soviet economy did not, however, yield the expected results. The mounting economic crises hit the regions hard. High hopes of increased welfare as a result of a loosening of the fiscal ties with the federal centre were dashed by the fact that a large number of federal subjects turned out to be dependent on federal transfers to cover their deficits. After a few attempts at attracting foreign investment and entering new markets, most regions therefore turned to the centre in search of subsidies and other help. Among the Northwest Russian federal subjects, Nenets and Arkhangelsk turned out to be heavily dependent on federal transfers, and after

Karelia's special budget regime was revoked in 1994, the republic also became a net recipient. Only Murmansk has been a net donor to the federal budget.

By the end of 1993, the 'Parade of Sovereignties' thus seemed to have disintegrated and its participants were mostly on their way back to the centre (the main exceptions being Chechnya and Tatarstan, who had still not assented to the new federation). Political power was concentrated along the axis of the executive vertical with Yeltsin controlling both the stick (the right to dismiss governors) and the carrot (the state coffer). On paper, Yeltsin seemed all but almighty.

1994-99: The Regions Consolidate their Position

Whilst on the face of it President Yeltsin seemed to have regained control after the 1993 showdown, the regions still had considerable room for manoeuvre. First of all, the lack of credible reform-oriented alternatives in the regions meant that the Yeltsin administration often had to strike a deal with the old nomenklatura when appointing a governor. Furthermore, the back-up control through the system of presidential representatives often misfired as the presidential representative 'went native', opting for co-operation with the local leaders rather than with distant Moscow. Despite erratic attempts at disciplining the regional leaders and centralising control, Moscow did not have resources to follow up on the development of centre-region relations. Moscow's mounting problems drew attention away from regional development, and most regions thus continued to live their own life with minimal interference from the centre.

In addition, the relationship between the presidential administration and the governors was not as clear-cut as it might have seemed in late 1993. Although the governors owed their power to the centre, the 1996 presidential campaign demonstrated the Kremlin's continued dependence on regional support. Only a couple of months before the elections, Yeltsin trailed far behind his main opponent on the opinion polls, and it is conventional wisdom that regional leaders played a key role in organising his re-election. In return, the regional leaders received 'rewards' such as contracts, subsidies and regional development programmes. This helped boost the authority of the regional heads, and contributed to strengthening their self-confidence.

The 'Parade of Governors'

The 1996 presidential election marked a watershed in Russian centre-region relations, as it paved the way for organising the long postponed gubernatorial elections. Before the presidential election, only about a dozen regions had won the right to organise popular elections. Within a year, all federal subjects but Karachayevo-Cherkessia had popularly elected governors/presidents.

The gubernatorial elections had several important implications. First of all, it meant a crucial change within the regions as the governors could now refer to popular mandate rather than presidential decree as their source of legitimacy. This clearly reduced the governors' dependence upon the Kremlin, and the status of the governors thus became more equal to that of the republican presidents. The elections also heralded a shift in the alignment of forces in the centre itself. Both the composition and the real status of the Federation Council underwent a change as, for the first time, the executive and the legislative branches of power were formed in accordance with the 1993 Constitution.

As already mentioned, three out of four regional heads in Northwestern Russia were appointed by Yeltsin (the exception being Stepanov in Karelia). Being such an appointee proved to be a mixed blessing in the forthcoming elections. On the one hand, the governors in office had the whole machinery of the power apparatus working for them, often controlled the media, and possessed financial and other levers. On the other hand, their hitherto dependence upon Kremlin did not necessarily make them popular with the regional electorate.

The latter proved to be the case in Murmansk. Here the incumbent Yevgeniy Komarov had been in office since November 1991 and enjoyed substantial economic and other support from the Kremlin in the run-up to the elections. Prime Minister Viktor Chernomyrdin even visited Murmansk to discuss a power-sharing agreement with Komarov on the eve of the elections.[28] Nevertheless, Komarov was not able to bring victory home. In the second round of the November 1996 gubernatorial elections, he lost to former First Secretary of the Oblast Committee of the Communist Party of the Soviet Union (CPSU) and former Chairman of the Oblast Soviet (1990-93), Yuriy Yevdokimov (Yevdokimov received 43.5 per cent, against Komarov's 40.7 per cent of the vote).

In Arkhangelsk, by contrast, the incumbent managed to secure a popular mandate. The relative newcomer Anatoliy Yefremov had been in office for less than nine months,[29] and was thus probably less associated with the federal centre and the negative impact of economic and social reform at the regional level. Running against former First Secretary of the Oblast Committee of the CPSU and current member of the State Duma (representing the Communist Party of the Russian Federation (CPRF)) Yuriy Guskov, Yefremov, unlike his colleague in Murmansk, could also draw on the whole reformist electorate in the run-off. The result was a solid victory for Yefremov (62.0 per cent against Guskov's 28.8 per cent).

The incumbent governor of Nenets Autonomous Okrug, Vladimir Khabarov, had less luck defending his position. Khabarov, like Yefremov, was new in office, having been appointed in February 1996. In the elections, he was backed by the entire political establishment, including the presidential administration, the Communist Party and the influential local politician Artur Chilingarov, the Nenets representative in the State Duma. Nevertheless, the local electorate placed their hopes for a better life on the election of a new type of politician, businessman Vladimir Butov. In the run-off, Khabarov received 40.3 per cent of the vote, almost ten per cent less than Butov.[30]

Although the introduction of popularly elected governors in North-western Russia thus did not have an outcome entirely to the Kremlin's liking, it was quick to mend fences. Even before the run-off in Murmansk, the centre declared 'victory', stating that both candidates were 'supporters of reform' (Yuffe, 1999, p. 691). This pragmatism with respect to whom to support was not confined to the centre alone. Although elected with the backing of the oppositional Congress of Russian Communities, the new governor was quick to underline that he wanted to co-operate with the presidential administration.[31]

Nevertheless, the gubernatorial elections can be seen as a sort of 'Parade of Governors'. By the 'move away from a short administrative leash towards a loose and long financial one', the centre gave up the main control mechanism within the power vertical (Petrov, 1999, p. 23).

Further Concessions from the Centre: The Bilateral Agreements

In addition to relinquishing its direct control over the regional executive, the centre made further concessions to a number of regions through the conclusion of power-sharing agreements.[32] Between 1994 and 1998, Moscow signed altogether 46 such bilateral power-sharing agreements, the vast majority being adopted in the run-up to the presidential elections in the summer of 1996.[33] The bilateral agreements have been hailed as a success of Russian centre-region relations, demonstrating the flexibility and adaptability of the federal design. At the same time, it has been depicted as an illustration of the centre's weakness and willingness to compromise when faced by strong demands for regionalisation.

In Northwestern Russia, the Kremlin concluded such a bilateral power-sharing agreement with Murmansk in October 1997. Although all of the agreements follow a general pattern, they also incorporate provisions and address problems of special concern to the region in question. On the occasion of the signing of the bilateral agreement with Murmansk, President Yeltsin specifically pointed out that this treaty would help the centre and the oblast to jointly address the relocation of inhabitants of Murmansk to Russia's southern regions.[34]

Murmansk's agreement enumerates a long list of joint responsibilities,[35] but nevertheless reflects the relative weakness of the oblast vis-à-vis the centre. The agreement was clearly not as advantageous to the oblast as the early bilateral agreements of 1994-95, but rather reflected the centre's appreciation of some of the main concerns of the regional authorities. At the time when Murmansk got its bilateral agreement, the process of developing Russian federalism through the conclusion of such agreements was clearly on the wane and the attitude of regional politicians in Murmansk with respect to the importance of the treaty was also mixed.[36] The three other federal subjects of Northwestern Russia did not sign agreements with the centre.[37]

Legal Separatism

The bilateral agreements were an attempt at regulating the legal framework of centre-region relations through a deepening and elaboration of the existing framework (the Federal Treaty and the Constitution). Nevertheless, a number of federal subjects came to adopt legislation that contradicted federal law, either because the regional legislatures disagreed with the federal framework legislation, or simply because such legislation did not exist.[38]

The majority of the contradictions appeared in laws adopted by the national republics. The constitutions of all but two republics have been declared by the Constitutional Court to include provisions that violate the federal Constitution. Karelia represents one of the two exceptions to this rule (the other being Kalmykia), but when looking at the legislative process in general, Karelia hardly has a better track record than the others. For instance, the Karelian legislators have tried to introduce unsanctioned taxes at the republic level.[39]

Also the oblasts and krays have adopted statutes (*ustavy*) and other legislation that contradicts the federal framework. Some have, for example, claimed the right to determine the responsibilities of judicial and law-enforcement agencies or to revise federal borders, both of which are indisputably the prerogative of the federal government. One of the regions the statutes of which contradicted federal legislation was Arkhangelsk. The oblast arrogated for itself the right to structure the judiciary, even though Article 71 of the Constitution reserves this right for the federal government. Nenets, for its part, passed financial, hard currency, credit, and customs laws that violated the Constitution.[40]

After the 1997 spring reshuffle, when President Yeltsin brought some of the young reformers into the government, the new reform drive also manifested itself in the relationship with the regions. In an attempt to streamline centre-region relations, the federal government launched a campaign fronted by First Deputy Prime Minister Anatoliy Chubais to bring regional legislation into line with federal standards. The campaign, however, soon turned out to be another half-hearted attempt at disciplining the regions. When the young reformers once again were dismissed in March 1998, the campaign lost its political clout, although the process of judicial review continued.

Economic Separatism

The young reformers also tried to tackle economic separatism. The continued economic crisis and the lack of success of the federal authorities in handling this issue as well as reduced ability to fulfil their obligations towards the regions, had forced the regions to adopt measures that often ran contrary to federal interests. Some regions embarked upon radical reform, while others clung to a more traditional Soviet approach. In addition, a number of federal subjects had been able to negotiate special agreements in return for their loyalty (like the above-mentioned Karelian tax agreement). Such preferential treatment not only caused much envy among the less fortunate entities, but also further weakened the federal economy. The result was increasing economic differences between the federal subjects as well as escalating economic anarchy.

Regional attempts at withholding taxes or seizing control over federal property became widespread. One of the more creative approaches in this respect – although clearly directed more at drawing the centre's attention to the dire economic situation of the oblast rather than a serious proposal – was Arkhangelsk Governor Anatoliy Yefremov's announcement in 1997 of his intention to sell two submarines to 'friendly countries' to cover the federal government's 1.1 trillion rouble debt to one of the defence plants in Severodvinsk. Yefremov underlined the need to look to 'non-traditional approaches' to resolve the problem of non-payment.[41] More provoking was his introduction of price controls the following year to stem the rising cost of living for local residents in the aftermath of the August crisis.[42]

Although the Kremlin applauded regional self-help programmes, it became increasingly concerned about the growth in economic separatism apparent throughout the country.[43] In June 1997, Chubais stated that governors whose regions defaulted on payments to the federal pension fund risked dismissal.[44] The right to sack popularly elected governors lacked legal basis, and the threats were never implemented. Nevertheless, this incident serves to illustrate the centre's growing concern with lack of economic discipline – as well as its impotence.

The centre could no longer rely on direct control over the executive vertical and had to resort to the less reliable budgetary process when trying to combat economic separatism. This process is less than transparent, and the more the centre has been forced to rely on the budget as its main 'stick', the more criticism the system has drawn from the regional level. In the current system, taxes are collected in the regions and transmitted to the centre whence they are redistributed again between the regions in the form of transfers. Arkhangelsk Governor Anatoliy Yefremov has, as a number of other regional leaders, called for a change in the balance of centre-region relations whereby most of the money collected in taxes is to stay in the regions.[45]

The lack of transparency in the redistributive process has been seen as a serious problem, as it is not evident when and how much of the collected revenue would return to the regional budget. Murmansk Governor Yuriy Yevdokimov has claimed that whereas tax reductions and privileges in the budgetary process used to have a national tinge (i.e. the republics got preferential treatment) 'now the privileges are not connected with the status of the region, but how close its leader is to the Kremlin'.[46] Karelia's Prime Minister Sergey Katanandov,[47] who in a similar vein has underlined the need to reduce arbitrariness in the budgetary process, shared this view.[48]

Rhetoric vs. Political Practice in the Late Yeltsin Era

Although some of the momentum for streamlining the federal structure was lost with the fall of the young reformers, the subsequent governments of the late Yeltsin era felt a certain urgency with respect to centre-region developments. The newly nominated Prime Minister Yevgeniy Primakov opened his first speech to the State Duma by declaring that 'the new government must first and foremost pay special attention to preserving Russia as a single state. Today this is a lot more than a theoretical or a hypothetical issue. We are facing a serious threat of disintegration of our country' (Alexseev, 1999, p. 2). As Prime Minister, Primakov also favoured the centralisation of the federal state structure along the lines of regional associations (all federal subjects except Chechnya are members of associations organised along the lines of the old Soviet planning regions).[49] As in most of Primakov's tenure, however, actual politics did not follow rhetoric. Primakov himself admitted that although he would have liked to see the number of federal subjects reduced, such a move was not feasible in the short run.

In spite of political will to streamline, or even re-centralise the Federation, all attempts at implementing such a policy turned out to be partial and half-hearted (the sole exception being the disastrous war in Chechnya 1994-96). An apt example was the Kremlin's attempt in 1997 to reassert control over governors that it had lost the previous year. Amidst a noisy campaign against the Governor of Primore, Yevgeniy Nazdratenko, a presidential decree was adopted to boost the role of the presidential representatives. In the end, however, Yeltsin's decree did little to change centre-region relations. Although the Federation in some respects went through a consolidation process, and the secession of federal subjects gradually seemed less likely (again with the exception of Chechnya), the second half of the 1990s turned out to be a period of continued withering away of federal power in the subjects.

2000-: The Emergence of a New Tsar?

As the Yeltsin era was drawing to a close, regional governors started to look for his successor in order to join the winner's team in time. The governors seemed stronger than ever before, and having consolidated their power at the regional level, they now sought increased influence in Moscow. Yeltsin seemed more and more incapable of ruling the country, and the rapid turnover in governments further undermined the federal centre. The Federation Council was already 'theirs'; now the governors wanted to take on the State Duma. Several regionally based election blocs emerged, the most powerful being *Otechestvo* (Fatherland) headed by Moscow Mayor Yuriy Luzhkov, around which regional executives started to flock. A number of regional branches of Luzhkov's party were set up around regional leaders, including Murmansk Governor Yuriy Yevdokimov and Karelian Prime Minister Sergey Katanandov.

The Kremlin was not going to give up without fight, however, and directed its artillery at Luzhkov. By the end of 1999, it was evident that Luzhkov was losing ground and the new Prime Minister, Yeltsin's heir-designate Vladimir Putin, was on the ascendant. Sensing the shift of political winds, the governors were quick to realign themselves, either by joining the Kremlin sponsored (and Putin supported) *Yedinstvo* (Unity), or by openly declaring their support for Putin. On the eve of the December 1999 parliamentary elections, a number of Russian regional executives, including Nenets Governor Vladimir Butov, issued a statement calling on all of the country's political forces to support Prime Minister Putin.[50] Butov had initially planned to run for Yedinstvo himself, but had had to drop these plans when bloc leaders made clear that they would not allow anyone on the list who had previous criminal convictions (Butov had two). The

Kremlin loyalist Anatoliy Yefremov also dutifully switched from the old 'Party of Power' (Our Home is Russia) to the new one.

After Otechestvo's poor showing in the elections, the governors were falling over themselves to demonstrate their loyalty to the new president. In January 2000, the two former Luzhkov loyalists Yevdokimov and Katanandov joined the bandwagon, signing a statement adopted by the Northwestern Association in support of Putin's candidacy in the upcoming presidential elections.[51] The attempt to form a regional counterweight to the centre had thus failed.

The Advent of Putin

The unexpected resignation of President Yeltsin on New Year's Eve 1999 instigated a new dynamism in Russian centre-region relations. Yeltsin's successor, Vladimir Putin, had made his name fighting Chechen separatism, launching the second Chechen campaign in September 1999. First in his capacity of acting president, and then, from March 2000, as popularly elected president, Putin brought a new emphasis on increased state power and re-centralisation into Russian politics. In his first state-of-the-nation address, Putin thus pointed out that the 'competition for power' between the centre and the regions had been 'destructive'. According to Putin, Russia had not developed into a 'full blown federal state' but become 'a decentralised state'.[52] No sooner was his new government in place, than he embarked upon an ambitious plan to reform the federal structure. The various initiatives aimed at streamlining the federation can be subsumed under two headings: attempts at strengthening presidential authority and measures to re-constitutionalise the Russian Federation.

The first category includes Putin's attempt to re-claim control over federal agencies at the regional level, which increasingly had come under the regional leaders' influence during the late Yeltsin years. The above-mentioned 1997 decree tasking the presidential representatives with overseeing and co-ordinating the activities of these agencies did little to strengthen federal authority, as the vast majority of presidential representatives ended up as allies of the governors or republican presidents, often having been put in power at their recommendation (Smirnyagin, 2000). Underlining the need for a 'strong vertical', Putin therefore slashed the number of presidential representatives by introducing a new administrative layer between the centre and the regions, the federal okrugs, which were to be headed by presidential representatives. The establishment of seven new okrugs in May 2000 signified a re-centralisation of the presidential vertical, and thus an indirect re-centralisation of the Federation as such, whereas the regional leaders effectively lost the control they had amassed over federal agencies operating on their territories.

In addition to strengthening the vertical, Putin also set out to curb the legal powers of the regional leaders. In a reform package that was adopted in the summer of 2000, governors and republican presidents lost their *ex officio* representation in the Federation Council. The presidential administration argued that the practice of holding both positions simultaneously rendered the work of the Federation Council ineffective. While there was probably some truth in this, the passage of the 'Law on the Procedure of Forming the Federation Council' also implied that governors and republican presidents lost their parliamentarian immunity. This paved the way for the second piece of legislation, which gave the president the right to dismiss governors and republican presidents if they violated the Constitution or federal law (although he could only do so on the basis of a court ruling). The two laws were initially met with fierce resistance in the Federation Council, but as the pro-Putin State Duma overturned its veto, the members of the Federation Council gave in and passed both pieces of legislation in the second round.

Simultaneously, as part of a separate package of laws on the new taxation system, the Federation Council adopted legislation which strengthened the redistributive character of the federal budget. In this matter, the governors were more divided in their opposition, as the law was met with protests from the large 'donors', but welcomed by the poorer regions. Taken together, however, the above-mentioned measures all served to strengthen the federal centre, and more specifically, the federal executive.

The second main category of initiatives, which can be referred to as measures to re-constitutionalise the Russian Federation, was connected with the new emphasis on 'the dictatorship of law'. Putin has reiterated his ambition to have all regional laws brought into accordance with the Constitution and federal law (Putin had been responsible for centre-region relations in the presidential administration during the campaign against legal separatism in 1997). In May, Putin issued decrees ordering Bashkortostan, Amur and Ingushetia to bring their legislation in accordance with federal norms,[53] and in the following months he has overturned several gubernatorial decrees which were declared to be unconstitutional. Finally, Putin has also brought up the question of the status of the bilateral agreements and their legal basis within the Russian federal system.[54]

Whereas the outcome of President Putin's re-centralisation drive is still unclear – the limits of his power have been clearly demonstrated by the Kremlin's failure to secure the election of its candidates in important gubernatorial elections[55] – the president is undoubtedly building up an arsenal of weapons to keep the governors in line. This process will also have bearings on the status of the northwestern federal subjects.

Conclusion

With the exception of a short interlude under the 'Parade of Sovereignties', the regions of Northwestern Russia have not been among those who have set the agenda for the development of Russian centre-region relations. The ethnic argument pushed by Karelia and Nenets was less than convincing, but, more importantly, the economic argument from the early 1990s proved to be fundamentally wrong, at least in the short run. The decentralisation of the Soviet economy was not the panacea the regional leaders had thought, and as the economy continued to deteriorate throughout the 1990s, the regions' economic dependence on the federal centre grew.

As the fear of secessionism and a break-up of the Russian Federation abated, the element of design became more pronounced in Russian centre-region relations. The legislative framework was mostly in place by the onset of President Yeltsin's second term in office, and the latter half of the 1990s saw attempts at strengthening the political-administrative basis for Russian centre-region relations, the single most important achievement of which undoubtedly was the introduction of popularly elected governors. Nevertheless, the institutional basis remained weak, not so much for lack of a framework of formal institutions, as the persistence of the tradition of conducting politics outside the formal political-administrative structures. The combination of informal backroom politics with a vague federal redistributive system stimulated the development of patron-client relationships that characterised Russian centre-region relations at the turn of the millennium. Hence, whereas the governors in Northwestern Russia now enjoyed a popular mandate, and thus formally were not as dependent on the centre as they had been up to 1996, they nevertheless continued to actively court the centre in order to secure financial support and federal programmes.

The reliance on *ad hoc* and personalised relations became a hallmark of the Yeltsin era, something which clearly undermined the element of federal design in the devolution process. Instead, centre-region relations were built through lobbying, compromise, and horse trading. An important implication of these personalised relationships was that regional leaders tended to pursue their own parochial concerns vis-à-vis the centre rather than building horizontal coalitions.[56] For many republican presidents, 'sovereignty' became synonymous with federal non-interference in their internal affairs and a degree of economic autonomy, whereas oblast, kray and okrug leaders transformed their territories into separate fiefdoms (Sakwa, 2000).

Due to the combination of Yeltsin's personal style and the federal centre's increasing difficulties fulfilling its obligations towards the regions, the devolution of power often took place in a haphazard and *ad hoc* manner. Centre-region relations in Russia in the 1990s can therefore also be summed up as a period of withering away of state power, in which the federal subjects have often been forced to take upon themselves the responsibilities of the state because of its inability to deliver.

With the onset of the Putin regime, however, there seems to have been a shift in the way of conducting centre-region relations: Yeltsin's *laissez faire* attitude has been replaced by a new emphasis on formality and procedure (cf. 'the dictatorship of law'). It is, however, important to stress that the re-centralisation witnessed under Putin does not necessarily equate de-federalisation. Under Yeltsin, Russia had developed into a *de facto* confederation of independent regions, and strengthening the vertical and re-constitutionalising the Russian Federation can be seen as attempts at addressing some of the excesses in the devolution process under Yeltsin, and a return to the federal structure outlined in the Constitution. Whether this actually is Putin's aim, and whether he can succeed in restoring the Russian Federation to a single legal framework and a unified economic space, remains to be seen. Nevertheless, after a decade of devolution mainly by default, Russia now seems set to embark upon a path where centre-region relations are to be developed by design.

Notes

1. In its most extreme form, regionalisation may approach separatism. It is, however, useful to distinguish between extensive regionalisation aiming at a confederalisation of the state, and separatism, which implies full secession.
2. The term 'regions' is here used to denote federal subjects irrespective of whether they are ethnically or administrative-territorially defined.
3. The final draft of Gorbachev's new treaty, the so-called 'Nine plus One Federal Treaty', was approved on 15 August 1991, but was never signed due to the August Coup. The draft envisaged a more decentralised federal structure based on voluntary accession (Smith, 1995).
4. The North Ossetian ASSR had declared itself a union republic within the USSR on 20 July 1990. Declarations similar to the Karelian one were made by Komi on 30 August and Tatarstan on 31 August 1990.
5. *Deklaratsiya o gosudarstvennom suverenitete Karelskoy ASSR.*
6. The first okrug to unilaterally upgrade its administrative status was Chukchi Autonomous Okrug, which declared itself an autonomous republic in September 1990.
7. *Naryana vynder*, 29 September 1990.
8. *Pravda severa*, 15 November 1990.
9. *Naryana vynder*, 21 October 1990.
10. For a discussion of the conflict between Arkhangelsk and Nenets, see Blakkisrud (forthcoming).
11. As a result, territorially defined entities such as Arkhangelsk and Murmansk did not take active part in this process.
12. *Dogovor o razgranichenii predmetov vedeniya i polnomochiy mezhdu federalnymi organami gosudarstvennoy vlasti Rossiyskoy Federatsii i organami vlasti suverennykh respublik v sostave Rossiyskoy Federatsii ot 31 marta 1992*, Preambula.
13. *ibid.*, Art. 3.1.
14. The People's Congress was set up as part of Gorbachev's legislative *perestroika*. The People's Congress had 1,068 members and met on average twice a year. Between these sessions, the Supreme Soviet exercised legislative power, filling the role of a Russian parliament (Sakwa, 1993).
15. *Komsomolskaya pravda*, 7 July 1993.
16. The only republic that came close to realisation before being dissolved by the Kremlin was the Ural Republic, which was set up in Yekaterinburg.
17. *Konstitutsiya Rossiyskoy Federatsii*, Art. 5.4.
18. A majority voted against the draft in Adygeya, Bashkortostan, Dagestan, Karachayevo-Cherkessia, Mordovia, Tyva and Chuvashia, while the turnout did not meet the minimum requirement in Chechnya, Tatarstan, Udmurtia, Komi and Khakassia. In addition, 11 oblasts voted against the draft: Belgorod, Bryansk, Volgograd, Voronezh, Kaluga, Kursk, Lipetsk, Oryol, Smolensk, Tambov and Sverdlovsk (Blakkisrud, 1997).
19. As a result, elections were held in eight federal subjects. In all but one case, governors appointed by President Yeltsin were replaced with representatives from the local elite (Busygina, 1997).
20. The appointment of the former apparatchik Komarov as governor in Murmansk was met with protests from the local pro-reform movement (Yuffe, 1999).
21. Balakshin and Komarovskiy were both removed from office in February 1996. Komarovskiy had resigned once before, in April 1993, but was then reinstated by the presidential administration.

[22] The Federation Council's opposition led, however, to a rephrasing of the letter of resignation, where Balakshin was now said to have stepped down 'on his own request' (Yuffe, 1999, p. 433).

[23] *Konstitutsiya Rossiyskoy Federatsii*, Art. 83 k.

[24] On the introduction of presidential representatives, see for instance Stoner-Weiss (1997) or Busygina (1996).

[25] In addition to overseeing regional developments and reporting to the federal centre, the presidential representatives were to co-ordinate the activities of the various federal organs operating in the given subject. The number of such organs varies from subject to subject and over time, but in late 1999 there were 54 federal organs represented in Arkhangelsk (author's interview with the presidential representative in Arkhangelsk, Marina Belogubova, Arkhangelsk, 8 September 1999).

[26] Although more than 50 presidential representatives had been appointed by the end of 1993, only a handful of republics had received such representatives (Kabardino-Balkaria, Mordovia and Igushetia in 1991 and Chuvashia in 1992) (Busygina, 1996). After the adoption of the Constitution, the process was gradually speeded up. The first presidential representative to Karelia, former FSB Colonel Vladimir Zlobin, was appointed only in April 1998. At that point, all republics except Bashkortostan, Tatarstan, and Sakha had a presidential envoy (*EWI Russian Regional Report*, 16 April 1998).

[27] The former Chairman of the Karelian Supreme Soviet, Viktor Stepanov, was elected Prime Minister (i.e. head of the republic) in popular elections in 1994.

[28] In addition, the powerful Northern Fleet and several large enterprises backed the incumbent.

[29] Before his appointment, Yefremov had been Deputy Governor and the oblast's representative in Moscow.

[30] Butov trailed the incumbent by 18 per cent in the first round, but managed to sway the electorate through his promises of higher salaries and pensions (*Centre for Russian Studies Database*, 13 December 1996).

[31] *Centre for Russian Studies Database*, 4 December 1996.

[32] The treaties have been signed by Yeltsin (or in some cases the prime minister) and the regional executive, but were not subject to ratification by the federal or regional legislatures.

[33] Although the practice of signing power-sharing agreements has not formally been abandoned, no agreement has been signed since Moscow City concluded its agreement in June 1998.

[34] *Segodnya*, 31 October 1997.

[35] *Dogovor o razgranichenii predmetov vedeniya i polnomochiy mezhdu organami gosudarstvennoy vlasti Rossiyskoy Federatsii i organami gosudarstvennoy vlasti Murmanskoy oblasti.*

[36] Author's interview with Deputy Chair of Murmansk Oblast Duma, Igor Lebedev, and Deputy Governor Igor Chernychenko, Murmansk, 6 September 1999.

[37] Arkhangelsk began drafting an agreement, but negotiations seem to have stalled and the conclusion of such an agreement under the present regime seems unlikely. See Chapter 2 by Brynjulf Risnes for a more optimistic view on this issue.

[38] According to the Ministry of Justice, 2,400 of the approximately 50,000 normative acts that the Ministry had obtained from the federal subjects since 1995 were incompatible with federal legislation and the Constitution (*Rossiyskiy regionalnyy byulleten*, 14 February 2000).

[39] *Izvestiya*, 4 November 1997.
[40] *EWI Russian Regional Report*, 4 November 1997.
[41] *Jamestown Monitor*, 14 March 1997.
[42] *Centre for Russian Studies Database*, 10 September 1998.
[43] *ibid.*, 13 March 1997.
[44] *Jamestown Monitor*, 30 June 1997.
[45] *ibid.*, 4 September 1998.
[46] *Rossiyskiy regionalnyy byulleten*, 27 December 1999.
[47] Katanandov had replaced Viktor Stepanov as Karelian Prime Minister after the May 1998 elections.
[48] *Rossiyskiy regionalnyy byulleten*, 18 October 1999.
[49] The four northwestern federal subjects are members of the Northwestern Association, which also includes Komi, Vologda, Kirov, Leningrad, St Petersburg, Pskov and Kaliningrad.
[50] *Centre for Russian Studies Database*, 14 December 1999.
[51] *RFE/RL Newsline*, 13 January 2000.
[52] *ibid.*, 10 June 2000.
[53] *EWI Russian Regional Report*, 17 May 2000.
[54] According to a law adopted in June 1999 (*Rossiyskaya gazeta*, 30 June 1999), all of the existing agreements must be brought in compliance with the Russian Constitution by 2002 (see Chapter 2 by Brynjulf Risnes).
[55] Gennadiy Seleznyov lost to Boris Gromov in the Moscow Oblast gubernatorial elections in January 2000, and Deputy Prime Minister Valentina Matvienko had to withdraw from the St Petersburg gubernatorial elections in May.
[56] In the case of the northwestern regions, however, the co-operation within the Barents Euro-Arctic Region to a certain extent stimulated the growth of transregional co-operation (see Gorter-Grønvik, 1998).

4 Russian Regions in Transition: Centralisation through Decentralisation?

PER BOTOLF MAURSETH

Transition from a centrally planned to a market economy implies – by definition – a massive decentralisation of economic decision making. In the Soviet Union, one result of central planning was geographical decentralisation of economic activity to a large set of mono-industrial towns. For Russian regions in transition, an important question is whether centripetal market forces may alter the pre-existing industrial location. This chapter addresses regional economic development in Russia in general and the situation in Murmansk and Arkhangelsk Oblasts in particular.

The macroeconomic development in Russia conceals large regional differences and dramatic changes in internal relationships. Some authors have even questioned whether Russia can be regarded as one country in economic terms (Van Selm, 1998, pp. 617-618). During the Soviet period, economic planning – not market mechanisms – determined industrial location. In deciding where to locate industrial production and therefore hundreds of towns and millions of people, both economic and political motives influenced decision makers. In the Soviet Union, relative transport prices were lower than in market economies and planners paid less attention to transport efficiency. The result was a very transport-intensive economy that has become an important challenge for post-Soviet Russia. In market economies, transportation costs constitute an important determinant of industrial location, together with access to markets and raw materials. The imbalance between present industrial location and market forces may result in larger regional economic differences in Russia as well as considerable migration in the future.

The rest of this chapter is organised as follows: The following section reviews some stylised conclusions from theories of regional development in market economies. These are contrasted with industrial location in the Soviet economy. Thereafter, the macroeconomic development in post-Soviet Russia is shortly discussed. This serves as a background for the discussion of the general regional development in the subsequent section. The description of the macroeconomic development and the regional dynamics shed light on recent development in Murmansk and Arkhangelsk Oblasts, to be discussed thereafter.

Regional Economics and Economic Geography

It is a striking fact about spatial distribution of economic activity that it seems to cluster together instead of being scattered around. Some regions become centres of economic activity while others remain sparsely populated with little industrial production.

The traditional way of explaining regional economic specialisation is the theory of comparative advantage. Firms will tend to choose locations for their production where costs are smallest. Costs will be smallest in regions that have a comparative advantage for these firms' production. Thus, regions' comparative advantages predict their economic specialisation.[1]

The theory of comparative advantage does explain why regions and countries specialise in production of some goods and exchange these goods for other goods. Increasing returns to scale is another possible source of trade between regions and countries that can explain such intra-industry trade. When there are increasing returns in production, it is profitable to concentrate production of one good at a single production site. Increasing returns imply – by definition – lower unit costs in large-scale production. Thus, if there are increasing returns, total production and therefore consumption, may be higher if a region specialises in production of one good and buys other goods from other regions. This applies even if there are no comparative advantages between regions.[2]

In the case of increasing returns, market access becomes an important determinant of industrial location. For a firm to choose to locate to a small region, i.e. a small market, this region would have to have a cost advantage as compared to the larger one. One such cost advantage could be lower wage costs. Regions within a country usually have a common labour market, however. Thus, workers would tend to migrate to wherever wages are high instead of production being located where wages are low. Other types of cost advantages are necessary for firms to choose to establish themselves in smaller regions. Then we are back to the story of comparative advantages. In a market economy, therefore, production of goods that are subject to increasing returns will tend to be established nearby large markets. Production in smaller regions may be determined by comparative advantages.

Since population and therefore migration determines market size, it raises the question: How many and what regions become large and, hence, the host-region of industry that is subject to increasing returns? In simple formal models, the answer to the first part of the question depends on the degree of increasing returns and the importance of transportation costs. The answer to the second part of the question is far more intriguing. The answer seems to be that coincidences and history matter. If one region happens to get large in the first place, it will be an attractive production site for more industries and therefore stay large. If one region is small in the first place, it will be unattractive and therefore stay small. To change a pre-existing geographical pattern of production, radical changes in an economy may be necessary. One such radical change may be an increase in transportation costs. In that case, it may become profitable to establish a new production plant for some goods to serve distant markets. A decrease in transportation costs may have the opposite effect.

In the above discussion of comparative advantages, transportation costs were disregarded. Transportation costs limit the ability to exploit comparative advantages and reductions of transportation costs induce further specialisation. In the case of increasing returns, transportation costs determine what regions become industrial centres and what regions become hinterlands. Changes in transportation costs may therefore have ambiguous effects on regional prosperity. Reduced transportation costs favour the concentration of the production of goods that are subject to increasing returns. For the location of such production, industrial centres may profit while peripheral regions may lose. Reduction in transportation costs will be to the benefit of regions that have specialised their production according to comparative advantage, however.

The theoretical discussion does not describe economic dynamics. What determines economic development in the long run? Will economic processes result in increasing differences between regions or will there be convergence? Interestingly, the answer to these questions also depends on whether there are increasing returns or not. Most theories of economic growth focus on the accumulation of (physical and human) capital. Investments today yield increased production capacity tomorrow. Traditional theories of economic growth assumed decreasing returns to individual factors of production. In that case, capital-rich regions would experience lower returns to investments than regions that are poor in capital. In a country with free capital movements, therefore, capital would flow to the poorest regions. As time passes by, the marginal productivity of capital was expected to decrease for all regions. To counteract decreasing returns to capital, technological progress is necessary. Thus, regional growth is regarded as being dependent on technological change. If technological progress occurs independently of capital accumulation, it will not change the relative position of rich versus poor regions and economic growth will be characterised by convergence. New theories of economic growth, however, argue that technological progress may occur as a result of investments. If this is the case, regional economic development may well result in divergence. The reason is that some regions may be lucky and get into a benign circle in which technological change breeds investments that in turn breeds new innovations. Other regions may become caught in a low-growth trap without investments and technological change.[3]

In the presence of so-called externalities, in which firms learn from other firms within the same location, human capital accumulation may depend on the size of regions. Thus, tendencies to decreasing returns on capital accumulation may be counteracted by agglomeration effects. Also for this reason, regional economic development may be characterised by divergence.

Regions in the USSR

The Soviet Union had extensive resources of oil, gas and coal. Since it limited its integration into the world economy, these resources were unusually lowly priced. Energy was not a scarce resource for Soviet economic planners. Energy and energy-intensive products like transportation were therefore used more intensively than in other countries. Even when transportation costs were taken into account, the lower prices of transport caused resource wastage compared to the optimal situation in an economy with world market prices.

The result was that the Soviet Union became one of the most transport intensive economies in the world. Figure 4.1 shows transport tonne-kilometres per unit of GDP (Gross Domestic Product) in the Soviet Union and some other countries. The figure reveals that the Soviet Union was extreme by all standards.

Figure 4.1 Transport, tonne-kilometres, per unit of GDP, 1988

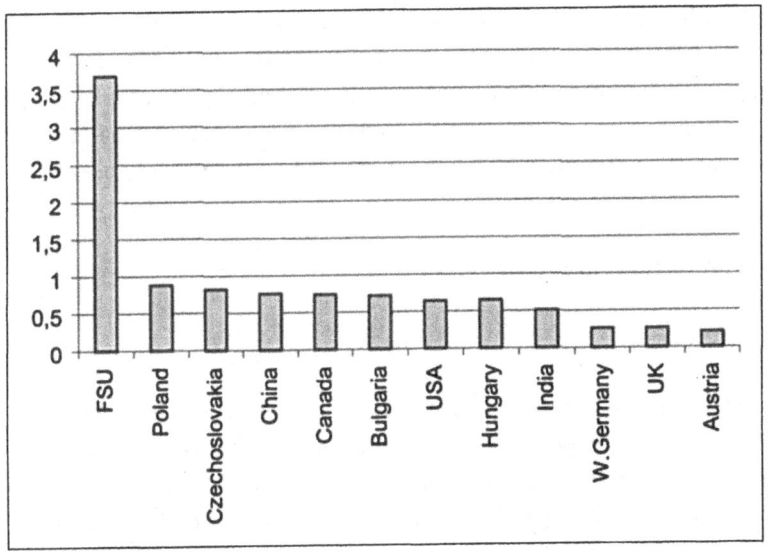

Source: Holt (1993).

It seems that the Soviet Union aggravated all factors that increase transport-intensity in other economies. Formerly planned economies range high in the figure. So does Canada, which is also a large country with a harsh climate. The combination of size, climate and economic system seemed to produce the most extreme result in the case of the Soviet Union. Besides the extreme transport intensity, Soviet industrial location also had other peculiarities as compared to western market economies. Industrial location in the Soviet Union was characterised by very large combines of production facilities concentrated in towns without other forms of economic activity. This was partly a result of subsidised transportation. As explained above, for production that is subject to increasing returns, low transportation costs constitute a centripetal force in the economy. Since Soviet planners did not face real prices for transport, it seemed effective to concentrate all production in one plant. The typical Soviet industrial town is therefore one that is highly specialised in large-scale production of one, or a very few, industrial products. As will become clear, this is a major challenge for post-Soviet Russia when transportation costs are increasing and relative prices on goods and raw materials change dramatically towards world market prices.

The large differences in industrial structure in the Soviet Union produced differences in standards of living across the union, although they were smaller than between market economies with similar differences in economic structure. A regional breakdown for the RSFSR is not available, but in 1989 average monthly salaries in the richest Soviet republic, Estonia, were 112 per cent of the Soviet average while average salaries in the poorest republic, Azerbaijan, were 74 per cent of the Soviet average.[4]

Recent Macroeconomic Development

Economic Crisis

This section gives a crude overview of the recent economic development in Russia and of major policy reforms in the transition to a market economy. Figure 4.2 reveals the dynamics in Russian GDP[5] and industrial production from 1980 to 1999. The figure indicates a dramatic development. Real GDP declined by 44 per cent in the period while industrial production more than halved. After the break-up of the Soviet Union, Russia has become a poor country.

The figure indicates that the decrease in industrial production may have decelerated after 1993. In 1997, there was modest growth in the Russian economy, with GDP growing at 0.8 per cent and industrial production at 2 per cent. In 1998, the contraction continued with a decrease in GDP of 4.6 per cent and 5.2 per cent in industrial output. As will be commented on below, there was growth in the Russian economy in 1999 (and also in the first half of 2000).

Figure 4.2 seems to indicate a deceleration of GDP contraction in Russia, but no structural break in the development the last two years. This however, may be misleading. After the rouble-crisis in August 1998, Russia changed its exchange rate regime, essentially from a fixed exchange rate to a floating one (see below).

Figure 4.2 Real GDP and industrial production 1980-99, 1989 = 100

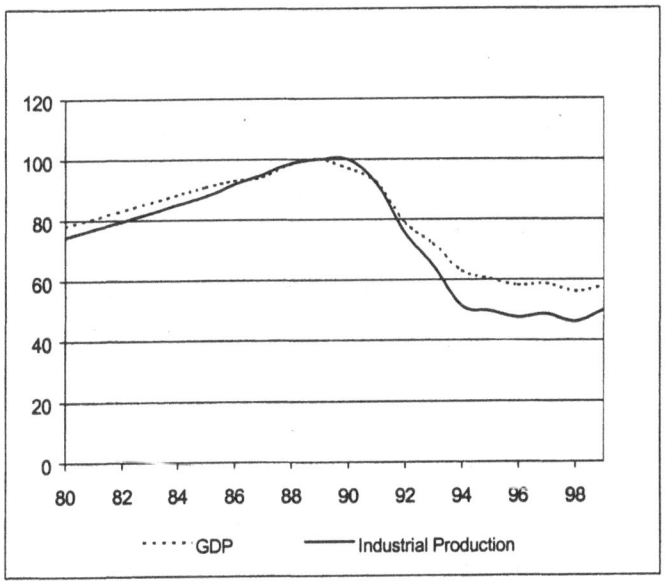

Source: United Nations (1999) and *Russian Economic Trends, Monthly Update,* July 2000.

The 1998 devaluation was regarded as a major defeat for Russian stabilisation policy. The reason was that a tight monetary policy in order to keep the rouble within the predetermined 'rouble-corridor' was regarded as an essential ingredient in deflating the economy. This had been achieved since 1995, and economic growth from 1997 was regarded as a deserved result of monetary stabilisation. Monthly inflation (Consumer Price Index (CPI)) in Russia is graphed in Figure 4.3.

Figure 4.3 Change in CPI from same period the year before

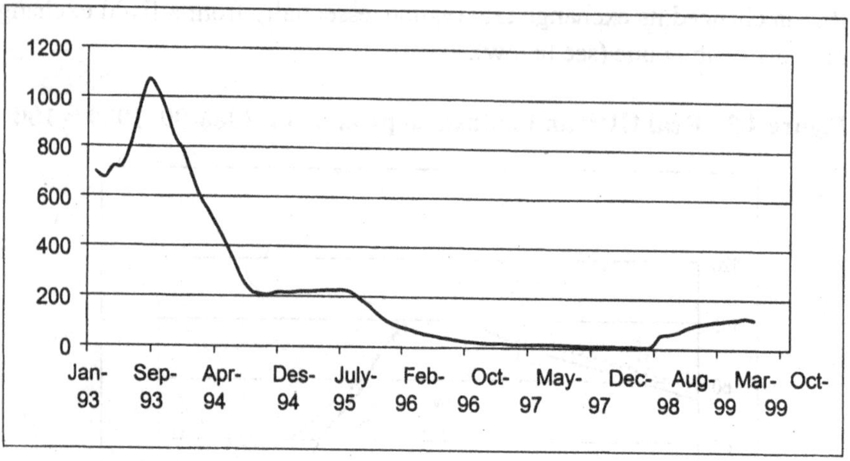

[Graph showing CPI change from Jan-93 to Oct-99, peaking around 1000+ in Sep-93, declining sharply through 1994-1995, flattening near 0 through 1996-1998, with a slight rise after Aug-98.]

Source: EcoWin (1999).

Economic Reforms

During the period of severe economic crisis since the dissolution of the Soviet Union, the Russian economy has undergone radical economic reforms. The main reform elements have been:[6]

- *Price liberalisation.* In 1992, most prices were set free and enterprises were allowed to set prices according to their own will. Only some prices, mainly transport, energy and some consumer prices, were still regulated. This was a shock therapy for the economy and immediately resulted in very high inflation (see Figure 4.3).
- *Trade liberalisation.* Trade liberalisation had started already during the last years of the Soviet period. From 1992 onwards, regulations on imports were first lifted and thereafter, as domestic prices on raw materials increased, export regulations and tariffs were reduced.
- *Privatisation.* Since 1992, Russia has accomplished the largest privatisation programme ever. As of April 1995, three-quarters of Russian industry were privately owned. This was achieved through voucher privatisation in which the workers and managers in state owned firms amongst other options could acquire up to 51 per cent

of the shares in the companies. After 1995, privatisation has continued at a slower pace through sales of shares, mainly to domestic banks.
- *Tax reform.* The Soviet economy did not have a tax collection system in the usual sense. In order to avoid financial collapse, a tax system was hastily introduced in 1991 and 1992. Over time, the Russian tax system got increasingly complex with a large number of taxes and opportunities for negotiations and tax evasion. This applied both to firms and persons and to the relations between the federation and the federal subjects.
- *Legislation.* Since 1992, Russia has adopted a large number of market-oriented laws to facilitate the introduction of a market economy. They apply to competition, bankruptcy, stock markets, financial regulation, privatisation, international trade and inward foreign direct investments.[7] The problem in Russia has not been a lack of laws, but the widespread disregard of them.

After ten years of reform, Russia has now achieved more or less consistent legislation for a market economy. Pending reforms (as of July 2000) concern private property of land and foreign participation in the exploitation of natural resources. In the spring of 2000, tax collection became more effective and stringent. Among the most urgent challenges is the reduction of organised crime, corruption and opportunistic exploitation of the existing legal framework. Even if Russian economic reform has been far less successful than was expected in 1992, it has transformed the economy from a centrally planned one to a decentralised one. Most economic decisions are now made by consumers, workers, firms, farmers and local and regional authorities instead of the central planning authorities as they were before.[8]

The August 1998 Devaluation – One Step Back and Two Forwards?

After the devaluation in August 1998, the rouble depreciated 80 per cent in seven weeks. It was feared that the result would be renewed hyperinflation, accelerated economic contraction and continued economic crisis for years to come. The devaluation was a result of investors' lack of confidence in the Russian government. Specifically, it was very large capital outflow in the weeks before the devaluation that forced the Central Bank to devaluate.[9]

One year after the rouble crisis, surprised observers asked themselves, perhaps for the first time since the break-up of the Soviet Union: 'What went right?' In fact, none of the grim predictions turned out to be true: [10]

- The rouble has stabilised at a floating level of about RUR 25-30 to the US Dollar. From the end of August 1998 to April 1999, the rouble depreciated about 25 per cent, but from April to August 1999, the rouble in fact appreciated modestly. The first months of 2000, the rouble was stable.
- Inflation did not accelerate. The consumer prices adjusted fully to the devaluation, and from August 1998 to August 1999 the CPI increased by 120 per cent. This was a once and for all increase, however, and it has not triggered hyperinflation. One of the reasons for this was that wages and pensions only partially adjusted to increasing prices. Real wages decreased by 36 per cent from the July 1998 level to the same month in 1999. Monthly nominal pensions increased modestly by ten per cent in the period.
- The Russian trade balance improved markedly during 1999. For the first half of 1999, this was mainly a result of decreased imports since also exports decreased. In the second half of 1999, exports increased markedly.
- Most important is probably the fact that the devaluation and the following depreciation have resulted in economic growth. In 1999, Russian GDP increased by 3.2 per cent.

Thus, it seems that the devaluation of the rouble was a lucky accident. It resulted in a needed adjustment of the currency and it did not – because of disciplined monetary policy and only partial adjustment of wages and pensions – destabilise the economy. The Russian economy is still in serious crisis, but in 1999 and the first half of the year 2000 there were several important signs of improvement.

One very important improvement in the Russian economy in 1999 was a modest re-monetisation of the economy. Since the beginning of the transition, Russia has witnessed steady growth in payments arrears. Non-payments have been widespread between firms, from firms to its employees, from the state to its employees and from firms to the state (Ivanova and Wyplosz, 1999). In August 1999, aggregate wage arrears had fallen to the level of March 1996, before the start of intensive growth in such arrears. Wage arrears continued to fall during 1999.

As will be argued below, the devaluation of the rouble and the subsequent export-led growth have important implications for regional development. Since Russian regions differ in economic structure, the effects of macroeconomic shocks differ.

Regional Development

As noted above, there were large differences between the Soviet Republics during the Soviet period. In this section, we discuss regional development in Russia after the dissolution of the Soviet Union. Have economic differences increased or decreased with the introduction of a decentralised economy? What are the policy responses to recent changes? Which regions are winners and which are losers in the transition to a market economy? Is it possible to develop a taxonomy of different types of Russian regions, or is the pattern one of 89 distinct regions with little in common?

Different data sets on regional economic development are used. Coherent data on the economic development in Russia are hardly available. There are several reasons for this. First, the statistical authorities in Russia (Goskomstat) have been in transformation since the break-up of the Soviet Union. In the Soviet period, not all data were public and some were used for propagandist purposes. Furthermore, the national accounting system has changed from the use of Net Material Output to the Western system of national accounts. Second, Goskomstat has been provided with little resources to facilitate these changes. Third, Russia has undergone dramatic events the last ten years which make statistics less reliable. The data used in this section are from different sources that are described in the appendix to this chapter. All data are from published sources.

Regional Distribution of Per Capita Income

As discussed above, theories of regional economic development in market economies give varying predictions of the evolution of income differences between regions and countries. These are long run theories, however. They may predict future development, but they cannot explain the flux in Russian regions since the break-up of the Soviet Union.

Figures 4.4 and 4.5 illustrate two different aspects of the dynamics of income distribution among Russian regions. The first figure graphs the relative real income in 78 Russian regions in 1995 and in 1997. The data are from Bylov (1998). Nominal incomes in both years are weighted by a price index for each region. The price index used is the official subsistence level in each region. The resulting numbers thus give an impression of real income in the Russian regions. These figures are then divided by the Russian average. The resulting figures are relative real income for each region. The figure indicates that there is a neat correlation between incomes in the two years. In particular, the figure illustrates that Moscow has forged ahead of the Russian average and has become a relatively rich city. Moscow had a nominal per capita income in 1997 at 4.5 times the Russian average and a real income of about 3.5 times the Russian average.

Figure 4.4   Correlation between income in 1995 and 1997

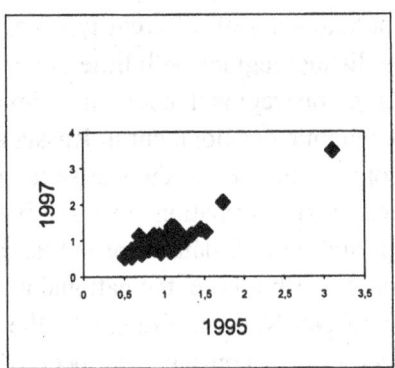

Figure 4.5 repudiates the impression given in the Figure 4.4. This latter figure is constructed by assigning each region their rank (from zero to 50) as compared to other regions. The main effect of this is to compress the visual impression of the extreme observations. Moscow ranks as number 50 and its immediate follower is Tyumen, while the real difference between Moscow and other Russian regions are revealed in Figure 4.4. Figure 4.5 gives a picture of noisy regional development. There is a positive correlation between ranking in 1995 and in 1997, but not a very clear one. Thus, according to these data, Russian regional development is not characterised by a steady ranking of regions. Instead, there is considerable leap-

frogging. Some regions lagged behind while others forged ahead in the short period from 1995 to 1997.[11]

Figure 4.5 Ranking of regions in 1995 and 1997

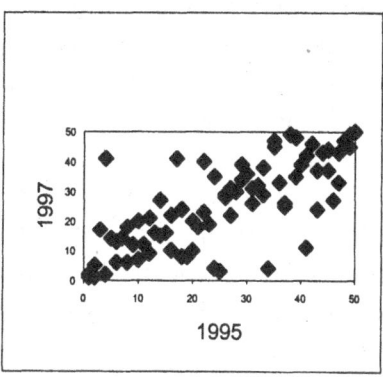

The two figures above do not give much information about whether economic differences between Russian regions are increasing or not. They indicate a neat correlation between real income per capita in 1995 and in 1997, but only a weak correlation in each region's ranking compared to other regions. To evaluate the dynamics of regional income distribution, another data set, stretching from 1993 to 1995, was used together with the data set used to construct Figures 4.4 and 4.5.[12] The two data sets are probably not completely comparable. The latter contains data on nominal income in 1993, 1994 and 1995, and price indices for 19 consumables for 1995. By constructing relative real incomes in the same matter as described above, a time series of five years is obtained (1993, 1994, 1995, 1996, 1997).[13] In this chapter, the first data set (from 1995-97) is used most frequently since it is probably the most reliable one. In Figure 4.6 below, however, we make use of the 1993 data from the latter data set together with the 1995 and the 1997 data from the first data set presented. The constructed observational unit used in Figure 4.6 is the logarithm of each region's real income relative to the Russian average. The purpose of this data construction is to adjust for different averages (between the two data sets) and possibly other disturbances. Figure 4.6 consists of so-called Kernel density estimates of the distribution for the three years.[14]

To the extent that the data reveal the real distribution of income in Russian regions, the figure indicates both typical patterns of income distribution and peculiar Russian facets: As in other countries, the distribution is seemingly (log) normal. This finding applies also for regions in Western Europe and for other large countries.[15] Particular for Russia, however, is the fact that the distribution *widens* over time. The tail gets thicker while the middle range is reduced (the very long right hand tail is due to Moscow's position as the stable number one in terms of income per capita). Furthermore, the figure indicates that the distribution is getting more skewed: There is an emerging peak for regions that are somewhat richer than the average while the distribution loses regions marginally poorer than average. If this is a long-run trend, it indicates that Russia may end up with a cluster of relatively rich regions and a more uniform distribution of poorer regions. This may have both political and economical consequences since it indicates that the interest of the median region may deviate from the left-hand side of the distributions (the poorest regions).

The standard deviation of the distribution of (log) relative incomes confirms the impression of increased differences. The standard deviation in 1993 was 0.22, in 1995 it was 0.26, in 1996 it was 0.28, and in 1997 it was 0.27. Thus, differences increased from 1993 onwards and have stabilised at a higher level in recent years. Hanson (2000) reports that regional differences increased in 1998 but decreased in the first half of 1999.

The Political Response: Fiscal Federalism

What is the political answer to the development outlined in the above subsection? In this subsection, some aspects of the federal budgetary system, including the federal tax system and transfers to the regions, are discussed.

The Soviet Union was formally a federation in the sense that the Soviet republics, and also the different parts of the Russian Socialist Federal Soviet Republic (RSFSR), had some legal autonomy. In reality, the Soviet regime was highly hierarchical and characterised by centralised decision making. Federalism, in the sense of a formal power sharing between the centre and the regions that reflects real decentralisation of power, is a post-Soviet phenomenon in Russia. There are three main levels of government in Russia: Federal government, regional government (republics, oblasts, krays) and local government (rayons and towns). The political development of Russian federalism has been analysed at length elsewhere (e.g. in Blakkisrud (1997); Hønneland (1999); and Chapter 3 in this book, by Helge Blakkisrud). Here, the discussion focuses on economic aspects.

Figure 4.6 Kernel estimates of the regional distribution of income per capita

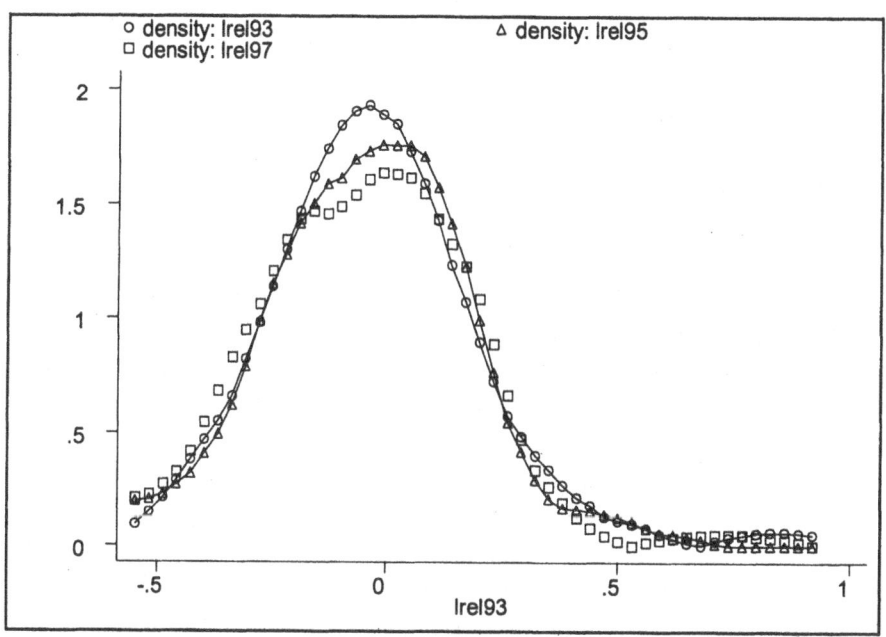

Source: Bylov (1998) and Centre of Economic Analysis (1995a) and (1995b).

In well-functioning market economies, fiscal federalism is regarded as a Pareto-improving device that helps adjust public services and taxes to local preferences. Ideally, the balance of power between local and central authorities should reflect the distinction between common and local needs. Central authorities should ideally be responsible for national public goods, while local authorities should take care of the local ones. In addition, federal authorities should be responsible for macroeconomic stabilisation and inter-regional distribution. Public revenue should be generated and shared between vertical levels of authorities according to predetermined, fixed and transparent rules. The optimal local autonomy over taxes is disputed, but in the literature there seems to be agreement that there should be some local independence in revenue generation. Additional local revenues should not be taxed away by higher levels of government. Furthermore, for reasons of efficiency, local taxes should be imposed on immobile tax bases, while tax rates on mobile tax bases should be equalised across the federation.[16]

To a certain degree, one can argue that the Russian federalism reflects the above principles. Systems of fiscal federalism are based on three main aspects. The first is the division of responsibilities between federal, regional and local responsibilities. The second is the income generating system, mainly the tax system. The third are transfers between the federal and the regional authorities.

Responsibilities

The division of responsibilities between levels of government in Russia partly reflects principles of fiscal federalism. Sub-federal governments are responsible for covering expenditures such as health, primary education and housing subsidies.[17] The federal government is responsible for macro economic stabilisation, inter-regional distribution and the provision of national public goods, such as defence. This applies to the most important sectors, although different levels of authority share responsibility in some areas (OECD, 2000). Earlier in the transition period, there were some signs of fiscal disintegration. Some regional authorities started to provide goods that were clearly federal responsibilities, like issuing 'surrogate money' (e.g. Nizhniy Novgorod, Bashkortostan and, in particular, Sverdlovsk). Other regions have raised export or import tariffs on their own. Even more dramatically, there have been attempts at limiting free trade between regions *within* the Federation (Van Selm, 1998). However, recent trends indicate that such regional attempts are getting less, not more, widespread. Some regions – mainly republics like Tatarstan, Bashkortostan and Sakha – have obtained particularly generous power-sharing agreements with the federal government that decentralise numerous rights and responsibilities that are otherwise federal. In the spring of 2000, it seemed that the Putin administration was seeking to limit the autonomy obtained by Tatarstan and Bashkortostan. Recently, bilateral power-sharing agreements between regions and the federal authorities have become common, but most of them are of limited importance (OECD, 1997). For Murmansk Oblast, instance, the power-sharing agreement is regarded as being too diffuse to have any crucial implications for local policy making (see also Chapter 2 by Brynjulf Risnes and Chapter 3 by Helge Blakkisrud).[18] Several regions have been appointed *Special Economic Zones*. Most such zones are believed not to function at all (OECD, 1997). The legislative status of the different economic zones is unclear. For most practical purposes, therefore, the division of responsibilities between federal, regional and local authorities seems to be in accordance with principles of economic federalism. Furthermore, it does not seem that regional independence efforts have seriously threatened the federalist division of responsibilities in Russia in recent years (with the exception of the events in Chechnya).

Taxes

Revenue-generating mechanisms such as taxes and the property rights to natural resources, however, Russia has only gradually adjusted to principles of economic federalism. The legal devices for fiscal federalism in Russia are the 1992 Federal Treaty, the 1993 Constitution, bilateral agreements between federation subjects and the federal authorities, the tax system and the annual federal budgets. Because of the many different legal regulations in federal-regional relations, of which some are internally inconsistent (Hønneland, 1999), and because of the many bilateral treaties between individual federal subjects and the Federation, fiscal federalism on the revenue side is far from transparent and rule based.

The Russian tax system has undergone dramatic changes in recent years. In the early years of the transition period, a large number of new taxes were introduced. This was partly a response to the budgetary deficit after Russian firms were privatised. Previously, the main source of state income was profits from state-owned companies. After privatisation, this source dried up. In addition, the economic crisis eroded the tax base of the firms. The many taxes and the increasingly complicated tax system became an important hindrance to investments and the establishment of new firms. The political response was for a long time not a major tax reform, but overloading the system with tax exemptions, special treatment and privileges for special groups. From the start of transition to 1998, the Russian tax system was very inefficient and constituted a major hindrance to economic recovery. In 1998, a revised tax system was approved which is more transparent and much less complicated than the previous system.

The new tax system consists of local, regional and federal taxes. It is therefore an important ingredient in transforming Russian federalism into a more transparent and rule-based system. For most taxes, tax rates are predetermined and tax receipts are shared between local, regional and federal authorities according to law. The most important taxes are the VAT (of which 85 per cent is transferred to the federal budget), corporate profit tax (of which 81 per cent is transferred to the federal budget) and the personal income tax (of which 3 per cent is transferred to the federal budget). For the federal budget, the main additional taxes are foreign trade taxes and excises. The total tax burden in Russia is not particularly heavy by international standards. For 2000, the total tax receipts are expected to constitute 12.9 per cent of GDP. The VAT rate is proposed at 20 per cent in 2000 and the tax rate on profits at 30 per cent. The new system implies a 13 per cent flat tax on personal income.[19] Even if the new tax system seems to be an important step towards a simpler, more transparent and fair tax system, its details are yet to be settled.

Even though rules for public income generation and sharing have become clear and transparent, there are claims that local and regional income independence is very limited. The reason is that most regional and local taxes are set through federally determined maximum rates.

Transfers

Transfers from federal authorities to the regions is the third aspect of fiscal federalism. Federal support to the regions constitutes some 10-12 per cent of the total federal budget. One very important part of federal transfers to the regions is the 'Federal Fund for Financial Support of the Regions'. This fund was set up in 1994 in order to establish a more coherent framework to channel resources to the most needy regions. The fund is partly financed through VAT receipts. In 1997, this fund made up 75 per cent of total federal support to the regions. A. McAuley (1997) analyses the distribution of total net federal transfers to the regions based on data from 1995. He finds that net transfers reflect a high concern for equity and social needs since more support is transferred to regions that are poorer than the average compared to other regions. He also finds that this applies to the retention of tax receipts. Another explanatory variable for transfers to the regions is the status of the federal subjects. The ethnically defined regions are, almost without exception, net receivers of federal support, according to McAuley. Previous studies of federal support to Russian regions have revealed that in the immediate years after the dissolution of the Soviet Union, there was little evidence that redistribution was a concern for Russian policy makers. Thus, McAuley argues that transfers from the fund for support to the regions are governed by need in the regions rather than other motives.

Figure 4.7 illustrates the findings of McAuley. The figure graphs the relationship between the share of transfers from the federal regional support fund in the actual regional budget revenues in 1997 (vertical axis) and the log of relative real net income per capita in 1997. Income figures are the logarithms of real income *relative to the Russian average*, so figures below zero are for regions having a real income less than the average and figures above zero are for real incomes above the average. The figure seems to support the finding that regional redistribution is indeed a concern for transfers from the fund. The two positive outliers in the figure are Moscow (with a real income of 347 per cent of the Russian average and no support from the fund) and oil-producing Tyumen (with a real income twice the Russian average but with support from the fund making up about ten per cent of the budget revenues).[20]

Figure 4.7 Share of regional support fund in regional budget 1997

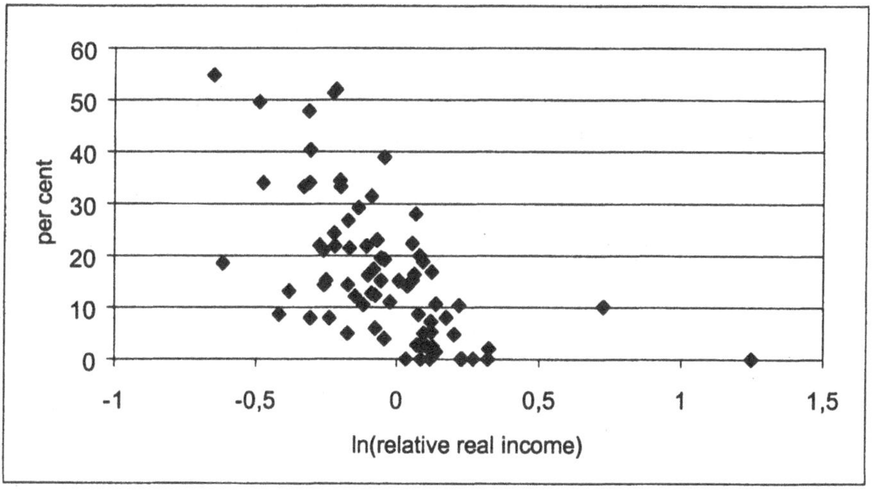

Source: Tabata (1998) and Bylov (1998).

It should be underlined that in addition to taxes and transfers, federal policies influence regional distribution through the localisation of federal activity. Furthermore, support from the funds constitutes a small part of

Russian GDP – ranging between one and two per cent. Hanson *et al.* (2000) analyse a broader concept of transfers between regions that is constituted of tax revenue remitted from the regions to the Federation less transfers from the federal budget to the regions. Also for this measure, transfers are significantly influenced by distribution motives (in the sense that 'rich' regions contribute more to the federal budget than do poorer regions).

Russian Regions: the Soviet Heritage

So far, there is only limited knowledge about the performance of Russian regions in the aftermath of the dissolution of the Soviet Union. Kirkow (1997b) summarises existing results in three main points:

- *History matters*. The location and specialisation of industrial production determines, to a large extent, the economic fortune of Russian regions.

- *The social context matters*. It seems to be important whether a region has an elitist political leadership or whether there is a network of civic engagement, co-operation and free flow of information.

- *The core-periphery relations matter*. Centre-periphery relations are important both between the regions and the federal centre, and also *within* the regions. Thus, both the location of a region and the degree of centralisation within the region matter for its economic development.

The inherited economic specialisation and structure of a region is found to be of importance in several studies. OECD (1995) discerns two types of Russian regions: *introvert* and *extrovert*. Introvert regions include provinces dominated by the military-industrial complex (mainly located in central European Russia and the Urals) and agro-industrial regions specialised in food production. Extrovert regions include resource-rich regions in sparsely populated northern areas and Siberia, the main commercial centres in Russia (Moscow, St Petersburg) and major points of entry into the Federation, for example the main ports. According to the OECD (1997), this taxonomy reflects both the economic potentials of the regions as well as their likely attitude towards economic reforms.

The extrovert regions are regions that typically have a potential for economic growth as a result of market-oriented reforms. Generally, Soviet industry was not internationally competitive, but Soviet production of raw materials was (Senik-Leygonie and Hughes, 1992). Russian exports have increasingly specialised in raw materials production, especially energy products like oil and gas.[21] Thus, regions specialised in raw material production have done better than average after the transition to a market economy started. OECD hypothesises that extrovert regions generally will favour economic reform as a consequence of their possible gain from it. Thus, such regions are more likely to have a liberal political leadership.

Introvert regions on the other hand, are regions that, at least in the short run, probably will experience severe problems. They are specialised in industries that are not competitive on international markets and are likely to be considerably downscaled in the Russian market economy. By use of input-output tables for the Soviet economy, Senik-Leygonie and Hughes (1992) found that for instance the Soviet food industry had large *negative* social rates of profit when factors of production were priced at international prices. Introvert regions are hypothesised to be more hostile towards radical economic reforms and in favour of a gradual and protectionist transition to a market economy.

It is important to emphasise, however, that the above taxonomy alone cannot explain the performance of Russian regions. There are relatively successful and unsuccessful regions of both types. Nizhniy Novgorod and Ulyanovsk are well known examples of an extrovert liberal region and an introvert protectionist region, respectively. For a while, they were both performing better than the average Russian region.

Econometric studies of the economic performance of Russian regions partially support the above classification. Sutherland and Hanson (1996) applied shift share analysis and found that growth and contraction in employment in 1993 were weakly correlated with industrial structure. Other significant explanatory factors were the regions' export performance (positive), the degree of dependence on military production (negative) and level of nominal wages (weakly negative). In a more eclectic study, Van Selm (1998, pp. 617-618) tests the hypothesis that both industrial structure and political regime influence economic performance in Russian regions. He finds clear evidence in favour of the former, but not of the latter, and he concludes that: 'Put very simply, regions with the right industries did better than regions with the wrong industries, but regions with the right policies did not do better than regions with the wrong policies.'

Econometric studies are dependent on available data on (preferably) all relevant explanatory variables for all regions. Several potentially relevant variables are lacking and some are unobservable. In most studies of Russian regional development, geographical data are lacking. Sachs (1997) presents evidence of the importance of geography for a sample of transition countries. He finds that geography is a major determinant of economic performance at the country level. Countries that are located near large Western European markets seem to do better than countries located further away from these markets.[22] Such geographical effects are probably also of importance in Russia. The mere size of Russia, being the largest country in the world, indicates that geography might be a very decisive factor for regional development. In the transition to a market economy, transport subsidies have been considerably reduced. Figure 4.8 below shows the development of real transportation costs in Russia. The graphed relationship is for the ratio between the producer price index for transportation and the composite producer price index. The graph demonstrates that transportation costs in the first years of transition increased more than the composite price index, but that this trend has been somewhat reversed in recent years. The overall impression from the figure is nevertheless that transportation has become considerably more expensive than it was during the Soviet period.

Figure 4.8   Real transportation costs

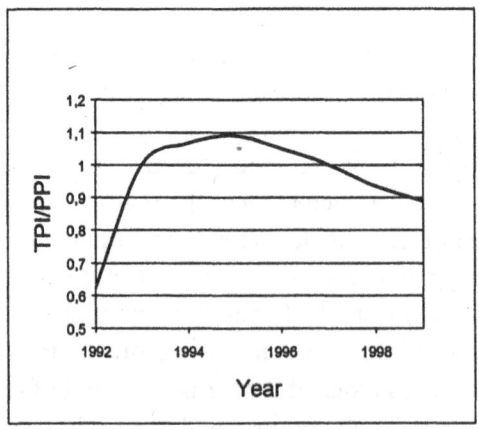

Source: *Russian Economic Trends*, No. 1, 1999.

In the theoretical discussion above, it was concluded that changes in transportation costs may have ambiguous effects on peripheral industrial production. Welfare may be reduced, but industrial production may increase or decrease as a consequence of increased transportation costs. In the Russian economy, this may be different. The reason is that the geographical distribution of economic activity was not a result of market mechanisms in the first place. Firstly, industrial location in the Soviet Union did not reflect concern for effective transportation. Secondly, industrial sites were very often enormous plants constructed to serve the whole Soviet market. Thus, the effects of increased transportation costs in Russia may be a combination of what models of economic geography imply and other effects. It is reasonable that increased transportation costs may give a potential for new production sites nearby large markets. When transportation costs increase, the profitability of peripheral industry will decrease and the profitability of central industry increase. Production in mono-industrial peripheral towns in Russia may therefore lose markets and become unprofitable. This is particularly probable since the mono-industrial towns are highly specialised. Local markets can therefore not sustain the local production, as would have been an option in the case of a more diverse industrial structure. For agricultural regions, self-sufficiency has become more common. This is not a viable strategy for mono-industrial towns. Thus, reductions in transport intensity of the Russian economy will more probably result in increased centralisation of industrial production rather than the opposite.

As indicated in the theoretical discussion above, migration may have a crucial impact on industrial development. Migration shapes regional market sizes. Russia is a single country with a common labour market, so mono-industrial towns may experience emigration when industrial production is downscaled. This will further erode prosperity in these towns. The population in a region constitutes its industry's home market. This applies particularly for supply industries to the local population. The possible link between economic performance and migration can be self-reinforcing: Emigration as a result of industrial decline further reduces the basis for industrial production by eroding the home market. Table 4.1 reports regression results on percentage growth in population and growth in income per capita in Russian regions. The source of the regional GDP data is the same as above. The source of the population data is Goskomstat (1999).[23] The table reveals a (weakly) significant positive relationship. Regions with a higher than average income per capita experience lower reductions in population than poorer regions.

If the reported results reflect migration as a result of changes in income, they should serve as a warning of potential dramatic changes in the Russian geography. Since economic performance in Russian regions differ dramatically, the resulting migration may lead to important changes in industrial location. Sutherland and Hanson (2000) analyse migration data directly. Their findings support the ones reported in Table 4.1. Outmigration from regions is influenced by, among other factors, real income and unemployment.

Table 4.1   Regression of change on population and change in income (heteroscedasticity consistent t-values in brackets)

Regression of change in population, 1998-99 $R^2 = 0.06$
Change in income per capita, 1995-97   0.94 (1.96)[a]
Constant   -0.36 (-5.80)[b]

[a] indicates significance at five per cent level.
[b] indicates significance at one per cent level.

Source: See text.

In summary, there seems to be a highly dynamic income distribution among Russian regions. In the crisis-ridden Russian economy, some regions are worse hit than others. Differences between income per capita increase. Previous research has revealed that the inherited industrial structure is one important explanatory factor for regional economic performance. In addition, geography and transportation costs probably play an important role. As migration data reveal, local demand in mono-industrial towns is being eroded. This can lead to a vicious downward spiral of emigration and reduced production in some regions.

A high degree of 'white noise' should be expected for Russian regions in transition. This reflects the fact that specific regional variables, that cannot be included in regression analyses, probably influence the economic performance of Russian regions. Also, the mechanisms that govern regional development in transition economies are weakly understood. As a complement to econometric studies, research on regional economic development in Russia also has to depend on case studies.

Murmansk and Arkhangelsk

This section describes the economic development of two oblasts in Northwestern Russia in light of the existing literature on regional economic performance in Russia. Murmansk and Arkhangelsk are both rich in resources and partly specialised in export industries. OECD (1997) classifies them both as typical extrovert regions. There are large differences between the two oblasts, however. Murmansk is a pure Soviet oblast. Before the Bolshevik revolution, the Kola Peninsula was scarcely populated and had no industrial production. During the Soviet period, Murmansk became an important centre for the Soviet fishing industry and the extraction of the rich mineral resources located there. In addition, Murmansk has a considerable military presence because of its ice-free harbours and geostrategic position. Murmansk ranks among the richest regions in Russia. As opposed to Murmansk, Arkhangelsk has a long pre-Soviet history. It was established in 1584 and was long an important commercial centre for trade between Russia and Western Europe (Kotilaine, 1999). The Arkhangelsk region was traditionally specialised in production of timber. During the Soviet period, a more diverse industrial structure was developed. Income per capita in Arkhangelsk is below the Russian average. (See Chapter 1 by Helge Blakkisrud and Geir Hønneland for a more detailed account of the history of the two oblasts.)

Industrial Structure in Murmansk

Figure 4.9 gives an impression of the long-term historical development in Murmansk and Arkhangelsk Oblasts since the establishment of the Soviet Union. The figure graphs the population in the two oblasts for various years since 1926. The figure reveals a dramatic growth in population in Murmansk over the period (the peak was in 1992). The Murmansk population in 1992 was 50 times as large as it was in 1926 (compared to an increase in the total Russian population in the same period of 60 per cent). This reflects an enormous industrial growth in this oblast during the period of central planning. The vast majority of the Murmansk population is urban: Only eight per cent of the population is situated in rural areas.

About one third of the working population in Murmansk Oblast works in industry. This share has become somewhat reduced in recent years. The share of employment by sector in 1991 and 1998 is described in Table 4.2.[24]

Figure 4.9 The population of Murmansk and Arkhangelsk Oblasts, 1926-99

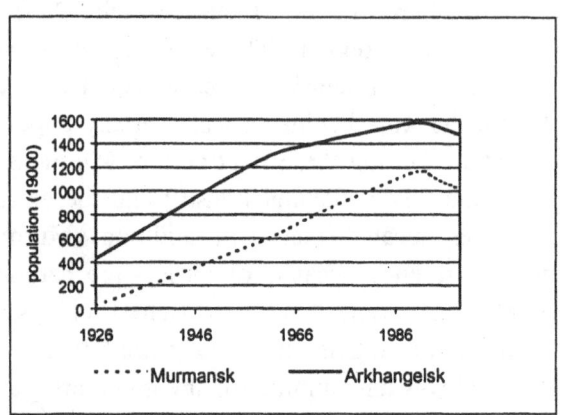

Source: Murmansk Regional Committee of State Statistics (1999a), Arkhangelsk Regional Committee of State Statistics (1998), Goskomstat (1999) and Maurseth (1997).

The table reveals two important characteristics of the Murmansk economy and its development in the transition to a market economy. Firstly, Murmansk was (and still is) a highly industrial area with a relatively high share of employment in industry. Secondly, the share of workers employed in industry has been significantly reduced in recent years and the corresponding share of services has increased, to almost two thirds of total employment in 1998. The decline in industrial employment is partly a consequence of the overall crisis in the Russian economy. It is, however, also a consequence of structural change in the economy. The Soviet economy was a highly industrial one and the Soviet Union had an extremely weak service sector as compared to western industrial countries at the same level of development. Thus, it is natural that decline in employment is larger in industry than in services.[25]

Table 4.2 Employment by sector in Murmansk Oblast, 1991 and 1998, per cent

Sector	1991	1998
Industry	33.6	27.2
Agriculture and forestry	2.3	1.8
Construction	15.5	4.7
Services	48.8	66.2

Source: Murmansk Regional Committee of State Statistics (1996) and (1999a).

Murmansk industry is highly specialised in a few branches. Figure 4.10 shows the composition of industrial production by value in 1997.

Figure 4.10 Structure of Murmansk Oblast industrial production, 1997

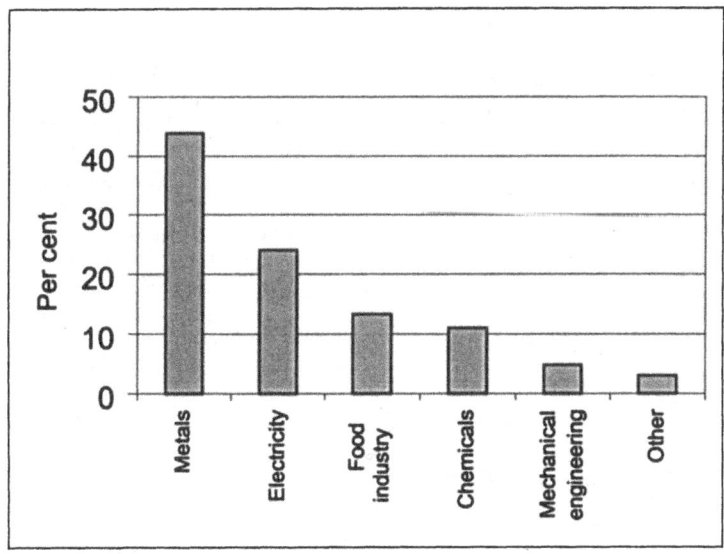

Source: Hønneland and Jørgensen (1999b).

The economic geography of Murmansk Oblast is typical of Soviet mono-industrial specialisation. Several large towns are solely dependent on a single or a very few companies within the same industrial branch. These mono-industrial towns are extremely vulnerable to changing economic conditions. When an industry is hit by price reductions or marketing problems, the economic foundation for these communities may become eroded. Table 4.3 demonstrates that Murmansk Oblast is indeed characterised by a high concentration of mono-industrial towns. The table shows the number of employees in the main company in several towns and the total population in each municipality. The table shows that the 'dependency rate', defined as the ratio of the number of employees in the largest company in each town to the number of inhabitants, is extremely high for cities in Murmansk, in fact more than 20 per cent in all the listed towns.[26] In Murmansk, there are also six so-called 'closed cities' built up as support facilities for the military sectors. (Hønneland and Jørgensen (1999b); see also Chapter 7 by Anne-Kristin Jørgensen.)

Table 4.3 Employment by main firm and population in some Murmansk towns

Town	Employment in main company	Population in municipality	Main product
Kovdor	5,000 + 2,500[a]	28,000	Iron-concentrate, apatite
Apatity	18,000	82,000	Apatite-concentrate
Olenegorsk	5,500	33,800	Iron-concentrate
Lovozero	4,000	19,000	Loparthite
Polyarnye Zori	6,000	18,000	Nuclear power
Monchegorsk	10,000	65,500	Nickel
Pechenga	8,500	20,000 + 22,000[b]	Nickel

[a]Two firms
[b]Population in Nikel and Zapolyarnyy

Source: Maurseth (1997).

Industrial Structure in Arkhangelsk

Arkhangelsk Oblast has a long pre-Soviet history. Thus, the industrial structure and the economic geography of Arkhangelsk are different from those in Murmansk. The population in Arkhangelsk over time is shown in Figure 4.9 above. The development is parallel to the one in Murmansk, except for the fact that Arkhangelsk had a population of more than 400,000 in 1926. The Arkhangelsk population is more scattered than the Murmansk one, with 25 per cent being situated in rural areas.

Arkhangelsk is as industrialised as Murmansk. One third of the working population was employed in industry in 1993. Arkhangelsk has a large forestry industry, and consequently a large proportion of employment, 8.8 per cent, is in agriculture, mainly in forestry.

Figure 4.11 shows that Arkhangelsk is extremely specialised in forestry-related industries (cutting, woodwork, pulp and paper). This made up nearly half of industrial production in 1994. Food industry (mainly fish products) and mechanical engineering are two other important industries.

Figure 4.11 Structure of Arkhangelsk Oblast industrial production, 1994

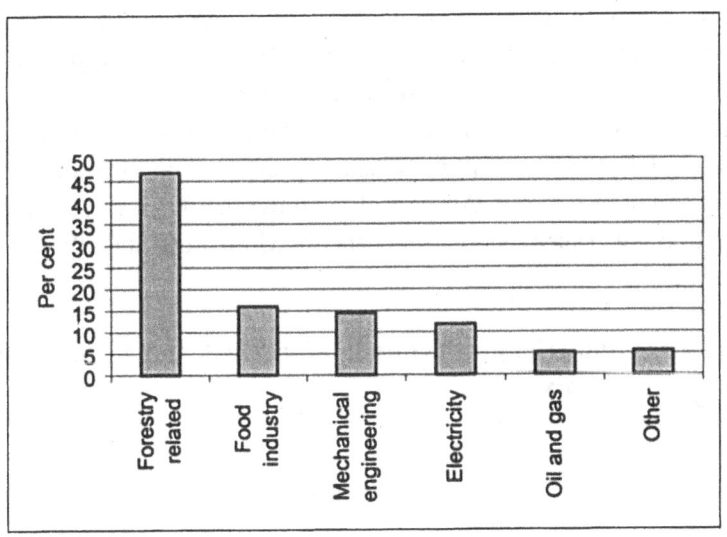

Source: Maurseth (1997).

The industrial specialisation of Arkhangelsk is one reason why its economic geography is different from that of Murmansk. The forestry-related industry is more scattered than the industry in Murmansk is. The rest of Arkhangelsk industry is also less specialised than industry in Murmansk is. Arkhangelsk has a large mechanical engineering industry connected to its shipbuilding yards in Severodvinsk (see Chapter 7 by Anne-Kristin Jørgensen). In recent years, there has been some optimism related to potential oil and gas extraction both onshore in Arkhangelsk and in the adjacent Republic of Komi and offshore in the Barents Sea (see Chapter 5 by Arild Moe). It is hoped that the shipbuilding yards in Severodvinsk, which in the Soviet period were highly militarised, will successfully restructure towards civilian production through supplies to oil extraction, in particular offshore in the Barents Sea.[27]

Industrial Decline: Murmansk and Arkhangelsk in the Transition to a Market Economy

Murmansk and Arkhangelsk are both hard hit by the crisis in the Russian economy. Figure 4.12 shows the development in industrial production in the two oblasts. The corresponding data for Russia as a whole is included for comparison. The figure shows that both Murmansk and Arkhangelsk have done better than the Russian average. Their industrial production has stabilised at a level somewhat higher than 60 per cent of the 1991 level as compared to 50 per cent for Russia as a whole. The figure, however, does not conceal the dramatic fall in industrial production in the transition period both in Murmansk and in Arkhangelsk. Between 1991 and 1998, industrial production decreased by 35 per cent in Murmansk and 39 per cent in Arkhangelsk.

Figure 4.12 Industrial production in Murmansk and Arkhangelsk Oblasts

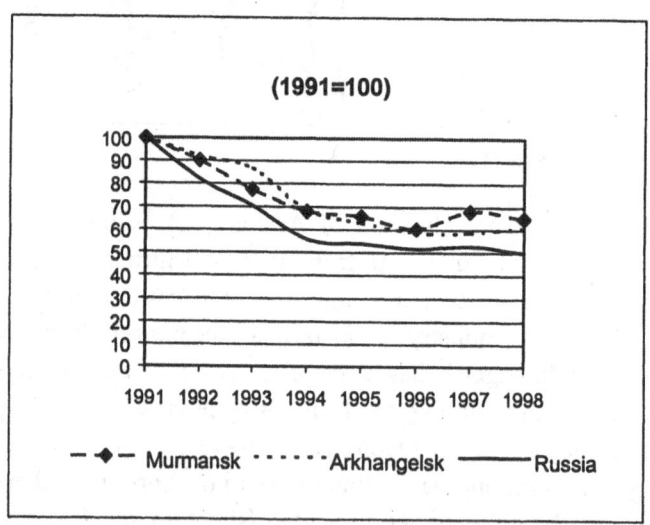

Source: Murmansk Regional Committee of State Statistics (1999a), Arkhangelsk Regional Committee of State Statistics (1999) and United Nations (1999).

Both Murmansk and Arkhangelsk industries produce partly for world markets and partly for domestic markets. In Murmansk, much of the extracted metals and minerals are exported while its large (but considerably downscaled) fish processing industry is mainly serving domestic markets (see Chapter 6 by Geir Hønneland). In Arkhangelsk, round and sawn timber is divided between international and domestic markets, as are oil and gas, while other industrial goods, mainly processed goods and consumables, are sold on domestic markets. Figures 4.13 and 4.14 below show the development in the production of some important industrial goods in Murmansk and Arkhangelsk in the period from 1993 to 1998.[28] The figures reflect the severe problems of the Russian processing and consumer industry in the transition period and the fact that the production of raw materials has decreased less than the overall industrial production. This reflects the general problem of the low Russian competitiveness on international markets.

Figure 4.13 Output of some industrial products in Murmansk Oblast, 1998

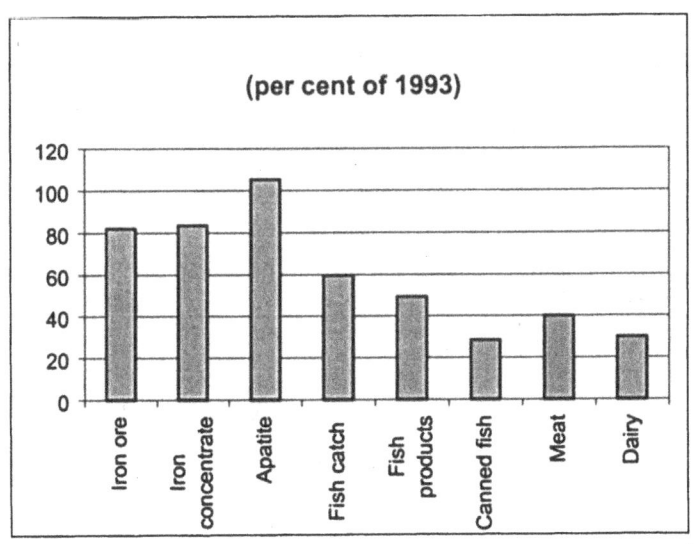

Source: Murmansk Regional Committee of State Statistics (1999a).

Figure 4.13 shows that the largest decline in industrial production in Murmansk has occurred in industries serving the domestic consumer market. The fishing industry and production of consumables such as dairy and meat products have been reduced to less than 50 per cent of their 1993 level over a five-year period. Production of raw materials like iron ore, iron-concentrate and apatite, on the other hand, performs better. The production of apatite even increased over the period. The same pattern is seen even more clearly in the case of Arkhangelsk. Since energy prices in the Soviet Union were very low as compared to world market prices, Russian integration into the world economy has increased the price of oil dramatically and therefore increased profits in oil production. For Arkhangelsk (including Nenets), this has stimulated *increased* production of oil and gas since 1993. Traditional production of raw materials and semi-manufactured goods, such as timber, sawn timber and paper, has almost halved since 1993. Also for Arkhangelsk, the production of consumables for the domestic market is worse hit than other branches. This applies to fish products, dairy products and the meat industry.

Figure 4.14 Output of some industrial products in Arkhangelsk Oblast, 1998

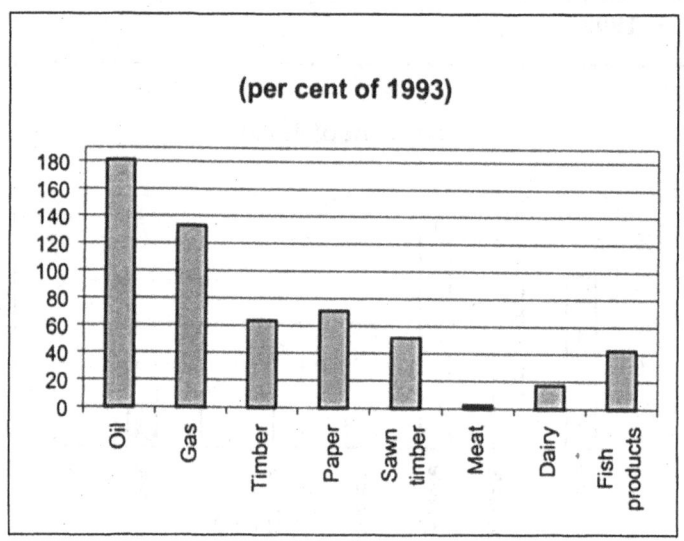

Source: Arkhangelsk Regional Committee of State Statistics (1999).

Uneven Consequences of the Crisis

Thus, industrial production in Murmansk and Arkhangelsk mimics the typical post-Soviet Russian development: There has been a dramatic overall decline in industrial production. This decline is not evenly distributed across industrial branches or geographically. Raw materials extraction and export-oriented production are generally doing better than industrial production for the home market.

Since Soviet industry was geographically specialised in mono-industrial towns, some areas are hit harder than others. The problem of mono-industrial towns may soon be illustrated in the case of Pechenga and Monchegorsk in Murmansk Oblast. The important nickel production plants in these towns were established for extraction of local nickel ores and further processing. As the local mines emptied, nickel ore has been transported along the Northern Sea Route from Norilsk in Siberia to the plants on the Kola Peninsula. This is an expensive and inefficient logistic solution initiated in order to keep production going in Murmansk Oblast. The transport of nickel ore is particularly costly because the ore is shipped on nuclear icebreakers. Increasing transportation costs and more profit-oriented production raise the question whether the nickel production sites in Murmansk Oblast are sustainable. In fact, it seems that the management of the parent company RAO Norilsk Nikel has decided to downscale production in Murmansk Oblast.[29] If this is the case, more than 8,000 workers will be directly affected, but since production of nickel forms the economic basis in these towns, all inhabitants in Nikel, Zapolyarnyy and Monchegorsk will be affected. In the worst case scenario, this will affect more than 100,000 people in these three cities. As such, the situation in these Murmansk towns is very typical of traditional Soviet mono-industrial towns.

Table 4.1 showed that population changes in Russian regions were significantly related to economic performance. Decline in population has been stronger in poor regions than in relatively wealthy ones. Figure 4.9 shows that Murmansk and Arkhangelsk are exceptions to this general rule. Population decline has been more dramatic in Murmansk than in Arkhangelsk, even though Murmansk ranks far above Arkhangelsk in relative income per inhabitant. After its peak in 1992, the population of Murmansk has declined by 12.6 per cent. In Arkhangelsk, the reduction in population has been 5.8 per cent. In Russia in total, the population decreased by 1.6 from 1992 to 1999. There are several reasons why migration from Murmansk is particularly high. First, the climate in Murmansk is harsh. Second, the very short history of Murmansk means that a high share of the population has relatives in other regions in the country. These peculiarities of the Murmansk population indicate that its elasticity with respect to changing living conditions is particularly high. Thus, continued economic decline may be followed by larger migration in years to come.[30]

The general decline of the Russian population is a consequence of the dramatic economic crisis in the country.[31] Here it is of interest to note the possible consequences for regional economic development. A declining population implies a decreasing home market for the local industry. This has two implications for a region's industrial potential. First, it reduces the market for local supply industries. Second, it reduces the incentives for location of other industries in the region and increases the incentives for such industries to locate to larger regions. For Murmansk Oblast in particular, population decline represents a major threat to future industrial development.

Recent Trends

As noted above, the August 1998 devaluation of the rouble stimulated growth in some Russian industries. At the time of writing, it is too early to judge whether the devaluation will result in a sustained recovery of the Russian economy. A look at the regional development in Murmansk and Arkhangelsk supplements nuances to the effects of the devaluation. Aggregate industrial production in Murmansk in the first five months of 1999 was 5.7 per cent higher than during the same period the year before. In Arkhangelsk, industrial production increased by 79 per cent from the third to the fourth quarter of 1998 and again by 18 per cent in the first quarter in 1999. In the second quarter, however, there was a decline as compared to the first quarter by 4.6 per cent. It is interesting to note that both in Murmansk and Arkhangelsk, the increase in production applied both to export-oriented production and production for the Russian home market. Production of goods like construction materials and bread (for the Russian market only) increased, as did export-oriented production of apatite (in Murmansk) and timber (in Arkhangelsk). Thus, it seems that the shift in exchange rate regime has stimulated export-oriented production, import-competing production and protected industries. The devaluation of the rouble does not make Russian industrial location more efficient and cannot hinder a relocation of markets and production in line with market forces. Thus, in 1999 the reduction of nickel production in Murmansk Oblast continued.[32]

Concluding Remarks

Extremely centralised decision making, low perceived transportation costs and remote sources of raw materials contributed to a decentralised economic geography in the Soviet Union. During the Soviet period, large mono-industrial towns were established all over the country. The typical Soviet region is like Murmansk Oblast with its large industrial towns situated nearby local raw materials. In the Soviet period, centripetal forces that have depopulated western peripheral regions were not in operation. Paradoxically, the introduction of decentralised economic decision making may put these centripetal forces back into operation. For purely Soviet type regions like Murmansk, the effect of this may be large differences between the towns within the region. Some municipalities find that their main industrial production closes down. Thus, large-scale migration from such communities may continue. Other towns, such as Apatity, may prove industrially competitive on international markets. The very specialised industrial towns in Russia will therefore experience uneven developments according to their inherited industrial specialisation. For regions like Arkhangelsk, even if this region is poorer than the Russian average, challenges may be less severe. Arkhangelsk has an industrial structure fitted to serve the domestic market. As such, its development may run in tandem with the general Russian economy.

Appendix

The data on regional income per capita used in this chapter are from two different sources. The first data set is from the Centre of Economic Analysis (1995a, 1995b). This data set reports average nominal income per capita in Russian regions in December 1993, March 1994 and March 1995 (and for points of time in between). This data set also reports the average cost of a bundle of 19 consumer goods in the Russian economy. The second data set is from Bylov (1998). Bylov reports data on regional income per capita on annual terms in 1995, 1996 and 1997. From 1995 onwards, Goskomstat revised its regional price indexes in order to make them better reflect subsistence minimum. The price index used from 1995 onwards is based on 25 consumer goods of which only some of the 19 goods included in 1995 index are included. The new consumer goods basket has an official status as 'minimum subsistence requirement'. Another important difference between the two price indexes is that the former had a limited geographical coverage of regions' capitals only, while the latter is intended to reflect average cost of living in the whole regions. All regions except Chechnya and Ingushetia are included (okrugs are included in oblasts or krays).

The correlation matrixes between nominal income per capita, the price indexes and the constructed real income per capita numbers in the various years are reported in Table 4.A1 on the next page. Data from the first data set are surrounded by internal lines.

Table 4.A1 Correlation Matrix

	nom. income 93	nom. income 94	nom. income 95	nom. income 95	nom. income 96	nom. income 97
nom. income 93	1.00					
nom. income 94	0.97	1.00				
nom. income 95	0.88	0.90	1.00			
nom. income 95	0.87	0.86	0.81	1.00		
nom. income 96	0.81	0.79	0.73	0.98	1.00	
nom. income 97	0.76	0.76	0.70	0.96	0.98	1.00
	Price 19 goods, 95	Price 25 goods, 95	Price 25 goods, 96	Price 25 goods, 97		
Price 19 goods, 95	1.00					
Price 25 goods, 95	0.93	1.00				
Price 25 goods, 96	0.90	0.97	1.00			
Price 25 goods, 97	0.84	0.89	0.94	1.00		
	Real income 93	Real income 94	Real income 95	Real income 95	Real income 96	Real income 97
Real income 93	1.00					
Real income 94	0.92	1.00				
Real income 95	0.77	0.80	1.00			
Real income 95	0.64	0.60	0.65	1.00		
Real income 96	0.58	0.50	0.53	0.95	1.00	
Real income 97	0.58	0.55	0.52	0.91	0.94	1.00

Source: See text.

Notes

1. Krugman and Obstfeld (1988) give an introduction to theories of comparative advantages.
2. Fujita *et al.* (1999) provide a broad introduction to economic geography. See also Krugman (1991).
3. Barro and Sala-I-Martin (1995) and Aghion and Howitt (1998) provide surveys of economic growth theory. Trade may be important for long-term economic development. The theories of *product cycles* hypothesise that technologically advanced countries develop and produce new products. As products mature and new vintages are added, less advanced countries take over production of matured vintages. For transition countries, the potential for taking over mature products from OECD countries is a possible development strategy. Both the Czech Republic and Poland have benefited from foreign direct investments in car production. For product cycle theories, see Aghion and Howitt (1998).
4. IMF, World Bank, OECD and EBRD (1991)
5. Data before 1990 are for Net Material Product, NMP.
6. For an overview of economic reforms in Russia, see Boone and Fedorov (1997), Åslund (1995) and Ponte Ferreira (1995). Ickes (forthcoming) discusses reforms in Russia with particular attention to the Soviet heritage.
7. Maurseth (1996) presents and discusses the legal framework for foreign economic activity up to 1996. Boone and Fedorov (1997) discuss the legislative process in general.
8. It is important, however, that much economic decision making is greatly distorted. One reason for this is the widespread corruption, rent seeking behaviour and organised crime in Russia. Gaddy and Ickes (1998) analyse how rent seeking influences the restructuring of firms. Chand and Moene (1999) present a dynamic model in which rent-seeking behaviour produces a low welfare equilibrium.
9. See *Russian Economic Trends*, Monthly Update, September 1998, or Hanson (1999) for a discussion of the crisis.
10. See *Russian Economic Trends*, Monthly Update, September 1999. See also *Russian Economic Trends*, Monthly Update, April 2000.
11. Again it should be underlined, however, that data on Russian economic development are notoriously of bad quality.
12. These data are from the Centre for Economic Analysis (1995a) and (1995b).
13. The methodological problem consists in the fact that there is only a weak correlation between the two series. For the two data sets for 1995, for instance, the correlation coefficient is only 0.64. In the appendix, the full correlation matrix between the data is provided. It is not possible to judge whether the discrepancies between the series are because of the low quality of the data or because the use of price indices was changed in 1995. The index used up until 1995 was constructed on the basis of 19 consumables while the index used from 1995 onwards is based on 25 consumables. Mikheeva (1999) uses regional data on physical production for specific branches of industry. Her results are very similar to the ones presented here.
14. Kernel density estimates are a form of advanced histograms in which the bars are made moving averages of each other. The idea is that such estimates smoothen random disturbances in the empirical distribution and thus reveal a more correct underlying distribution. See Härdle (1990) for an introduction.
15. Quah (1996) reports similar findings for different samples of Western European countries.
16. See Oates (1999) and Zhuravskaya (1999).

17 Zhuravskaya (1999) and OECD (2000).
18 Author's interviews in Murmansk, September 1999.
19 *Russian Economic Trends*, Monthly Update, October 1999 and May 2000.
20 A Tobit-regression, that takes into account the logically lower bound of the share of the fund in regional budgets at zero, revealed a very significant effect of (the log of) relative income with a coefficient of –40 and a p-value of 0.000. However, the explanatory power of this regression in terms of the pseudo R^2 was only 0.07.
21 Maurseth (1997) and *Russian Economic Trends*, Monthly Update, January 1997.
22 Maurseth (1999) presents similar evidence for Western European regions. Regions that are located nearby large markets seem to do better than other regions. In Western Europe, however, the tendency towards clustering has reduced in recent years.
23 Again, change in (the log of) income per capita *relative* to the Russian average was used.
24 For comparisons of industrial structure during the Soviet period and performance after the transition to a market economy, it is quite customary to use the share of employment instead of the share of value added, because value added shares are sensitive to price changes, which have been great in the transition period. Thus, the numbers reported in Table 4.2 may give a more accurate impression of the macro-structure of the economy in Murmansk than the structure of regional gross product would do.
25 Maurseth (1996) discusses this aspect of transition in somewhat greater detail.
26 It should be noted, however, that traditional Soviet plants were over-scaled because they were direct suppliers of some social services.
27 Russian oil and gas production is one of the Russian industries with the highest potential profitability in the long run (Senik-Leygonie and Hughes, 1992). Russian decision makers long hesitated in determining the extent and terms for allowing foreign direct investment in this sector.
28 Note that there had been a large decline in industrial production even before 1993 (see Figure 4.2). The period from 1993-98 in Figures 4.13 and 4.14 was chosen because this is the longest time series for industrial production in Arkhangelsk. To make the two series comparable, the same period was chosen for Murmansk.
29 *Nordlys*, 6 November 1999.
30 In fact, close to 30 per cent of the respondents in a study of living conditions answered that they planned to migrate. See Hansen and Tønnessen (1998).
31 See, in particular, *Russian Economic Trends*, Monthly Update, February 1999, and Hansen and Tønnessen (1998) for the case of the Kola Peninsula. Hansen and Tønnessen also discuss migration from Murmansk Oblast.
32 Murmansk Regional Committee of State Statistics (1999b) og Arkhangelsk Regional Committee of State Statistics (1999).

PART III
SECTORAL STUDIES: RESOURCE MANAGEMENT AND MILITARY PRESENCE

PART II

5 Offshore Developments: The Compatibility of Federal Decisions and Regional Concerns

ARILD MOE

The purpose of this chapter is to document the status of offshore petroleum activities and review recent developments through the prism of centre-periphery relations in Russia.[1] How have the petroleum resources affected relations between the regions and the federal centre, and to what extent have the regions influenced developments within this issue area – the development of offshore petroleum resources? The analysis deals particularly thoroughly with Murmansk Oblast, although Arkhangelsk Oblast and Nenets Autonomous Okrug are also touched upon. In Arkhangelsk, and particularly in Nenets, it is the development of onshore resources that is of primary concern. The development of these resources, particularly in the Timan-Pechora Basin, has its own set of problems, which falls outside the scope of this chapter.

The Barents Sea has long been considered an interesting area for petroleum activity. In the Russian part of the sea, enormous gas deposits and substantial oil resources have now been proven, and the first real licensing process in the area has just started. The resources are located mostly outside 12 nautical miles from the coasts, which means that they are under exclusive federal jurisdiction, according to Russian law. This contrasts with onshore resources that are under the joint management of the Federation and the respective region. Nevertheless, the development of offshore resources clearly affects regional interests, and the regions themselves may potentially influence such developments in a variety of ways, even if they do not participate directly in the resource management process.

The Soviet Union initiated seismic surveys in the Barents Sea in the early 1970s, spurred on by the theories of Soviet geologists, who maintained that the area contained significant petroleum resources. After 1978, extensive surveys, concentrated mainly in the area between Novaya Zemlya and the Kola Peninsula, were performed. Exploration drilling began in 1981 in the southeastern portion of the Barents Sea, which also is referred to as the Pechora Sea. The drilling took place on the Dresvyanskaya structure at the mouth of the Pechora River, from the platform Sevastopol, based on a converted Liberty ship anchored in shallow waters. In order to carry out operations in deeper waters, imported technology was needed. Special attention was devoted to the purchase of three drilling ships from Finland in 1979. Two of them, *Valentin Shashin* and *Viktor Muravlenko*, delivered in 1981 and 1982, came to play a key role in subsequent exploration efforts. These ships were designed for arctic drilling down to 6,000 m in water depths of 300 m.[2] In addition to the two drilling ships, three semi-submersible rigs – *Shelf 5, 6,* and *7*, built in Vyborg – and two jack-ups – *Kolskaya* and *Murmanskaya*, built by Rauma-Reppola in Finland – were employed. Thus, by the beginning of the 1990s altogether seven drilling rigs were operating in the Russian sector of the Barents Sea (Moe, 1994).

These rigs had carried out drilling on a total of 21 structures by 1991; 41 wells were drilled, of which 26 were completed (six were abandoned, and nine were put into 'conservation'). This is a small number compared to the number of drilling units, even if one takes into account the short work season and the inexperience of the crews. The discovery rate was very good, however, and nine interesting fields were discovered, including the giant Shtokmanovskoye gas and condensate field (in 1988) in the northwestern part of the Russian Barents Sea and the significant Prirazlomnoye (in 1989) and several small oil fields in the Pechora Sea.

Thus, by the end of the Soviet period it appeared as if the stage was set for major petroleum activities in the Russian Barents Sea. A significant resource potential had been identified, the competence and equipment of Soviet organisations working in the field had reached a reasonable level, and an emerging openness towards international co-operation seemed to guarantee that any remaining obstacles would be overcome by the parties involved.

With the dissolution of the USSR and the fundamental changes in the economic and political system in Russia, one would have expected that the regions adjacent to the offshore petroleum resources now would be in a position to influence developments on the continental shelf more directly, to their own benefit.

The Resource Potential of the Russian Sector of the Barents Sea

Both seismic surveying and exploration drilling were curtailed from the early 1990s, because of funding problems and the reorganisation of the oil and gas sector. Thus, the amount of drilling dropped from a top level of roughly 19,000 m in 1988 to 2,000 m in 1996. Seismic surveying dropped concomitantly. This decline in activity is reflected in annual additions to resources since 1990, which have been less than during the years of peak activity, but nevertheless substantial.

In the structures where detailed seismic exploration has been conducted, estimated resources (category C3) are set at 4,500 million tonnes of oil equivalent (Malovitskiy *et al.*, 1998, p. 10). Russian expectations are that the reserve numbers may increase considerably with more exploration. The geological organisations active in the area expect there to be a total of 24 billion tonnes oil of exploitable hydrocarbons in the Russian sector of the Barents and Pechora Seas. Of this, 3.4 billion tonnes are forecast in the Pechora Sea and 20.6 billion tonnes in the rest of the Barents Sea. In the Pechora Sea, the expected share of oil and condensate of total hydrocarbon resources is 45 per cent, whereas in the rest of the Barents Sea it is only 6.1 per cent. Thus, the Pechora Sea is considered to be promising for both oil and gas, whereas the Barents Sea is considered to be mainly gas-bearing.

At present, 16 oil- and gas-bearing or potential oil- and gas-bearing areas have been identified in the Russian sector of the Barents and Pechora Seas (*ibid.*). The dividing line between the concepts 'interesting structure' and 'field' is not totally clear, and consequently the numbers vary, but it has been reported that ten fields have been discovered, five in the Barents and five in the Pechora Sea. The Pechora Sea contains three oil fields (Prirazlomnoye, Varandey-More [Severo-Varandeyskoye], and Medynskoye-More); one oil and condensate field (Severo-Gulyayevskoye); and one gas and condensate field (Pomorskoye). The Barents Sea contains three gas fields (Murmanskoye, Severo-Kildinskoye, and Ludlovskoye) and two gas and condensate fields (Shtokmanovskoye and Ledovoye). Three of the discoveries were made after 1991 – Ledovoye, Varandey-More and

Medynskoye-More. The Severo-Dolginskaya and Yuzhno-Dolginskaya in the Pechora Sea are sometimes also referred to as fields, but the final testing of wells that have been drilled has not been completed. In addition to the offshore fields, there are two small fields on Kolguyev Island.

Figure 5.1 Interesting hydrocarbon fields and structures in Russian Barents and Kara Seas

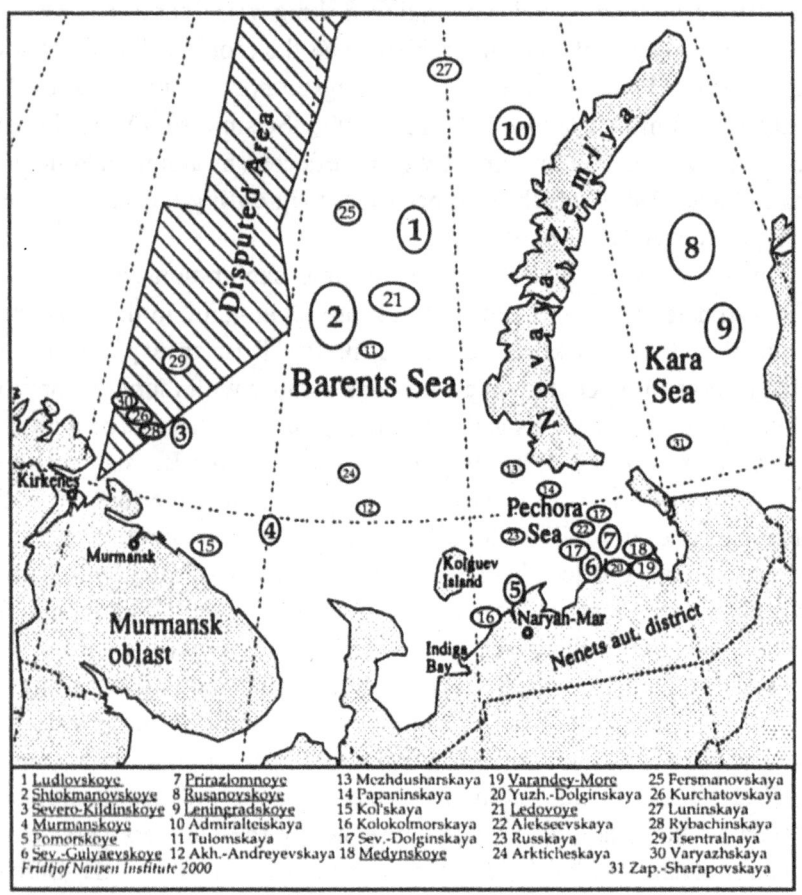

Underlined names represent *fields with exploitable reserves* (according to Russian definition), others are *promising structures*.

The Pechora Sea shelf is an extension of the onshore Timan-Pechora petroleum province. The latter is fairly well mapped. Extrapolating results from onshore exploration to the shelf, it is thought that the Pechora shelf may contain a vast number of oil fields. However, the average size will be small, with less than 30 fields expected to contain more than 10 mt (million tonnes).[3] The most recent Russian estimate of total exploitable oil reserves in the Pechora Sea suggests reserves of 400 mt.[4] This resource base could support an annual production level of 15 to 20 mt, making it a significant oil-producing region, comparable to, for example, the Republic of Komi. Almost all the hydrocarbons in the Pechora Sea are found in structures in shallow waters, at depths of less than 50 m, and most at depths of less than 20 m (Nikitin, 1999).

The largest field identified in the Pechora Sea is Prirazlomnoye, located 57 km offshore. Drilling on the structure started in 1989; it is now believed to contain as much as 100 mt of recoverable oil, sufficient to support an output of 7.5 mt annually (Nikitin *et al.*, 1999a, p. 8). The two other oil fields discovered in the Pechora Sea – Varandey-More and Medynskoye-More – are close to shore, 20 and 23 km, respectively. Preliminary estimates put recoverable oil reserves (category C1-3) at 20.5 and 85.9 million tonnes in the respective fields.[5] It is also expected that gas will be found in many small offshore fields in the Pechora Sea, but that average quantities will be too small to make them commercially viable.

Proven reserves of gas in the Barents and Kara Seas are approximately 6.6 trillion cubic meters (TCM). The Shtokmanovskoye gas and condensate field, located 650 km northeast of Murmansk and 550 km from the shore, was discovered in 1988. It is one of the largest offshore gas fields in the world, with proven natural gas reserves of 3,200 billion cubic meters (BCM). This is about twice as much as in the Troll field in the North Sea, which presently is the biggest productive offshore gas field in the world. Shtokmanovskoye also contains condensate, 22 mt,[6,7] which enhances its commercial attraction. Annual production from the Shtokmanovskoye field alone could amount to 50-100 BCM. After the discovery of Shtokmanovskoye, two other giants, Ledovoye and Ludlovskoye, were identified in the same part of the Barents Sea. With regard to natural gas, it is not the total volume that is most interesting about the Barents Sea deposits, but rather the fact that substantial volumes are concentrated in very large fields. In addition to the Barents Sea giants, two super-giants, both larger than Shtokmanovskoye, Leningradskoye and Rusanovskoye, have been discovered in the Kara Sea.

No drilling has yet been carried out in the offshore area that is disputed between Russia and Norway.[8] But analyses based on seismic surveying conducted prior to 1982, when a moratorium on seismic surveys was imposed, indicate that there may be commercially viable reserves in the area. In 1999, the Russian Ministry of Natural Resources ordered Russian seismic companies to submit reinterpreted data on the disputed area.[9] The prevalent attitude among specialists in the Murmansk geological organisations seems to be that prospects are favourable for finding exploitable resources there, and from time to time rumours surface about the location of large oil fields in this area.[10] However, there is little understanding of the Norwegian negotiating position – that co-operation in exploration and production can only be established once a firm delimitation line has been drawn.[11]

Even if only the most moderate estimates are considered, it is clear that the Barents, Pechora and Kara Seas are substantial petroleum provinces. However, this is not sufficient grounds for concluding that substantial development projects are justified or will be initiated. Other driving forces and constraints on development must be considered before anything can be said about the probability or timing of development.

There is no oil or gas production taking place offshore as of today, with the exception of a very limited production in the beach zone of Kolguyev Island. Production has taken place at this site since 1987, and in 1998 some 22,000 tonnes of oil were produced. The most imminent 'real' offshore project is clearly the Prirazlomnoye field in the Pechora Sea. This project will be discussed later along with the Shtokmanovskoye project.

Regional Interests

According to the Constitution of the Russian Federation, Russian mineral resources are the property of the state. But a major factor is that they are *managed* jointly by state authorities at the federal level, and regional authorities at the regional level (see Kryukov and Moe (1998) and Chapter 2 by Brynjulf Risnes). However, the hydrocarbon resources on the Russian Arctic shelf (i.e. those located beyond 12 nautical miles from the shore) do not belong in the category of joint management, being managed exclusively by the federal authorities. Nevertheless, the adjacent coastal regions, Murmansk and Arkhangelsk Oblasts and Nenets Autonomous Okrug, have an interest in influencing the further development on the shelf in order to maximise regional benefits and protect the local environment. Below, we shall attempt to identify the real as well as the perceived interests of the two oblasts. The analysis is structured around key factors that we believe play an important role when regional interests are defined.

The Organisational Basis for Offshore Development

Murmansk Oblast possesses an industrial complex capable of supporting offshore hydrocarbon development, reflecting the role of Murmansk as a staging ground for exploration of the Arctic shelf during the Soviet period. It was home to several geological and geophysical organisations in possession of both the competence and the equipment necessary to carry out this work. All of these organisations still exist:

- AMNGR, or Arktikmorneftegazrazvedka (Arctic Marine Oil and Gas Exploration Company)
- MAGE (Marine Arctic Geological Expedition)
- Trest Sevmorneftegeofizika (Northern Marine Oil and Geophysics Trust)
- AMIGE (Arctic Marine Engineering and Geological Expedition) – a geological company
- NIIMorgeofizika (Murmansk Research Institute for Marine Geophysics)
- Soyuzmorgeo (Scientific Production Association for Offshore Geology and Geophysics) – a co-ordinating body of the Ministry of Fuel and Energy, recently moved to Gelendzhik in Krasnodar Kray

When the exploration activity on the Arctic shelf was at its peak in the late 1980s, Arktikmorneftegazrazvedka (AMNGR) clearly harboured ambitions of securing a leading position in the subsequent development phase, and of transforming itself into an oil company. After the activity lost momentum in the early 1990s, several of the exploration organisations in Murmansk Oblast have taken part in co-operative projects with foreign partners, as a survival strategy. In some cases, the ultimate objective has been to compete for production licences on the shelf. MAGE, Sevmorneftegeofizika, and AMNGR (51 per cent) formed the company Pechormorneft, together with Finnish Neste and Kværner Masa Yards (49 per cent), with the objective of participating in offshore activities. The Norwegian Institute for Continental

Shelf Research (IKU) has co-operated with NIIMorgeofizika, and the Norwegian geophysical company Fugro-Geoteam has a joint venture with MAGE, known as Sevoteam, that has encompassed co-operation in Russian waters as well as abroad.

The organisations constituting the offshore complex still employ thousands of people in aggregate, but as their funding and activity have diminished, so has the number of employees. Some of the organisations have experienced personnel cutbacks of 50 per cent or more. MAGE reduced its staff from well over one thousand to 300.[12] AMNGR's physical capabilities have also been sharply reduced. Only one jack-up rig (*Murmanskaya*) is currently in operation in the Barents and Kara Sea area. Three semi-submersible rigs (the *Shelfs*) have been sold, and one jack-up (*Kolskaya*) has been leased and now operates abroad, as do the organisation's two drilling ships (*Viktor Muravlenko* and *Valentin Shashin*).[13] The equipment that has been leased out can of course be returned to the Barents Sea if the conditions change. AMNGR is still a fully owned state enterprise, but claims to have received no state funding for the last four years. The organisation has survived by leasing out its equipment and by taking on occasional assignments for Gazprom. AMNGR is also involved in the only production of oil currently taking place on the Arctic shelf, in the beach zone at Kolguyev Island. However, this production is fairly limited, and while it provides some income, is not reported to be particularly favourable from an economic point of view.

For these companies, the key to accelerating developments on the continental shelf is to create greater possibilities for foreign involvement. The companies may try to obtain the right to invite their own investors to take part in further exploration. However, there seems to be a prevailing perception within the organisations that their time has passed. The situation is quite different today from what it was in the early 1990s, since the organisations have shrunk, and so much of remaining capacity is now tied up abroad.

Arkhangelsk Oblast also has a significant oil and gas sector, but the activity has traditionally been directed towards exploration and development of onshore rather than offshore resources. The bulk of the regional expertise in this field was concentrated in the state-owned geological organisation Arkhangelskgeologiya, which has since become an oil exploration company controlled by Lukoil under the name Arkhangelskgeoldobycha. The company currently is engaged in both exploration and exploitation of oil deposits in Nenets Autonomous Okrug. However, Arkhangelskgeoldobycha has neither the experience nor the expertise or equipment, necessary for playing a role in the development of offshore resources.

Nevertheless, after the break-up of the Soviet Union, the Arkhangelsk region began to challenge Murmansk's status as the 'Arctic offshore capital'. This is closely connected with an effort to convert the large military shipyards in the area to offshore-oriented production (see Chapter 7 by Anne-Kristin Jørgensen).

The Establishment of Rosshelf

The production of offshore equipment was singled out at an early stage as the most promising conversion option for the shipyards. Although the yards did not possess any expertise in this particular field, they were technologically advanced and their engineers were experienced in the field of marine technology.[14]

The need to ensure financial support from the government, and the wish on the part of the defence industry to gain some influence over assignments, was the rationale behind the establishment of the Rosshelf joint-stock company. On 29 May 1992, Rosshelf was registered in Severodvinsk. It included the military shipyards as well as a handful of defence design bureaus as the main partners. Via Rosshelf, the yards attempted to assume the role of offshore operator, and ultimately to obtain licenses for the development of the shelf.

At the time, a consortium of Western companies established in 1989 – Arctic Star – in which AMNGR had become a participant, had carried out a feasibility study for Shtokmanovskoye in agreement with the Soviet oil and gas ministry. The companies in this group possessed considerable offshore experience and they were led to understand that the consortium would be given permission to develop the field.[15] Rosshelf decided to carry out its own feasibility study for the development of the Shtokmanovskoye and Prirazlomnoye fields, in order to compete for both licenses. Despite the attempts to pass Rosshelf off as an offshore oil company, the idea that the enterprise alone could obtain the licenses was clearly unrealistic. However, arguments regarding the necessity of protecting Russian state interests and the national industry were supported by many government officials, and by striking a deal with Gazprom, which was awarded a controlling share in Rosshelf, the latter succeeded in obtaining combined exploration and production licenses valid until 2018 both for Prirazlomnoye and Shtokmanovskoye.[16] In November 1992, President Yeltsin signed a decree granting Rosshelf the right to develop the two fields and instructing the company to work out a long-term programme for the development of the Arctic shelf. In December, the 'Arctic Star' consortium was dissolved.

A long-term programme for the development of the Arctic fields, which was one of the licensing requirements specified in the presidential decree, was prepared in 1994. According to this programme, the Prirazlomnoye and Shtokmanovskoye fields were to be developed in 1998–99 and 2003–05, respectively. By 2010, ten additional oil fields were to be developed in the Pechora Sea. The programme envisaged the construction of (among other things) 17 drilling rigs and platforms, 30 other surface and underwater facilities and a fleet of ice-breaking oil tankers. As the main contractor, the Severodvinsk yards would receive enough orders to stay in operation for decades. Indeed, it was estimated that the number of new jobs in the offshore industry as a whole would reach 140,000 within eight to ten years from the beginning of the programme's implementation.

Other Industrial Spin-off Effects from Offshore Development

From the above, it remains unclear to what extent companies based in the coastal regions will be able to participate directly in the development process as license holders/operators. What is clear, however, is that if large-scale development is going to take place, there will be substantial regional spin-off effects that will give rise to new economic activity. There will be a need for supply and service bases, landing and reloading facilities, and possibly also refineries and the production of equipment. The 'Law on the Continental Shelf' from 1995 codifies preference for projects that utilise and develop local infrastructure as well as Russian industrial capacity in general. Even if this law can be read as a clear policy statement, the actual implementation of the cited provisions will be an issue of negotiation when licenses are awarded. Gazprom has recently announced that 70 per cent of the construction work for Shtokmanovskoye will be given to Russian enterprises (Glukhova *et al.*, 1999).

The geographic location and characteristics of Murmansk Oblast is a great advantage in this respect. Along the northern coast of the Kola Peninsula, there are a multitude of fjords and bays that are usually ice free in winter.[17] The port of Teriberka, some 50 km northeast of Murmansk, seems most promising as a landing point for gas from Shtokmanovskoye and other gas and condensate fields in the Barents Sea. If the gas is to be brought ashore in Teriberka, a 547 km long triple-gas pipeline will be constructed, which will run from the Shtokmanovskoye field to the coast, possibly with extensions to other fields.[18] The establishment of a liquified natural gas (LNG) facility has also been considered.

Because of the shallowness of the Pechora Sea, development of oil fields in this area will probably require the construction of a reloading port for oil somewhere along the Kola coast. The Gulf of Pechenga, not far from the Norwegian border, is one possible location for this port. A pre-feasibility study was completed in 1996 by AOOT Giprospetsgaz and the Norwegian consultants Barlindhaug, which envisages the construction of a crude oil terminal in the Bay of Liinakhamari, which is located in the Gulf of Pechenga, as well as construction of an LNG plant and methanol plant.[19] There has been much attention devoted to these plans in Murmansk Oblast, and the study was commissioned by the regional administration. Gazprom representatives stated in April 1998 that the port should be ready to operate by 2002,[20] but no activity besides planning has occurred thus far, and apparently alternative locations further east are being considered.

If the Shtokmanovskoye field is developed, the Kola Peninsula will be the natural location for base and service facilities, and the construction of a service base in the Kola Bay, right across from the city of Murmansk, was initiated as early as the late 1980s (Bergesen et al., 1987). However, the work on the service base was abandoned in the early 1990s. There has also been some hope that the service assignments might help revive the naval shipyards in Murmansk Oblast. Currently, the question of the location of base facilities for the oil fields in the Pechora Sea is higher on the agenda, since these fields will most likely be developed before any in the western part of the Russian Barents Sea.

For Arkhangelsk Oblast and Nenets Autonomous Okrug, the most likely spin-off effects from the development of the shelf will be linked to exploitation of deposits in the Pechora Sea. These may include landing and reloading points for oil, as well as refineries and supply bases. For several years, various proposals for terminals have been discussed, primarily to serve the onshore fields that are likely to come on-stream first, but which also could be integrated with pipelines from offshore fields. Several points along the Nenets coast have been evaluated, although no final solution has been reached. Powerful forces want to connect the onshore fields to the Russian oil pipeline network controlled by the oil pipeline monopoly Transneft, further complicating the issue.

A conflict may arise concerning the location of bases for the development of the Prirazlomnoye and other deposits in the Pechora Sea. Both Murmansk and Arkhangelsk Oblasts, as well as Nenets Autonomous Okrug are attempting to promote themselves as suitable base locations. Several factors enter into the equation. Most importantly, an adequate infrastructure has to be in place, and the distance from the fields to the base should be as short as possible. The first of these criteria is sufficiently important to render the chances of Nenets slim. The okrug has no road or rail connections with the rest of Arkhangelsk Oblast. However, to the extent that Lukoil becomes an active player in offshore developments, it may seek to combine operations with an already very strong position in Nenets onshore. Arkhangelsk City and Murmansk are both conceivable as locations for supply bases. However, the distance to Murmansk is shorter, although not by much. An even more important point in Murmansk's favour is the fact that the White Sea freezes and is only navigable with icebreaker assistance in winter. Thus, it seems that Murmansk is the most likely choice.

Energy Supplies to the Regions

Ensuring an adequate supply of energy for the cold season is a perennial challenge throughout the Russian North. In recent years, there have been serious difficulties in providing sufficient heat, gas, and electricity supplies to consumers in both Murmansk and Arkhangelsk Oblasts.[21] Every autumn, the regional newspapers print articles on the situation concerning supplies of *mazut* (the heavy fuel oil used in many district heating plants) and gas virtually every day. These difficulties affect almost every inhabitant in the area as well as the local industry, and there is constant pressure on the regional politicians to do something about them.

Traditionally, there has been a supply problem with regard to energy in these areas – not enough energy was available locally – which was compounded by poorly developed infrastructure for its transportation and distribution, as well as by technical problems. Today, however, the problem is mainly a financial one: neither the regions as such nor the individual consumers are able to pay fully for the required energy, and thus energy supplies are halted periodically. However, many regional politicians still seem to think in terms of the planned economy, where paying for power was rarely a problem, while the outstripping of supply by demand was. Thus, they seem to regard the frequent energy crises first and foremost as a question of an insufficient supply of oil and gas. This distortion strongly influences their views on development of 'their own' hydrocarbon resources. It is envisaged as vital that the regions gain direct access to such resources, in order to ease the perceived shortages in supply. As a consequence, opportunities for regional control over development, as well as the geographic location of deposits to be developed, are aspects that tend to be over-emphasised at the regional level.

Gas pipelines connecting Murmansk and Arkhangelsk to the Russian pipeline network have been discussed for many years, but progress on these projects has been extremely slow. There are conflicting reports on the status of the projects. Reportedly, some work has been done in the Republic of Karelia, but the last stretch to Murmansk is only in an early planning stage. The short-term objective of this pipeline is to improve the gas supply to Murmansk. However, if the Shtokmanovskoye field is developed, the gas will flow in the opposite direction to markets in the south. In the summer of 2000, work was being carried out on the stretch Nyuksenitsa-Arkhangelsk,[22] and this project seems much closer to completion.

Regional priorities are intricately interconnected with jurisdictional questions involving shelf resources. The location of a given oil or gas deposit determines the extent to which regional authorities have a voice in the development process, as well as their share in the resource itself.

According to the 'Law on the Continental Shelf', oil and gas on the Russian shelf is under exclusive federal management. Resources located within the 12 nautical miles from shore, however, fall within the shared jurisdiction of the adjacent subject of the federation and the federal authorities, as do onshore resources (see Chapter 2 by Brynjulf Risnes). Financially, this joint jurisdiction implies that 60 per cent of the revenue from resource exploitation are to be assigned to the regional budget, whereas the remaining 40 per cent go into the federal budget. Moreover, if the subject in question is an autonomous okrug, which forms a territorial part of an oblast or a kray, the aforementioned 40 per cent is to be split between the oblast/kray and federal budgets.[23]

Murmansk Oblast has attempted to extend its influence to resources located within 200 miles from the coast. In an appendix to the bilateral agreement between the Russian Federation and Murmansk Oblast on the delimitation of authority between federal organs and those of the oblast,[24] the management of resources within the 200-mile economic zone, extending from the Murman Coast, is referred to as 'joint execution' – *sovmestnoye vedeniye*. It is not quite clear what this term means, but according to Murmansk officials it at least means *soglasovaniye* – co-ordination.[25]

None of the oil and gas fields thus far discovered in the Barents Sea are located within the 12-mile coastal zone of Murmansk Oblast, but some 'interesting geological structures' have purportedly been identified along the eastern Kola coast – *Kolskiy monklinal*. These are said to be similar to structures in the Timan-Pechora province, and they form the continuation of promising structures on the Norwegian side. Some experts believe that the prospects for making new discoveries in this area are quite good. However, no conclusions can be drawn until thorough exploration, including drilling, has been performed.

With respect to Arkhangelsk Oblast, it can be assumed that the large onshore oil deposits in Nenets Autonomous Okrug make development of the resources on the shelf a lesser priority to the Arkhangelsk authorities. Admittedly, the fact that Nenets gets the lion's share of revenues from oil located on its territory may be considered a counter-argument. However, the same situation will apply to offshore deposits within the coastal zone, since these are located in the Pechora Sea, which borders on Nenets. The fact that onshore resources are more accessible and less costly to develop than resources on the shelf is a weighty argument in their favour. Furthermore, there are indications of oil deposits onshore in an area not far from the city of Arkhangelsk – *Mezenskaya sinekliza*. Exploration drilling is expected to start there in 2001.[26] If the results are promising, development of these resources will probably receive the highest priority from the regional authorities.

Status of Development Projects

Thus far, Rosshelf/Gazprom's ambitious plans have only been realised to a very limited degree. Out of six new floating units that were to be constructed by the year 2000, including the production platform for Prirazlomnoye, none have been completed, and in some cases construction has not even started. The construction of the Prirazlomnoye platform at the great Sevmash shipyard in Severodvinsk was scheduled to take three years, starting in 1995, but in November 1998 Boris Nikitin, General Director of Rosshelf, stated that the Prirazlomnoye platform was only 19 per cent complete.[27] Plans for the parallel construction of two smaller drilling rigs have also been greatly delayed. The foundation for one of them – the jack-up Arkticheskaya – was launched in July 1999, but much work remains to be done on the rig. It is supposed to commence operations in 2001, although 'this will only happen if normal financing is provided from the commissioner'.[28] No work has been done on the other rig.

It has proven difficult to attract sufficient financial resources to the project. Initially, Gazprom and the Australian oil company BHP planned to cover 15 per cent each of the cost, with the International Finance Corporation (under the World Bank) providing 40 per cent; the remaining 30 per cent were to be covered by commercial loans from Russian and foreign banks. In early 1997, the total investments to develop the field were estimated at USD 1.5 billion.[29] But BHP announced in the autumn of 1997 that it wanted to reduce its share in the Prirazlomnoye project and abandoned active participation early in 1999, assuming a 'non-working' interest in the project.[30] A German company, Wintershall AG (a subsidiary of BASF), has become a new partner in the project.[31] The exact scope of its participation is still unclear, but it seems to be primarily of a financial nature.

The pace of development for this project is highly uncertain. Until recently, 2002 has been mentioned as a start-up year for production, but this is unrealistic. Aside from the financial problems, the Russian partner is in need of technical expertise from an experienced offshore company in order to develop and operate the field, at least initially, and it is doubtful whether Wintershall can perform this role alone. Gazprom reportedly has approached several companies to take part in the project, apparently without success so far. Nevertheless, despite these uncertainties, it is likely that

Prirazlomnoye will become the first active offshore project in the Barents and Kara Seas area.

The technical difficulties in developing the Shtokmanovskoye field are substantial. First is the distance to land, but great water depths (some 280 to 380 m), drifting ice, and high waves can also pose problems. The productive layers are located between 1,380 and 2,340 m.[32] However, technical evaluations of the site indicate that the field can be developed with existing technology, but Gazprom, which in reality controls the project, would need the participation of foreign companies with offshore experience, both for the technical and financial aspects of the project. A group comprising Norsk Hydro, Fortum, Conoco, and Total Fina is currently assisting Gazprom. Their work includes improvement of the geological data, development solutions and commercial evaluation of the market for gas and condensate from the field.

Gazprom officially maintains that it plans to start building one of several platforms in 2001 and that a production level of 60 BCM can be attained in 2010-12.[33] The building of the platform is estimated to cost USD 10 billion and the accompanying pipeline down to Volkhov east of St Petersburg USD 8 billion (Glukhova *et al.*, 1999). With the inclusion of the adjacent Ledovoye and Ludlovskoye fields, Gazprom envisages an 'offshore gas production centre' with an annual production capacity of 90 BCM (Nikitin *et al.*, 1999a). That would be almost twice the volume presently exported from the entire Norwegian continental shelf.

The exact transportation route for gas extracted from the Shtokmanovskoye field has not been decided. The plan thus far discussed most seriously entails a pipeline to Teriberka, east of Murmansk, with one line extending to the city of Murmansk. But other landing points, notably the Pechenga terminal (see below) have also been mentioned. Another pipeline might transport gas southwards via Belomorsk and Petrozavodsk. The gas thus could find its way to European markets via Finland and Sweden or directly to Germany through a pipeline under the Baltic Sea. The establishment of a LNG plant near Murmansk is also being considered. Such a project would provide the basis for exports overseas, particularly to the U.S. market.

Licensing

Legal Framework

Russia has a licensing system for hydrocarbon resources based on the 'Law on Subsurface Resources' (1992, revised several times later). The system prescribed in the law is not fundamentally different from, for example, the Norwegian system, including tenders for exploration and development licenses, payment for the use of underground resources, and provisions for mandatory work on the licensed blocks. The system is general, and intended to apply to all kinds of mineral resources, both on- and offshore. The actual jurisdiction over resources would differ, however, depending on whether the resources are on- or offshore (see below).

In various negotiations between Russian and foreign partners, production-sharing agreements (PSAs) became the favoured mode of co-operation. However, the legal basis for such agreements was delayed for a long time in the Russian Parliament. Draft laws went through several 'readings' in the State Duma, and a law was finally adopted and came into force on 11 January 1996.

Production-sharing contracts are most commonly used in developing countries with an insufficient legal framework for 'ordinary' operations by foreign oil companies, and are also used as a way to 'train' domestic oil companies in countries where production is just starting and there is no experienced oil industry. PSAs also relieve the host country of the burden of financing exploration and development. They offer a simple tax regime and provide a way of 'getting started'. The basic principles for a PSA are a contract between a (foreign) oil company and the government of the country in question for joint exploration and production in a given area. A national oil company usually represents the government. This company supplies acreage (the production site), while the foreign partner supplies capital, technology, or whatever is specified in the agreement. Thus, the foreign partner assumes the entire direct financial risk. The proceeds from the project are divided between the partners. The actual proportions are established in each contract, but there is usually one proportion until the foreign company has recovered all its costs (e.g. 50/50) and another subsequent rate by which the national oil company gains a larger share (e.g. 30/70) (Jones, 1988).

Clearly, two of the general reasons for employing PSAs – an inexperienced oil industry and lack of a legal framework – do not square well with conditions in Russia. Firstly, the country has a huge and experienced oil industry, which only in exceptional instances perceives any technical need to co-operate with foreign oil companies. Secondly, the country is already developing a regular licensing system, and an emphasis on PSAs could be regarded as a step in the wrong direction. However, there is little disagreement regarding the third reason for PSAs – the need to attract investment resources. The main idea here is to establish a stable and predictable framework for investors by giving the agreements a strong legal basis and protection. It is precisely this fundamental issue that has caused most controversy in Russia. The law included provisions that would give one side the possibility of changing the provisions of the agreement as a result of changing circumstances.[34] Precisely what kind of circumstances were not spelled out, but some members of the State Duma indicated that, for example, a marked increase in the world market price for oil could justify changes in the PSA. This uncertainty was a major concern for foreign partners.

Another clause was that only fields designated by the State Duma could be developed as PSAs. Only in May 1997 was the first such list approved by the State Duma. The list did not include all the fields where initial negotiations for PSAs had taken place.[35] Thus, the PSA law did not remove all uncertainties and, consequently, obstacles to foreign participation. The lack of political consensus regarding the development of the oil sector in general and the role of foreign capital and companies in particular was still manifest.

With regard to offshore development, the reasoning behind PSAs seemed to fit well. The enormous financing requirements as well as the inexperience of the Russian industry in this sector would seem to make PSAs highly interesting from the Russian point of view. Nevertheless, offshore projects were not automatically placed on the PSA list, although the Prirazlomnoye project was on the first list. Outside investors could find some comfort, however, in the fact that a license granted according to the 'Law on Subsurface Resources' may at a later point be converted to a PSA.

Licensing in the Barents Sea

The first exploration and production licenses in the Barents Sea were issued in 1992, for Shtokmanovskoye and Prirazlomnoye, as noted above. These licenses were not awarded according to the formulae discussed above, but as administrative decisions, without any open tenders, counter to the provisions in the new legislation. Since 1993, there has been talk of opening the Barents Sea for regular tenders for exploration and development licenses. These plans, however, failed to materialise or were postponed. In the meantime, several licenses for geological exploration were awarded to AMNGR in 1993 and Gazprom in 1995 in the same manner. Later the Finnish-Russian joint venture Pechormorneft was awarded exploration licenses for two blocks. These exploration licenses gave no guarantees of preferential treatment if development licenses were later awarded, but holders of exploration licenses would of course be in a better position to evaluate the prospects of the respective blocks when deciding if they would apply for a development license. Nevertheless, the exploration licenses remain unattractive.

A 'Concept for the Development of Hydrocarbon Resources in the Barents Sea Province' was adopted by the Russian government as early as 1995. But only in 1998 did the Ministry of Fuel and Energy and the Ministry of Natural Resources publish a new and more detailed development programme for the period 1998-2005, which included open tenders (Garipov, 1998).[36] The plan had been developed in consultation with all affected authorities, including the military. The announcement of the programme provided grounds for believing that the Russian authorities were now committed to increased foreign involvement. The plan envisioned the participation of several companies, including foreign ones, in tenders for development and exploration rights in the Barents and Pechora Seas as the main principle for development. However, some areas where 'special state interests, of a geological-economic or other nature' were concerned, would be subject to closed bidding rounds, where only Russian companies would be allowed to participate. Put bluntly, this would mean that the most promising structures and fields, as well as fields in areas considered to be of particular military importance, would be off-limits to foreigners.

The programme envisaged the organisation of four open licensing rounds between 1997 and 2005, including numerous blocks (*uchastki*). The start of the licensing rounds was delayed, and the first tender was announced only in November 1998, with the details for participation published in February 1999. The scope of the tender was far smaller than originally planned. The most attractive blocks – Medinskoye-More and Varandey-More – were reserved for Russian companies, whereas two smaller and less interesting blocks – Pomorskiy and Kolokolmorskiy – were open to foreign companies.

The organisation of the tender was, surprisingly, left to Yuzhmorgeologiya, a geological organisation based in Gelendzhik in Krasnodar on the Black Sea. According to a joint decision by the Ministries of Fuel and Energy and Natural Resources, all organisations carrying out exploration activities offshore would be required to turn over all data and information, old and new, to a new federal organisation, Rosmorgeoinfo (also based in Gelendzhik), or otherwise risk losing their operating license.[37] Thus, copies of the geological information hitherto stored in Murmansk were to be transferred to Gelendzhik.

The scope and set-up of the tender generated considerable criticism in Murmansk. The Governor of Murmansk Oblast, Yuriy Yevdokimov, launched a harsh public attack on the Ministry of Natural Resources, as well as on the Ministry of Fuel and Energy, for compromising the interests of the region and failing to consult with the regional authorities. He was enraged that two fields high on the priority list of Murmansk, Murmanskoye and Kolskaya, had been excluded, as well as by the fact that the tender was to take place in Gelendzhik. If the 'errors' were not corrected, he threatened to develop Murmanskoye and Kolskaya without consulting the federal authorities.[38]

Through these decisions – the content of the tender as well as the transfer of the geological data to Gelendzhik – the looming conflict between the federal authorities, in particular the Ministry of Natural Resources, and Murmansk Oblast, caused by years of impatience, came to the surface. One might question which decision was most frustrating for the oblast officials, the exclusion of Murmanskoye and Kolskaya or the exclusion of themselves from the tender process. Murmanskoye had been mentioned as a possible regional supply source as early as 1987, but dropped from public attention after the discovery of Shtokmanovskoye.

This reflected not only scale differences, but also the fact that the Murmanskoye deposit turned out to have a very complicated geology. According to a centrally placed participant in the exploration process, the field has no commercial prospects – the cost of extracting relatively small volumes would be prohibitive (Ostistyy, 1999). The Kolskaya block is so little explored that the presence of hydrocarbons remains uncertain, representing a single 'spot' in a long geological range. Consequently, placing these two blocks on the tender list would not have looked good and would have attracted neither Russian nor foreign oil companies (*ibid.*).

Results of the First Tender

Even though several companies were rumoured to be interested, only one company placed a bid, the Murmansk drilling organisation AMNGR.[39] This was clearly disappointing for the organisers, but not entirely unexpected. The most surprising 'no-show' was Gazprom/Rosshelf, which declared that they would not bid in tenders for rights to hydrocarbon sections of the Barents Sea that it already had invested in developing.[40] Gazprom/Rosshelf demanded to be included in the license or compensated. As mentioned earlier, Gazprom has been carrying out some activity on both Varandey-More and Medinskoye-More based on exploration licenses.[41] By March 2000, however, Gazprom/Rosshelf withdrew their claim, something that permitted the results of the first licensing round to be finalised. This happened in June 2000.

AMNGR clearly has the support of the regional authorities in Murmansk in the effort to increase activity on the continental shelf. However, the organisation does not have the financial strength required. It is therefore expected that it will seek foreign partners. Although foreign companies did not express an interest in the fields during the first licensing round, they may well consider a joint project with AMNGR. However, they will probably not risk a conflict with Gazprom, and will require at least tacit approval from those quarters before they establish any joint project with AMNGR. Second, as with other major projects in the oil sector, foreign companies will probably demand that the project be organised as a PSA. AMNGR expects that the Russian government will recommend that the fields be included on the PSA list. However, a decision of the State Duma is required for this to actually occur, and that process is relatively unpredictable. We would expect the pressure exerted by the Murmansk Oblast authorities to be a crucial factor in this process.

Outlook

It is expected that the second licensing round will be announced during 2000. For the regional authorities, it now seems better to support some exploration activity on the tracts that will come up for tender in later rounds, thus increasing the information base on the structures, reducing the risk and making the tenders attractive for a wider range of companies. Some money was set aside by the regional administration and the Ministry of Natural Resources to carry out exploration in 2000. However, a comprehensive programme would require more. It is suggested that, at a minimum, it would take two years of seismic exploration (at a cost of around USD 500,000) of the structures along the Kola coast to select suitable structures for drilling. Exploration drilling would require another two years. Subsequently, if positive finds were made, production could start some seven to eight years from now (Ostistyy, 1999). Two licenses for geological studies of these structures were put up for tender in February 2000. In order to evaluate the possible pace of development, however, it is not sufficient to look at the licensing programme, we must also turn to the interests of the involved parties.

Overall Demand Picture

In addition to such factors as the geology of offshore structures, the availability of financing, regional politics and the capabilities of Rosshelf to independently explore and produce offshore hydrocarbons, an essential component in any decisions regarding the development of offshore mineral resources in the Russian Barents Sea is domestic and world demand for oil and gas. The situation, in fact, can be quite different for oil and gas, respectively. In the oil market, the supply side consists of a large number of relatively small producers, with the development of one additional source not affecting the market substantially. In this environment, in principle, each project is considered on its own merits. There may be political constraints but there is no strong, co-ordinated national policy with regard to the development of oil fields. Russian oil companies, that to all intents and purposes are private and guided by commercial and strategic considerations at a company level, now make the real decisions.

Gas is entirely different. The gas market is characterised by a demand constraint, at least in the short to mid-term. It is clear that the development of offshore gas fields in the Barents Sea is not necessary to ensure adequate gas supplies for Russia as a whole, at least not within the foreseeable future. Therefore, we must consider whether Barents Sea gas deposits have any special market characteristics that might make their development advantageous on an international scale, despite abundant supplies at the national level.

From an international perspective, increasing the supply of natural gas through the development of Barents Sea deposits would be desirable. However, it is quite clear that the increased volume of regional consumption would not justify development of such a large field as Shtokmanovskoye, even if deliveries were paid in full. Development therefore will depend on export outlook. The location of the source will suggest the construction of a new transport corridor (e.g. through Finland and the Baltic Sea or Sweden to continental Europe). Such a new corridor would provide for a certain diversification of the gas market, in the sense that it would become less dependent on the other two main channels for Russian gas – via Ukraine-Slovakia and Belarus-Poland, respectively. However, a third pipeline corridor is also conceivable even without gas from the Barents Sea. It could merely be an extension of the Northern Lights network that brings gas from Siberia to the St Petersburg region.[42]

Gas from the Barents Sea would thus represent a reduction of the heavy reliance on West Siberian gas sources. However, would the market be prepared to buy substantially larger volumes of Russian gas than it does at present? It is impossible to answer such a question with much certainty, but it seems reasonable to believe that the market might be favourably disposed towards a source distinctive from West Siberia. There are no comparative cost estimates available for the Yamal fields and the Barents Sea, but a project in the Barents Sea might be expected to be more costly than an onshore project, even though the latter probably will include an undersea pipeline (under Baydaratskaya Bay) and a longer total pipeline distance. Thus, it is highly uncertain whether the 'diversification value' will offset increased development costs.

However, three other circumstances must be taken into consideration. Gazprom has clearly understood that it cannot develop a field like Shtokmanovskoye on its own. It lacks the requisite technology, experience and financial resources. In the ongoing preparatory work, Gazprom has included several other companies – Norsk Hydro, Neste/Fortum, Conoco, and Total. The work carried out by this group includes market evaluations, improvement of the geological data, as well as technical solutions. Thus far, the status of the group is informal, but the foreign companies clearly expect to become formal partners when the field is developed, and Gazprom is signalling that it wants to develop the field in partnership with others (Semenyaka, 1999). Several of the companies also have interests as potential gas purchasers. This could mean that market access for Shtokmanovskoye gas will be better than for other Russian gas.[43] In any event, the development of Shtokmanovskoye without a long-term commitment from the demand side for this particular gas is unthinkable.

The possibility of establishing a LNG plant on the Murman coast adds to the attractiveness of the project. That might provide access to markets beyond the reach of pipelines – for example, the United States. However, the difficulties of establishing a profitable LNG project in the region have already been demonstrated by the Norwegian Snow White project off the coast of Finnmark. The most certain element of the Shtokmanovskoye project in market terms is the export of condensate, which is in high demand in international markets, and would enhance the overall economic return from the field.

As is clear from the preceding discussion, it is exceedingly difficult to quantify the arguments for and against Shtokmanovskoye, but it does not seem that there are sufficiently strong reasons for pushing for immediate development. Nonetheless, both for Gazprom and the foreign companies involved, Shtokmanovskoye and the adjacent fields are an option that will materialise one day. As such, they merit attention and the use of some resources for the improvement of the development plan, but such preparatory work must not be confused with a real start-up.

Conclusions

Russia lacks a national plan for the development of its energy resources. What it has is an 'Energy Strategy', with forecasts of demand and assessments of the possibility of covering that demand through various energy sources under different scenarios. The present strategy was adopted in 1995 and covers the period until 2010. However, the strategy is far from an operational plan. Instead, it is more an attempt at forecasting developments. Detailed assessments of both driving forces and constraints upon the development of particular regions and fields must be undertaken on a region-by-region basis, as there is no integrated policy addressing these issues at the national level.

A recurrent theme in this chapter has been the role of the regional level. The regional authorities are a power in and of themselves, but they also work at the national level, where regional considerations, especially in the form of economic development and employment, are a concern. However, the regions of interest here – Murmansk and Arkhangelsk Oblasts and Nenets Autonomous Okrug – do not have uniform interests and priorities, and this probably weakens their influence in Moscow.

In recent years, the policy of the federal Russian authorities has primarily acted as a constraint on the development of the Arctic shelf. In a nutshell, their attitude seems to be that it is in Russia's long-term interest to minimise foreign involvement in the process, even if this means that the benefits will be postponed. Meanwhile, efforts can be concentrated on exploiting more readily accessible onshore resources.

Decision makers in the regions bordering on the Barents Sea have a different view, and consider the benefits that would accrue to the regions from increased activity on the shelf to be great. However, changes in the political climate towards greater protectionism can be observed here as well, and the 'wait-and-see' argument even carries some weight in the regions – at least in certain specific cases.

The regional authorities in Murmansk Oblast would like to see an increase in activity on the shelf as soon as possible. Development of the Shtokmanovskoye field is probably a top priority, since all spin-off effects from this project would benefit the Murmansk region exclusively, and since this is perceived as important for increasing the supply of gas to the oblast itself. It also seems that the oblast is highly interested in development of the Prirazlomnoye field, since Murmansk appears to be the most likely location for bases, as well as for a reloading port.

To the extent that foreign partners are needed to ensure the rapid development of other fields, we assume that the regional authorities will welcome their involvement. Ideally, the partnership would be with one or several of the regional offshore organisations, but it would not be in the region's interest to hamper development by other operators. The regional reactions to the exclusion of Murmanskoye and Kolskaya from the recent tender show that there is a strong wish to develop deposits in zones of 'joint execution'.

The position of Arkhangelsk Oblast is less clear. It appears that the development of the shelf is viewed as important in this region as well, but Russian leadership may be considered more of a priority in that process than it is in the one in Murmansk. The presence of onshore resources in the region can make it acceptable to proceed more slowly on the shelf. From the point of view of Arkhangelsk, it is paramount that Rosshelf is allowed to retain a leading role in the project. In general, it may be in the interest of Arkhangelsk Oblast for foreign companies to play a lesser role in the development of the shelf, if Russian control over projects implies more contracts for the naval shipyards. With respect to the development of the Shtokmanovskoye field, Rosshelf/Gazprom have announced their intentions to build the platform in Severodvinsk, and heavy involvement of foreign companies might prove detrimental to these plans. All in all, Arkhangelsk Oblast seems to have less to lose and more to gain by a 'wait-and-see' strategy than does Murmansk Oblast.

In the current situation, it seems clear that the naval shipyards are a constraint on the development of the shelf. It has been concluded that both the Prirazlomnoye and the Shtokmanovskoye fields can be developed with existing technology, and it goes without saying that the process could have proceeded more rapidly if experienced contractors had been hired to deliver the necessary supplies and equipment. Conversion of the yards has proved both time consuming and costly. Even more importantly, the foreign companies that would have to be involved for the process to gain momentum would probably have been more interested in participating if contracts for equipment were awarded on a competitive basis.

This does not mean that the yards cannot, in the future, be turned into an asset in the development process. Some of the fields on the Arctic shelf cannot be developed with current technology, and there is a possibility that defence enterprises and design bureaux specialising in marine technology will at least be able to contribute to new technological solutions.

Interestingly, even if Gazprom in many ways controls Rosshelf, the gas giant has also chosen to establish its own subsidiary – Gazflot – as a 'contracting department' for offshore rigs and vessels (Paliy et al., 1999). This gives Gazprom more flexibility in choosing development schemes than Rosshelf alone can provide. At present, Gazflot has one drilling ship in operation – 'Gazprom 1' – and the Arkticheskaya platform under construction in Severodvinsk will also belong to this division of Gazprom (*ibid.*). Recently, it has been announced that Gazflot has become the operator of a project to develop offshore gas resources in shallow waters in the Ob bay,[44] underscoring its role as an alternative to Rosshelf.

The role of the military is not quite clear. No one seems to doubt that the Northern Fleet has much say in offshore developments in the Russian Barents Sea, and it has traditionally been seen as negatively inclined towards almost any development. But with the establishment of the development plan for the Barents Sea, the military has appeared to accept fairly extensive development. Still, the power to impose restrictions, in particular on licenses, probably remains.

However, it is possible that the military may have changed its position in a substantive way. Whereas previously the military could detach itself from the regional economy, it is now more closely integrated into that economy.[45] The prevailing economic crisis also affects the military, and developments that would improve the economic situation would benefit the military as well. In Murmansk Oblast, the governor has worked hard to secure support at the national level, as well as from other regions, for improving the financing of the Northern Fleet (see Chapter 7 by Anne-Kristin Jørgensen). He should expect some reciprocity in the form of the military not obstructing his efforts to improve economic conditions in the region through oil and gas development. In addition, the argument of regional authorities that offshore development will improve the regional energy supply is also one that is expected to go down well with military officials, as the armed forces in the region have experienced serious energy shortages.

It is widely believed that there has been a conflict within the federal administration over offshore tenders. The Ministry of Fuel and Energy has supported open tenders and also the inclusion of more attractive fields in order to increase interest. According to former Minister of Natural Resources, V. P. Orlov, 'the speed of work to conquer the hydrocarbon resources in the Barents Sea does not correspond to the economic requirements of Russia and the real production capacities in the region' (Orlov, 1998, p. 4).

Gazprom has been the main force working against such developments. It is likely that the company management viewed the alliance with Rosshelf as a way to extend its gas monopoly to the shelf, correctly assuming that Moscow would welcome an actor promising to solve the social and economic problems prevailing in the regional defence complex. Gazprom wants to retain its leading position in the development of offshore resources, not only gas but also oil.[46] However, the company has many options and can afford to postpone extensive offshore development until it is in a better position to benefit from such development. An important issue is the emergence of other strong Russian actors on the scene. If Lukoil, which apparently is active studying northern offshore possibilities, decides to take part in the licensing round, it may force Gazprom to reconsider its strategy.

Despite the interest of the three involved Russian regions in increased activity on the shelf, it seems likely that development of offshore hydrocarbons in the Barents Sea will go very slowly, at least over the near term. This clearly demonstrates the power of the opponents of such development at present. Over the longer term, the outlook for development in the Barents and Pechora Seas will be shaped mainly by changes in the strength of the various forces outside the regions, but the three regions may influence the process. If the regions are able to formulate and present a co-ordinated vision of offshore development, then their prospective influence on federal decision makers will be enhanced.

The 'game' between the regional and the federal level with regard to offshore development is not clear-cut. Rather, it is a situation where the regional level to some extent can influence decisions made at the federal level. In this chapter, I have reviewed important components of the regional 'powers' with regard to these issues.

Institutional capacity is one major component. Although the offshore exploration organisations are not owned or formally controlled by the regional authorities, they nonetheless have a strong regional basis. Development of the offshore resources is impossible without the use of the existing organisations, but beyond these organisations the regional authorities have, not unexpectedly, limited expertise in these issues.

Limited jurisdiction has often been put forward as a reason why the regional level is not likely to influence offshore development directly. Indeed, the law is clear on this point, establishing management of resources outside 12 nautical miles as a federal prerogative. As we have seen, Murmansk Oblast has pressed for acknowledgement of a say also in these waters. In addition, the strong emphasis put on the use of regional industrial capacities in any large offshore project will eventually also involve the regional authorities.

A third key issue is the availability of *financial resources*. Regional authorities have the possibility of using the regionally based organisations to carry out surveys and exploration. Murmansk Oblast has done so, albeit only to a limited extent. However, it is a costly exercise. Sufficient money for such work is not to be found at the federal level either. It will have to come from the oil industry, whether Russian or foreign. Companies will of course only invest in such activities if it is likely that they will get a share in the exploitation of the resources at a later point. With regard to resources beyond 12 nautical miles, the regional administrations are in no position to provide such assurance directly; they may, however, co-operate with the oil industry in lobbying for a more vigorous exploration and development programme offshore.

In sum, the influence that the regional level can exert over offshore development is more of a negative than a positive kind. The regional level will have to be consulted on major decisions regarding offshore development, such as the development of bases and landing sites. The federal level will have difficulty forcing through decisions against the will of the adjacent regions, but the regions have very few possibilities of accelerating developments offshore on their own. However, by allying themselves with forces at the federal level that support speeding up developments, they may exert greater influence. If or when a situation arises where the federal level supports an accelerated Arctic exploration and development programme, the regions can be expected to negotiate solutions with the federal authorities that will give them reasonable benefits from offshore developments. Such developments are also likely to enhance the general position of the affected regions vs. the centre.

Notes

1. This chapter is a revised and shortened version of Moe and Jørgensen (2000).
2. For more details on the period before 1987, see Bergesen et al. (1987).
3. This assessment is based on Belonin and Podolski (1995), as quoted in Bjørkvoll and Sandvik (1997, p. 42).
4. This figure was stated by B. Nikitin, a Gazprom official, during a discussion in the Presidium of the Russian Academy of Sciences in 1997 (quoted in *Vestnik Rossiyskoy akademii nauk*, Vol. 67, 1997, p. 906). This is more than earlier assessments. Gazprom expects that 1.1 billion tonnes of exploitable oil reserves already exist for the Barents Sea as a whole (including the Pechora Sea), and that the potential is much larger (see *Russian Petroleum Investor*, May 1998 and Zorin (1997)).
5. 'Resolution of the Government of the Russian Federation No. 1586-r, 3 November, 1998, and Resolution of the Ministry of Natural Resources', No. 3, 3 February 1999; *Ekonomicheskiye i pravovyye voprosy nedropolzovaniya v Rossii*, No. 3, 9 February 1999, pp. 5-6.
6. Recent statements from Rosshelf give an even higher number for gas reserves – 4,000 BCM (*Upstream*, 19 November 1999).
7. *Vestnik Rossiyskoy akademii nauk*, Vol. 67, 1997, p. 906.
8. Norway and the Soviet Union, and later Russia, have been negotiating since 1974 over a delimitation line for the continental shelf and economic zones in the Barents Sea. Norway holds that the boundary should be drawn according to the median-line principle, whereas Russia maintains that a sector-line principle should be applied. These two claims leave a sizeable disputed area between the two countries (some 155,000 km^2), much larger than the Norwegian shelf in the North Sea (see Moe, 1994).
9. The Murmansk Arctic Geophysical Expedition also carried out some work on the fringes of the disputed area about 10 years ago; see interview with OAO MAGE General Director G. Kazanin in *Politika-Ekonomika-Finansy* (Murmansk), No. 1-2, 2000, p. 21.
10. A recent example of such speculation presented as fact can be found in an article by a Lukoil publication (*Neftegas*, 11, 1999). The article also advocates the use of decommissioned platforms from the North Sea in this area.
11. In Russian publications, the disputed area is often referred to as a 'zone of joint economic interests between Russia and Norway' (e.g. *Gazovaya promyshlennost*, No. 7, 1999, p. 7).
12. Moe (1994, p. 22).
13. *Murmanskiy vestnik*, 13 January 1999.
14. According to Yuriy Kondrashov, Assistant Chief Engineer at Sevmash, building the platform for the exploitation of the Prirazlomnoye field is complicated, 'but completely within the capacity of those who for years have been fulfilling analogous tasks when building submarines' (Fattakhov, 1995, p. 13).
15. See Moe (1994, p. 135). Arctic Star ultimately consisted of Norsk Hydro, Conoco, and the Finnish companies Imatran Voima, Metra and Neste, with AMNGR as the Russian partner.
16. *Perechen nedropolzovateley, poluchivshikh litsenzii na polzovaniye nedrami dlya poiskov, otsenki, razvedki, i razrabotki mestorozhdeniy uglevodorodnogo syrya*, Roskomnedra and Rosgeolfond, Moscow, 1995.
17. This favourable site characteristic was the rationale behind the establishment of the Northern Fleet, which has six submarine bases in this area.
18. Notably Ledovoye, Ludlovskoye and Fersmanovskaya (Nikitin et al., 1999b, p. 12).

[19] *The Northern Seaport (TNS) Pechenga. Pre-feasibility Study – Phase 1.* Barlindhaug/-Giprospetsgaz, Tromsø, 1996.
[20] *Reuters News Service – Eastern Europe*, 16 April 1998.
[21] In December 1998, for example, it was reported that people in Arkhangelsk preferred to rent apartments in the city's old wooden houses rather than in modern blocks of apartments equipped with modern conveniences. The reason was that the old houses are equipped with stoves; thus, the inconvenience of having no indoor plumbing was outweighed by the fact that it was possible to stay warm (*Nash sever*, December 1998).
[22] *Pravda severa*, 21 June 2000.
[23] *Zakon o nedrakh*, 1992, Art. 42 (subsequently revised several times).
[24] *Dogovor o razgranichenii predmetov vedeniya i polnomochiy mezhdu organami gosudarstvennoy vlasti Rossiyskoy Federatsii i organami gosudarstvennoy vlasti Murmanskoy Oblasti*, 30 October 1997, Art. 2.
[25] *Murmanskiy vestnik*, 22 January 1999.
[26] *Pravda severa*, 15 June 2000.
[27] *Interfax*, 20 November 1998.
[28] *Severnyy rabochiy*, 22 July 1999.
[29] *Russian Petroleum Investor*, February 1997, p. 52. According to Gazprom, the price of the platform alone is expected to be USD 800 million (*BBC Monitoring International Reports*, 11 February 1999).
[30] *Russian Petroleum Investor*, October 1997.
[31] *FT International Gas Report*, 2 April 1999.
[32] *ibid.*
[33] *Reuters News Service – Eastern Europe*, 24 September 1998. Gazprom recently has announced that it would like to see production start as early as 2006 (*Upstream*, 19 November 1999).
[34] For an analysis of the law, see Makhlina (1996).
[35] In a number of cases, preliminary agreements between Russian and foreign companies had been signed in anticipation that the project in question would be accepted as a PSA.
[36] A 'Concept for Development of Hydrocarbon Resources in the Barents Sea Province' was adopted by the Russian government as far back as 1995.
[37] In 1998, 'The Russian Information-Analytical Centre for Research and Development of the Continental Shelf, the World Ocean, and the Special Economic Zone', *Rosmorgeoinfo* for short, was established in Gelendzhik. It consisted in part of Soyuzmorgeo, which had been a Murmansk-based, all-Union geological organisation for the entire continental shelf, but which was transferred as a very reduced institution to Gelendzhik in 1998. Both organisations became part of the Geological Organisation of the Southern Continental Shelf – Yuzhmorgeologiya (*Murmanskiy vestnik*, 22 January 1999).
[38] *Murmanskiy vestnik*, 19 December 1998.
[39] ITAR-TASS, 20 July 1999.
[40] *Interfax*, 6 July 1999. According to Boris Nikitin, General Director of Rosshelf and member of Gazprom's management board, Gazprom has spent about USD 90 million on drilling in the Prirazlomoye area (*Interfax*, 20 November 1998).
[41] The Finnish-Russian joint venture Pechornomeft in fact had exploration licenses for both blocks that were included in the open tender – Kolokolomorskiy and Pomorskiy. On the basis of seismic exploration done in 1997-1998 and re-analysis of data, they decided not to apply for a development license, but one of the partners – AMNGR – decided to go for it alone.

[42] Fortum (Neste) and Gazprom have established a 50/50 joint venture – North Transgas Oy – to develop plans for a pipeline via the Baltic Sea to Germany. In connection with a feasibility study of the project, Gazprom's Boris Nikitin explicitly stated that the pipeline could either be a branch of the Yamal-Western Europe pipeline or could supply gas from Shtokmanovskoye (*Interfax*, 17 November 1998). In a recent Gazprom presentation, the project is mentioned without reference to the Barents Sea (*Gazovaya promyshlennost*, No. 7, pp. 37-39).

[43] However, the possibility of joint development (with Western partners) of other Russian gas fields should not be ruled out.

[44] *Polyarnaya pravda*, 18 July 2000.

[45] For a thorough analysis of the relationship between the military and civilian sector on the Kola Peninsula, see Hønneland and Jørgensen (1999b).

[46] E.g. *Russian Petroleum Investor*, February 1999, p. 42.

6 Centre-Periphery Tensions in the Management of Northwest Russian Fisheries

GEIR HØNNELAND

The fishery sector is one of the mainstays of Northwestern Russia's economy, and in particular that of Murmansk Oblast. The aim of this chapter is to present the system for regulating the activities of the Northwest Russian fishing fleet and discuss tensions between management bodies at the federal and the regional level.[1] The main question is whether there has been a transfer of management responsibility from the federal to the regional level following the disintegration of the Soviet Union.

The management of the Northwest Russian fisheries takes place within the wider framework of the bilateral Norwegian-Russian management regime for the Barents Sea fisheries. Hence, a brief description of this overall management system seems appropriate. Next, a presentation of the Northwest Russian fishing fleet is given, focusing on its development during the 1990s. In turn, my main discussion is devoted to the responses of fishery management bodies to the changes taking place in the fishing industry and in the general political framework over the last decade.

Background: The Management of the Barents Sea Fisheries

The Barents Sea comprises those parts of the Arctic Ocean lying between the North Cape on the Norwegian mainland, the South Cape on the Spitzbergen Island of the Svalbard Archipelago, and the Russian archipelagos Novaya Zemlya and Franz Josef Land. For the purpose of discussing the management of the fish resources in the Barents Sea, the fish banks to the west, north and east of Spitzbergen are usually also included. Both groundfish and pelagic species are traditionally important here. Economically, the

Norwegian Arctic cod is by far the most important species. Other groundfish species of importance are *haddock, redfish, saithe* and *Greenland halibut*. *Herring* and *capelin* are the key pelagic species in the area. As they serve as food to groundfish and marine mammals, they are crucial to the functioning of the ecosystem. In addition, there is a considerable *shrimp* fishery in the Barents Sea.

The Third UN Conference on the Law of the Sea (1975-82) resulted in a transition from multilateral negotiations for the Barents Sea fisheries under the auspices of the Northeast Atlantic Fisheries Commission (NEAFC) to bilateral negotiations between coastal states with sovereign rights to fish stocks. Norway and the Soviet Union entered into several bilateral fishery co-operation agreements in the mid-1970s. The most important ones related to the establishment of the management regime are the mutual agreements of 11 April 1975[2] on co-operation in the fisheries sector and of 15 October 1976[3] on mutual fisheries relations.

The Norwegian-Russian management regime for the Barents Sea fish stocks defines objectives and practices for co-operative management between the two states – in addition to management procedures at each of the administrative levels of the two countries – within the fields of *research*, *regulations* and *compliance control*. The first steps in the co-operation between Soviet/Russian and Norwegian scientists in the mapping of the Barents Sea fish resources were taken already in the 1950s. It is now institutionalised within the framework of ICES (the International Council for the Exploration of the Sea). The co-operation is generally characterised as successful (Stokke *et al.*, 1999). The participating research institute on the Russian side is PINRO.

The Joint Russian-Norwegian Fisheries Commission includes members of the two countries' fishery authorities, ministries of foreign affairs, marine scientists and representatives of fishermen's organisations. The Norwegian delegation to the commission is headed by the administrative leader of the Norwegian Ministry of Fisheries. The Russian delegation is headed by the First Deputy Chairman of the State Committee on Fisheries of the Russian Federation.[4] The Commission assembles at least once a year, establishing total allowable catches (TAC) for the joint fish stocks of the Barents Sea: cod, haddock and capelin. Cod and haddock are shared on a 50/50 basis, while the capelin quota is shared 60/40 in Norway's favour. In addition, quotas of the parties' exclusive stocks are exchanged. Russia has traditionally given a share of its cod quota to Norway in return for a share in Norway's quotas of redfish, herring and Greenland halibut (Stokke and Hoel, 1991). However, after the introduction of reforms in the Soviet Union in the late 1980s, the Russians have kept a larger portion of their cod quota. After the sessions in the Joint Commission, the two parties conduct further quota exchanges in bilateral negotiations with third countries. Traditionally, the Soviet Union/Russian Federation has given part of its Barents Sea cod quota to the Faeroe Islands, while Norway has transferred a share of its quota to the EU in exchange for quota shares in the North Sea.

Map 6.1 The Barents Sea

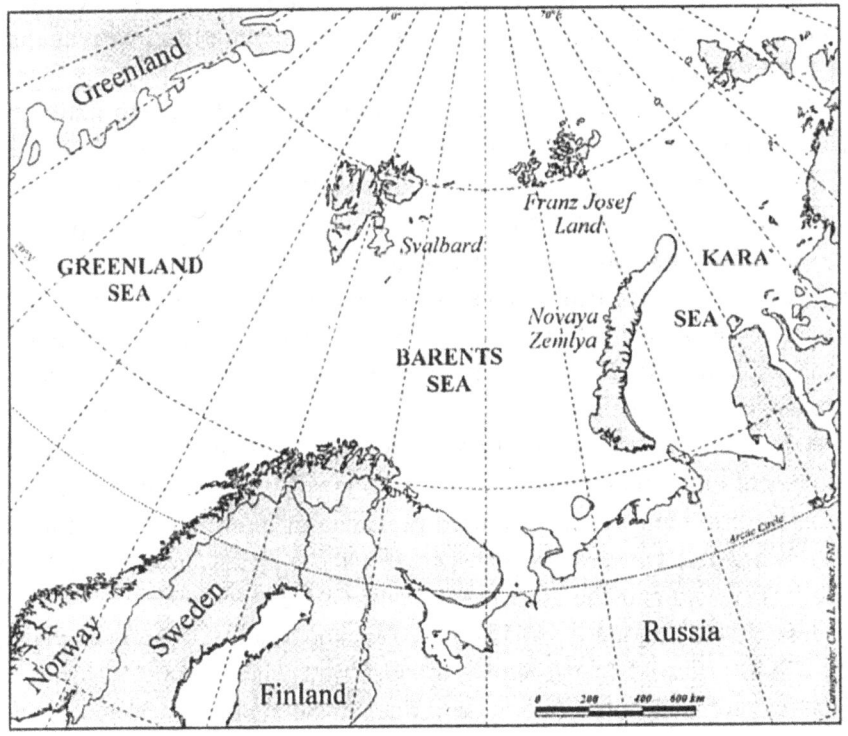

The Norwegian Coast Guard revealed a dramatic increase in underreporting from Russian vessels in the course of 1992, and took extra steps to calculate the total Russian catch in the Barents Sea for that year. By the end of 1992, Norwegian fishery authorities presented these figures to their Russian colleagues. They indicated overfishing of more than

100,000 tonnes by the Russians. Overfishing corresponded to a quarter of the total cod quota in the Barents Sea in 1992. Russia had 170,000 tonnes at its disposal, of a TAC of 396,000 tonnes, after internal quota exchanges with Norway. This estimate was supported by export statistics, which indicated that close to the total Russian cod quota in the Barents Sea had been exported to Norway. At the same time, considerable quantities had been exported to other Western countries. Some cod had also been landed in Murmansk. This sudden rise in overfishing co-incided with Russian fishermen starting to deliver the bulk of their catches abroad, primarily in Northern Norway. This direct export of their product simultaneously increased the incentives to fishermen to underreport their catches, and reduced the possibility for Russian authorities to keep track of the catches since control had traditionally been conducted in connection with landings of fish in Russian ports.

Towards the end of 1992, both Norwegian and Russian authorities had become aware of the shortcomings of the enforcement within Russian fisheries in the Barents Sea. At the 21st session of the Joint Commission in November 1993, the delegation leaders of the two parties jointly proposed the appointment of an expert group to consider the question of co-operation between the enforcement bodies of the two states. The expert group presented its recommendations in May 1993, and the proposed measures were soon implemented. The most important initiative was to establish a formal exchange of catch information. The Norwegian Directorate of Fisheries now regularly forwards data from all Russian landings in Norway to enforcement authorities in Murmansk. Additionally, inspection data may be submitted on request. An organised exchange of information about activities at sea has been established between the Russian enforcement body Murmanrybvod and the Norwegian Coast Guard. Moreover, an exchange of inspectors is regularly carried out. Most importantly, Russian inspectors have been allowed to participate as observers when inspectors from the Norwegian Fish Control (a branch of the Directorate of Fisheries, responsible for catch control ashore) inspect Russian vessels in Norwegian ports. Upon delivering its recommendations, the expert group was transformed into a permanent committee for Norwegian-Russian co-operation on enforcement and management issues under the Joint Commission. It has met at least once a year since 1993. The committee is headed by representatives of the Directorate of Fisheries (Norway) and Murmanrybvod (Russia). It also includes representatives of the Norwegian Coast Guard and Sevryba (see below) and PINRO in Russia.[5]

On the whole, Russian-Norwegian fisheries management co-operation proved to be fairly successful during the 1990s (Hoel, 1994; Stokke, 1995; Hønneland, 1998). Most stocks have grown steadily since the end of the 1980s. The capelin stock, with its rapid fluctuations, represents a departure from this tendency. While the stock soon recovered from something close to a total breakdown in 1985-86, a new setback came in 1992-93. Furthermore, the Greenland halibut stock has suffered a threatening decline since the early 1990s, and is now only taken as by-catch (except a limited direct fishery with passive gear). The TAC of Norwegian Arctic cod amounted to 700,000-850,000 tonnes in the mid-1990s. A decline in the stock has been observed since then. The quota was accordingly reduced from 850,000 tonnes in 1997 to 480,000 tonnes in 1999, and further to 390,000 tonnes for 2000.

The most serious problem in recent years within the co-operation process between Norwegian and Russian authorities has been the repeated refusals by Russian authorities of applications for joint Russian-Norwegian research cruises in the Russian Zone of the Barents Sea. However, it should be noted that these refusals come from Russian security services and environmental protection bodies, not from fishery management authorities. On the positive side, an extension of the regime to include co-operation between enforcement bodies from the two states has been made, and Norway and Russia took a common stance against Iceland in the dispute regarding the Barents Sea Loophole.[6]

The Northwest Russian Fishing Industry

Traditionally, the fish and marine mammals of the Barents Sea have constituted the foundations for settlement along its shores, particularly in Northern Norway and in the area around Arkhangelsk in Russia. The fishing industry of Northwestern Russia developed rapidly after the Russian Revolution in 1917. It is now largely concentrated on the Kola Peninsula. The Murmansk Trawl Fleet was established in 1920, and a development programme for the fisheries sector was launched in 1926 by the central Soviet power. The building of the Murmansk Fishing Combinate, which was to become the largest industrial fish processing complex in the Soviet

Union, was started via this government initiative. As in other industries in the Soviet Union, the *branch principle* was the guide used to organise the fisheries sector. This implied that the economic sphere of the union was divided into a certain number of branches that were all subordinated to their respective ministries. Apart from Khrushchev's attempts during the period 1957-64 to implement a *territorial* organisation of Soviet industry, the branch principle remained prevalent until the extensive post-Soviet privatisation project started in 1992.

Sevryba, the association of fishing companies in *the northern basin* of the Soviet Union, including all fishing activities in Murmansk and Arkhangelsk Oblasts and the (then) Autonomous Republic of Karelia,[7] was founded in 1965. It was given the status of General Directorate of the Soviet Ministry of Fisheries in Northwestern Russia.[8] After several less comprehensive reorganisation efforts, Sevryba was turned into a private joint-stock company in the autumn of 1992. As many as 23 companies covering various core activities (ranging from ship owners, on-shore processing factories, a shipyard, research institutions, sales and supply organisations and various other firms) founded the new company together. In April 1993, the Union of Private Fishery Enterprises in the North (Sever) was included in the A/O Sevryba structure. This union, founded in 1992, comprises more than 130 small private firms directly involved in or connected to the fishing industry in Northwestern Russia.[9]

The basic structure of the fishing companies was upheld within the new institutional framework. This implies that the majority of the approximately 450 fishing vessels located in Northwestern Russia are still controlled by a handful of fishing companies. The rest are distributed between *kolkhoz'*es (the collective fleet) and other small private fishing companies. The total number of vessels has been rather stable over the past decade since old vessels have only to a limited extent been taken out of service (even if they have passed their expected time of service), and few new vessels have been purchased. The existing fishing companies in Northwestern Russia can be grouped under three categories:

- **The large Sevryba fishing companies (traditional companies)** (Murmansk Trawl Fleet, Murmanrybprom (Murmansk Fish Production Association), Sevrybkholodflot (Northern Fish Freezer Fleet), Sevrybpromrazvedka (Northern Fishery Survey/Research Fleet), Arkhangelsk Trawl Fleet, Karelrybflot (Karelian Fishing Fleet)
- **The collective fishing fleet (*kolkhoz'*es)** (Murmansk Collective Fishing Fleet, Arkhangelsk Collective Fishing Fleet, Karelian Collective Fishing Fleet, a few independent collective fishing companies)
- **The small private fishing companies (including coastal fishing)** (The Union of Private Fishery Enterprises in the North, a few small independent fishing companies)

The traditional fishing companies are a typical legacy from the Soviet period. This fleet consists mainly of medium-size (50-70 meters) and large (over 70 meters) vessels, and each company owns between 30 and 95 vessels. All in all, they account for 250-300 vessels. Before the dissolution of the Soviet Union, their main activity was the exploitation of pelagic species in distant waters and pelagic and demersal species in the North Atlantic Ocean and the Barents Sea. Now they mainly fish for cod in the Barents Sea.

The *kolkhoz'*es in some respects have fleet structures similar to the traditional fishing companies, but are significantly smaller in number of vessels, ranging from one to ten vessels each. They account for around 80-100 vessels in total. Nearly all are mid-sized (50-70 meters). An important characteristic of the fishing *kolkhoz'*es is that they are far more diversified in their business activities than the other fishing companies, engaged to a larger extent than the others in the catch of pelagic species.

The small private companies (including the *coastal fishing* fleet) have the smallest fishing fleet, both in number and size, clearly limiting the cruising range of the vessels and also, in practice, the geographical markets for sale of the fish. At present, the fleet mainly consists of fresh/salt fish combination vessels and some round freezer and fresh fish vessels. It counts some 100 vessels, including approximately 30 coastal fishing vessels of less than 50 meters. The rest are mid-sized (50-70 meters). It should be noted that the Russian perception of 'coastal fishing' is somewhat different from that found in the neighbouring Scandinavian countries.

While a Norwegian 'coastal' fishing vessel normally has a crew of 1-3 persons and goes to port for delivery of catches every day, a Northwest Russian 'coastal' fishing vessel has a crew of more than a dozen and stays at sea for a couple of weeks before delivering the catch.

Table 6.1 Total catches of fish and marine mammals by vessels registered in Murmansk Oblast during the period 1991-97 (in 1,000 tonnes)

year	1991	1992	1993	1994	1995	1996	1997
catch	1061	855	639	533	447	432	401

Source: *Statisticheskiy yezhegodnik: Murmanskaya oblast v 1997 godu.*

The northern basin fisheries employed some 80,000 persons in the 1980s. The Murmansk Fish Combinate alone accounted for more than 6,000 employees in the land-based processing industry, while the largest fleet, the Murmansk Trawl Fleet, had more than 17,000 employees at its peak. A sharp reduction in catches, and subsequently in employees, set in at the beginning of the 1990s. Throughout the 1990s, the total annual catch of the fishing fleet based in Murmansk Oblast (accounting for the bulk of the Northwest Russian fishing fleet) has dropped year by year, from 1.06 million tonnes in 1991 to 0.4 million tonnes in 1997 (see Table 6.1). The main reason for this catch reduction is a major decline in fishing activities in distant waters by the fleet of Northwestern Russia as a result of increased fuel costs. Adding to the problems of the land-based processing industry in Murmansk, Russian landings of fish abroad increased markedly during the same period. Russian landings of cod to Norway (fished in both Norwegian and Russian waters), for instance, reached 94,000 tonnes in 1992, while in 1988 they had only totalled 10,000 tonnes. Thereafter, the Russian landings in Norway increased further to nearly 150,000 tonnes around the mid-1990s. Since that time, there has been some reduction. Russian deliveries of cod to Norway totalled 119,800 tonnes in 1998. The reason for this considerable increase in the export of fish is twofold. First, it became legally easier to import fish to Norway. Second, Northwest Russian fishermen had to compensate for both the termination of state subsidies and an overall reduction in total catches. The main result of the fact that most Russian-caught fish is landed in Norway is the loss of employment in Murmansk, both in the active fishing fleet and in processing industries ashore. The fish processing plants directed towards production of valuable bottom fish species, such as cod and haddock, have practically been at a standstill since the mid-1990s. The total employment in the northern fishery basin is believed to have dropped to some 35-40,000 people.[10]

Towards a Regionalised Management System?

The distribution of fish quotas during the Soviet era was carried out by Sevryba, which co-ordinated all of the Soviet northern fishing fleet's fishing activity, and was completely subordinated to the Soviet Ministry of Fisheries. This responsibility was transferred to a corporate organ, the Technical-Scientific Catch Council (TSCC) (*nauchno-promyslovyy soviet*) in 1990. The TSCC consists of representatives from Sevryba, federal authorities and marine scientists. Sevryba was, however, given such a strong position in this council that for all practical purposes it retained total control of the quota distribution. Furthermore, the strong ties between Sevryba and federal fishery authorities have persisted into the post-Soviet era. Top leaders in the fisheries administration in Moscow have, for instance, continued to be recruited from the association in Murmansk, and the preferences of Sevryba seldom diverge from those of the federal State Committee on Fisheries, which took over the responsibilities of the previous Soviet Ministry of Fisheries in the Russian Federation. Sevryba is thus a kind of federal representative in the region, rather than a representative for regional authorities.

However, when the quotas for 1993 were to be distributed, the Murmansk Oblast administration for the first time demanded to have a say in the matter. It attempted to gain control over a quota, which it intended to subsequently sell to fishing companies. The demand was turned down by the TSCC with the argument that only organisations actually possessing vessels could be allotted quotas. However, the oblast administration continued its efforts to gain control over the fisheries management, and entered into negotiations with the State Committee on Fisheries. Towards the end of 1993, the negotiations quite surprisingly led to an agreement to transfer the responsibility for managing the Russian part of the Barents Sea fish quota to the oblast/republican administrations in Murmansk, Arkhangelsk and Karelia. A Fisheries Department was set up in the Murmansk Oblast administration in November 1993, and similar bodies were established in Arkhangelsk Oblast and the Republic of Karelia during the spring of 1994.

Russian fisheries management appeared to be undergoing a process of regionalisation. This is how the events were presented in the international fisheries press, and by regional authorities in other countries demanding the same rights as the regions of Russia. However, although the agreement between the State Committee on Fisheries and the Murmansk Oblast administration is still in effect, it has not had the practical consequences many, especially in the West, had anticipated. Sevryba immediately denounced the agreement as contrary to federal law. Resources in the exclusive economic zone are, according to the Russian constitution, a federal responsibility (see Chapter 2 by Brynjulf Risnes). Furthermore, Sevryba correctly pointed out that the oblast administrations lacked the expertise and experience to take on responsibility for the complicated management process. The old procedures were followed during the quota distributions for 1994 and 1995, although the regional fisheries departments were given responsibility for distributing some very limited quota shares to the coastal fisheries. Since the distribution of quotas for 1996, the agreement has been implemented in the sense that the oblast administrations issue quota decrees. However, their role seems to be more secretarial; actual decision-making power continues to rest with the federal State Committee on Fisheries and partly still with its regional representative, Sevryba.

In connection with the distribution of quotas for 1997, a new system was introduced as an experiment in the northern basin. It involved new principles for distribution between the various structures at the regional level, as well as the reorganisation of the administrative bodies responsible for the allocation of quotas.[11] A main feature was that federal authorities to a larger extent than previously sought to use the distribution of fish quotas as a means of achieving overarching political objectives. Whereas 50 per cent of the total quota – now labelled the *technical quota* – was to be distributed according to the same principles as earlier, i.e. on the basis of number of vessels and previous years' catches, the remaining half was reserved for ship owners who somehow contributed to the more general societal goals of the fisheries policy of the Russian Federation. The so-called *social quota* of 20 per cent was to be distributed according to ship owners' contributions to the maintenance of the employment and social welfare of their employees, as well as the degree to which they complied with their tax obligations. The *stimulation quota*, also consisting of 20 per cent of the total quota, was to be allotted to ship owners who caught other species than cod and haddock, the economically most valuable ones. Hence, it was a means of stimulating catch *volume*, primarily through the catch of pelagic species such as herring and mackerel (in more southern ocean areas), rather than the mere financial efficiency of the enterprise. Finally, 10 per cent of the total quota was to be set aside as a *competition quota*. This was a paid quota share, reserved for Russian ship owners with a licence in the Barents Sea who had not been caught for serious violations of the fisheries regulations. The revenue from this arrangement was to be organised as a fund which in time would be used to stimulate fishing activities contributing to the fulfilment of regional and federal needs but not necessarily profitable at enterprise level.

Hence, the federal authorities aimed at utilising the fish quotas as means of supporting enterprises that contributed to the maintenance of employment, the social welfare of fishermen, food supplies to the Russian population, and tax revenues to regional and federal budgets. In practice, the new system would primarily favour the large, traditional Sevryba structures at the expense of smaller, newly established ship owners, mainly concentrating their catch effort on cod and haddock. In practice, however, the new system ended up not being implemented in the quota distribution of 1997. Institutional resistance from a considerable part of the industry as well as uncertainty as to the practical application of the new principles seem to be the main reasons for this non-implementation. A formal proposal was made by the Regional Fishery Council (see below) in Murmansk to increase the technical quota to 70 per cent as of 1998, and reduce the social and stimulation quotas to 10 per cent each. Much the same happened in the following years. The distributing bodies claimed that Moscow had not provided them with sufficiently elaborated criteria to perform their tasks. Again, the quotas were distributed in one bulk. The criteria for the social, stimulation and competition quotas were, however, taken into consideration.

The distribution *process* (see Table 6.2) was not radically changed; rather, it reflected a gradual adjustment to the political realities of the day. The TSCC still exists, and is still headed by the General Director of Sevryba. Its competence is, however, restricted to the distribution of the total quota between the federal subjects of Murmansk and Arkhangelsk

Table 6.2 The main decision-making bodies of Northwest Russian fisheries and governmental bodies and user groups represented

Decision-making body	Represented governmental bodies	Represented user groups
The Joint Norwegian-Russian Fisheries Commission (responsible for establishing TACs for the joint stocks in the Barents Sea)	• the State Committee on Fisheries (head of delegation) • the oblast/republican administrations of Murmansk, Arkhangelsk and Karelia • VNIRO (federal fisheries research institute) • regional fisheries research institutes from Murmansk and Arkhangelsk (PINRO, SevPINRO) • regional control bodies in Murmansk and Arkhangelsk (Murmanrybvod and Sevrybvod) • Sevryba	• the administration of Sevryba • Murmansk Trawl Fleet • Murmanrybprom • Arkhangelsk Trawl Fleeet • Karelrybflot • Murmansk Collective Fishing Fleet • Sever
TSCC (responsible for distributing quota shares between Murmansk, Arkhangelsk, Nenets and Karelia)	• Sevryba (leader) • the oblast/republican administrations of Murmansk, Arkhangelsk and Karelia • regional fisheries research institutes in Murmansk and Arkhangelsk (PINRO, SevPINRO) • regional control bodies in Murmansk and Arkhangelsk (Murmanrybvod and Sevrybvod)	• the administration of Sevryba • Murmansk Trawl Fleet • Murmanrybprom • Arkhangelsk Trawl Fleet • Karelrybflot • The collective fishing fleets of Murmansk, Arkhangelsk and Karelia • Sever
The Regional Fishery Councils (responsible for distributing quota shares between individual companies in the respective regional entities)	• the oblast/republican administration in the respective regional entities (leader) • Sevryba • research and control bodies from the respective regional entities	• the administration of Sevryba • the largest fishing companies in the respective regional entities • the collective fishing fleets of the respective regional entities • Sever

Oblasts, the Republic of Karelia, and since 1998 also Nenets Autonomous Okrug.[12] Within each region, *Regional Fishery Councils* are responsible for the further distribution among ship owners. These are headed by representatives (normally leaders) of the fisheries departments of the regional administration (i.e. the governors' apparatus). However, federal authorities still have to approve all decisions. Thus, the new system contributes to the implementation of the 1994 agreement (see above) inasmuch as governors' representatives head the regional bodies responsible for quota distribution among enterprises. On the other hand, it would be incorrect to assert that the reorganisation led to a regionalised fisheries management in Northwestern Russia. First, fish resources in the exclusive economic zone are still defined as *federal* property. Hence, federal authorities have to sanction all judgements at a regional level. Furthermore, although seriously weakened, Sevryba, their *de facto* representative organ in the region, still exerted decisive influence on certain management decisions.

Towards a Power-Based Management System?

Most of the period 1997-99 can be characterised as something close to a state of emergency in federal Russian fisheries management. In March 1997, President Yeltsin issued a decree that deprived the State Committee on Fisheries of its status as State Committee and subordinated it to the Ministry of Agriculture. A period of fierce opposition from the Fisheries Committee followed, and more than six months passed before the decision was implemented. Moreover, a governmental commission was established in April to evaluate the entire fisheries management of the Russian Federation.[13] Its mandate was to:

> define measures to secure state control and regulation in the exploitation and conservation of living resources and sale of fish products [...], to co-ordinate the activities of relevant federal executive organs in questions concerning the battle against crime in relation to the exploitation of living resources [...] and to secure co-ordination with the relevant executive organs of the federal subjects.[14]

The commission was headed by Deputy Prime Minister and Minister of Economy Yakov M. Urinson, while the leader of Russia's fisheries administration (now formally First Deputy Minister of Agriculture) was his deputy. A striking feature of the composition of the commission was the heavy representation of *power structures*, such as the Ministry of Internal Affairs, the federal security service (FSB), the tax police, the Border Guard and the state customs committee, and of *economic authorities* such as the Ministry of Economics, the Ministry of Finance and the Ministry of Foreign Economic Relations and Trade, at the expense of those authorities traditionally responsible for fisheries management.[15]

The commission does not seem to have had any decisive influence on Russia's fisheries management system, but it foreshadowed a new trend in the country's management culture. This trend was confirmed by a new decision with significant implications for the fisheries management, namely the decision of August 1997 to transfer enforcement responsibility at sea from the civilian bodies under the State Committee on Fisheries to the military Border Guard.[16] This led to a much greater general stir than the March and April events had. During the autumn of 1997, the battle between the Border Guard and the Fisheries Committee (now subordinated to the Ministry of Agriculture) was a major issue of contention in Russian politics, receiving due attention in the media and generally far outside traditional fisheries circles. The decision met harsh criticism from both the established fisheries management structures and from the fishing industry itself. In an open letter to President Yeltsin, the leaders of the Russian Pacific Ocean fishermen wrote:

> We are worried about the fact that the fisheries management in Russia is disintegrating year by year. Why ruin something that works? How come the Border Guard all of a sudden finds itself competent to handle fishery issues? Have they already plugged all holes in the border? Don't they have anything else to occupy themselves with? Probably, they are just trying to divert attention from what they are supposed to be doing. See who's supporting them! It's the eternal men of yesterday![17]

Protests also came from fishermen of the northern basin. A representative of the fishermen in Murmansk made the following statement: 'The situation in our fishing industry is still difficult. The last six months' disintegration also of the federal management organs renders it extremely alarming'.[18]

The most conspicuous feature of the debate was, however, the aggressive tone on the part of the Border Guard. It created an image of

Russia's fish resources being plundered, and blamed hitherto responsible organs for weak enforcement of regulations. Furthermore, parts of the press seemed to a large extent to have adopted the stance of the Border Guard. 'The Mafia Has Beaten the Fishery Inspection. Can the Border Guard Beat the Mafia?' read the major headline on the front page of *Izvestiya* 12 September 1997.[19] On the part of the Border Guard, it was asserted that the interests of the existing inspection system were too close to those of the fishing industry itself, and hence, that the civilian enforcement bodies were not in a position to enforce regulations effectively. In the future, however, no violator was to feel safe, the argument went: the fish resources of the fatherland would be protected by uniformed personnel, if necessary with weapon in hand.

The governmental structure of the Russian Federation was reorganised in connection with the economic and political crisis in the autumn of 1998. According to the 'Presidential Decree on the Structure of the Federal Bodies of the Executive Power'[20] of 24 September 1998, the Fisheries Committee regained its status as State Committee. Shortly after, the leader of the Committee, Aleksandr Rodin, was ousted. Rodin was, as his predecessors, a 'fishery man' who had climbed the career ladder *within* the Soviet/Russian fishery complex. His successor had a long track record from various power agencies, signalling a new direction in Russian fisheries management (i.e. confirming other signals from the preceding year; see above). The power struggle between the traditional fisheries management bodies and various power structures, in particular the Border Guard, is considered by actors in Northwest Russian fishing industry to reflect the more overall contest between the presidential administration and the federal government. The Border Guard was allegedly supported by the former in its quest for influence on fisheries management.

Compliance control in the Russian part of the Barents Sea has, until recently, been the sole responsibility of Murmanrybvod, the regional branch of Rosrybvod (Russian Fishery Inspection), which in turn is part of the federal State Committee on Fisheries.[21] In addition to ocean fisheries, Murmanrybvod has been responsible for controlling fishing in rivers and lakes on the Kola Peninsula. It has had 20 inspectors for control of the Barents Sea fisheries. However, in July 1998 the responsibility for enforcement in the Barents Sea was transferred to the military Border Guard after a lengthy dispute with civilian fishing authorities. Enforcement at sea was supposed to become more extensive as a result of the reform, since the Border Guard has considerably more vessels at its disposal than the two owned by Murmanrybvod. However, presence at sea by enforcement authorities has actually been further reduced recently as a result of the economic crisis in Russia. Although the Border Guard possesses more vessels than Murmanrybvod, it has so far not been able to utilise this potential since it cannot afford to buy fuel for them.[22]

More interesting in a discussion of management authority is the fact that a parallel enforcement structure has evolved in the Russian part of the Barents Sea. While the Border Guard was eventually given the responsibility for enforcement at sea, Murmanrybvod managed to retain all other enforcement operations, e.g. control of documents, catch control in harbours and closing and opening of fishing grounds. It is important for the old enforcement organ to keep as many of the previous tasks as possible since each transferred task means a reduction in funding. Paradoxically, inspectors from the Border Guard and Murmanrybvod have during 1998-99 conducted inspections more or less side by side in the ports of Murmansk Oblast. Murmanrybvod is still entitled to inspect in port whereas the Border Guard has been compelled to conduct the majority of its inspections here since it cannot afford the necessary fuel to inspect at sea (see Chapter 7 by Anne-Kristin Jørgensen). In time-honoured Russian tradition, the inspection activities of the two bodies are not co-ordinated.

Sevryba towards Revival or Comfortable Backwater?

To the extent that there was a conscious and substantial objective behind the 1994 agreement between the State Committee on Fisheries and the Murmansk Oblast administration, it might have been to separate management and industry interests from each other. Regional authorities were to take over management responsibilities whereas Sevryba was to retain its role as an association of industry enterprises. It soon turned out, however, that the member enterprises of Sevryba – i.e. all industry actors in Northwest Russian fisheries except the collective fleet[23] – no longer saw any role for the association as an overarching structure. In practice, they have operated as independent industrial actors since the transformation of Sevryba into a joint stock company in 1992.[24] The central administration of Sevryba has accordingly been compelled to reduce its staff from more than

800 people in the 'good old Soviet days' to some 50 at present. Stripped of its control over the fleet, it became all the more important for the remaining Sevryba administration to retain its role in the management process. The result was the battle between Sevryba and the Murmansk Oblast administration outlined above. Possessing all the experience and expertise that the oblast administration lacks, Sevryba first came out as the winner: although regional authorities had formally taken over the responsibility for fisheries management, they were in practice totally dependent upon the continuing co-operation of Sevryba in the management process.

In 1997, the Sevryba administration acquired its first vessel, Sevryba-1. It was then in a position to secure favourable quota conditions for it, registered it in Cyprus, and thus emerged as a small, but lucrative one-boat fishing company. At the same time, the management tasks were increasingly handed over to the oblast administration. The institutional identity of Sevryba was again changing; with the emerging possibilities for Sevryba 1 and several sister ships already under way, it seemed finally to be ready to let go of management responsibilities.[25]

Since mid-1999, a central topic of discussion in the Murmansk fisheries community has been the question of establishing a new 'basin management body', i.e. an official body in charge of managing the entire northern fisheries basin. The 'basin body' would be based on the remains of Sevryba and be placed *both* under the State Committee on Fisheries and the governors/president of the four federal subjects in Northwest Russia. The principal question is whether the new body – if established – will be granted more responsibility than has previously been the case in the region, i.e. will there be a more regionalised fisheries management process in Russia? Some seem primarily to want 'a strong hand' in the northern fisheries basin; many fishermen think that Sevryba in its present form is much too concerned with its commercial activities, making it unable to defend the interests of its members when required. There have been proposals to raise the status of the new Sevryba by appointing its leader deputy chairman of the State Committee on Fisheries. Others have even demanded that the new 'basin body' should both be in charge of quota allocation and of fisheries collaboration with Norway, without any interference from Moscow.[26] As of July 2000, the 'basin body' has not yet been established.

To sum up, in recent years there have been only minor changes in Northwest Russian fisheries management. Even though the decision has not yet been made, political signals indicate that a new management body will be created for the entire northern basin, based on Sevryba. Some central players have great ambitions for the 'basin body' and in Russian politics, needless to say, one cannot rule out even the most unexpected solution. Nevertheless, it would mean a *very* radical change in Russian fisheries policy if the new organisation were granted independent responsibility for quota distribution and management collaboration with Norway. Legally, this possibility cannot be excluded, although there are probably weighty arguments against such a solution being in accordance with federal law. In purely practical and political terms, it is hard to find good reasons for Moscow to thus relinquish power over an important natural resource. However, one must not disregard the possibility of a compromise, involving a certain shift of responsibility from the federal to the regional level. Still, this solution also does not seem very likely at present. The most probable outcome would in fact be the creation of the 'basin body', thus 'strengthening' the regional fisheries management with an organisation that is 'stronger' than Sevryba and the oblast administration today, while the federal authorities maintain control and sanction possibilities for decisions made in the region.

Conclusion

The most conspicuous feature in the development of Northwest Russian fisheries management over the last decade is the constant power struggle between various governmental bodies at the regional level, at the federal level and between the two levels. Moreover, there has been a more or less continuous change in the 'power balance' between various structures, leaving a considerable amount of insecurity as to who is at a specific time actually in charge; or rather: who is actually the strongest among those formally in charge? The general trend towards regionalisation in the early years of the Russian Federation spurred the administration of Murmansk Oblast to claim influence in the fisheries management, which had hitherto been the responsibility of federal authorities and its executive body in the region, Sevryba. The oblast administration gained such influence on paper, but as is often the case in Russia, this did not imply a *de facto* transfer of decision-making power. The result was first a period when both Sevryba and Murmansk Oblast administration claimed they were in charge of the quota distribution, then a compromise which still left the actual delimitation in responsibility somewhat unclear. The oblast administration seems to have settled with a limited influence on the management process whereas Sevryba at the moment seems more interested in doing business than in distributing quotas. Admittedly, the expected establishment of a new 'basin body' represents an element of uncertainty in this respect.

A similar state of flux appeared at the federal level – as well as in the enforcement sector of the regional level – when various 'power structures' started to demand increased influence over fisheries management in 1997. First, the old system continued to function for a long time after the reorganisation decrees were issued. Second, when the changes were actually implemented, a compromise evolved which secured the continued existence also of the old systems. Hence, the State Committee on Fisheries today consists of people from the old fishery complex, but under stronger influence of various 'power figures' than before. The Border Guard has in fact been given responsibility for enforcement at sea, but the civilian fishery inspection bodies under Rosrybvod have held on to all other previous tasks. In practice, the Border Guard has also been forced to operate mainly in the harbours of Murmansk Oblast due to scarce funding and high fuel prices. Inspectors from Murmanrybvod and the Border Guard thus conduct their inspections according to the same standards, operating in the same geographical areas towards the same groups of fishermen, but without any coordination between them. Again, the 'intruder' seems to have settled with part of the gain. However, Murmanrybvod seems more eager to keep as many of its remaining management tasks than the case has been with Sevryba during the last years of the 1990s. Nevertheless, the situation is so unstable that one cannot exclude the possibility that Sevryba again might emerge as an important actor in Northwest Russian fisheries management.

In sum, it is difficult to limit a discussion of management authorities in current Northwest Russian fisheries to a straightforward argument of centre-periphery tensions. Fisheries management is also influenced by other general tensions in Russian politics and society, such as the ones between the presidential administration and the government, the power structures and other parts of the executive branch, and perhaps most important in this case, the one between the old industrial complexes (here the fisheries complex) and the political-administrative branches of government. So far, the tension between the executive and legislative has not affected

Northwest Russian fisheries, probably due to the weak role of the regional dumas in the area.

Northwest Russian fisheries are certainly not regionalised in the sense that management authority has been transferred from the federal to the regional level. Nevertheless, an increased role for regional authorities can be witnessed as compared to the Soviet period. This has primarily taken place at the expense of the old fishery complex conglomerate in the region. Hence, it can be argued that management tasks have been transferred from one regional actor to another. On the other hand, the administration of Murmansk Oblast is more independent from federal fishery management authorities than Sevryba was (and still is, for that matter). It should also be observed that the new quota distribution system proposed by federal authorities in 1997 was halted by joint opposition from the regional level. More than anything, however, it should be noted that the current Northwest Russian fisheries management system is fragile in the sense that the power balance between the various actors may easily change according to the overall political development in Russia.

Notes

[1] The first part of this chapter is based on other publications by the author (Hønneland, 1998; 2000a), partly in co-operation with Frode Nilssen from the Norwegian Institute of Fisheries and Aquaculture Ltd. in Tromsø (Hønneland and Nilssen, 2000). The empirical material is mainly collected through interviews with representatives of Northwest Russian fisheries by the author, Mr. Nilssen and our co-operation partners from the Kola Science Centre of the Russian Academy of Sciences, Anatoliy Vasilev and Lyudmila Ivanova.

[2] St prp nr 86 (1974-75) Om samtykke til inngåelse av en avtale mellom Norge og Sovjetunionen om samarbeid innen fiskerinæringen.

[3] St prp nr 74 (1976-77) Om samtykke til ratifikasjon av en avtale mellom Regjeringen i Kongeriket Norge og Regjeringen i Unionen av Sovjetiske Sosialistiske Republikker om gjensidige fiskeriforbindelser.

[4] The changing status of this body is further described below.

[5] See Hønneland (2000b) for a more detailed discussion of the committee's achievements.

[6] Referring to the international waters in the northeastern part of the Barents Sea, where Icelandic and other vessels of various nationalities have caught considerable amounts of cod since the early 1990s. See Stokke (1998) for a discussion of the status of the Barents Sea Loophole.

[7] Accordingly, the northern fishery basin today comprises Murmansk and Arkhangelsk Oblasts, the Republic of Karelia and Nenets Autonomous Okrug.

8 Similar bodies were set up in the Far East ('Dalryba'), the Baltics (Zapryba), the Caspian Sea (Kaspryba) as well as the Azov Sea and the Black Sea (Azcherryba, later re-named Yugryba).
9 However, only 70 of these are involved in the catching of fish, and no more than 18 among them have a cod quota in the Barents Sea. Thus, most of the companies do not have fishing as their core activity, and they resort to the catching or selling of fish primarily to raise funds for other kinds of production or trade.
10 This figure is based on the estimate of Russian specialists; official statistics do not contain data on the total employment in the Northwest Russian fisheries sector.
11 *Vremennoye polozheniye o raspredelenii kvot vylova vodnykh bioresursov predpriyatiyam Severnogo rybokhozyaystvennogo basseyna v 1997 godu; Polozheniye o raspredelenii kvot vylova vodnykh biologicheskikh resursov mezhdu polzovatelyami.*
12 Minor shares of the total Barents Sea cod quota are transferred to Leningrad and Kaliningrad Oblasts and set aside for scientific purposes or 'basin needs'.
13 *Postanovleniye pravitelstva Rossiyskoy Federatsii: O Pravitelstvennoy komissii po koordinatsii deyatelnosti i operativnomu resheniyu voprosov v sfere okhrany zhivykh resursov territorialnykh vod, kontinentalnogo shelfa, isklyuchitelnoy ekonomicheskoy zony Rossiyskoy Federatsii, Kaspiyskogo i Azovskogo morey.*
14 *ibid.*, p. 3287.
15 Admittedly, the somewhat 'softer' Ministry of Natural Resources and State Committee on Ecology were also represented.
16 Enforcement had been performed by regional enforcement bodies (such as 'Murmanrybvod' in the Barents Sea) under the State Committee on Fisheries; cf. the discussion below. See Hønneland (1998) for a more detailed description of the Russian fisheries enforcement system.
17 *Izvestiya*, 4 October 1997.
18 *Polyarnaya pravda*, 19 September 1997.
19 *Izvestiya*, 12 September 1997.
20 *O strukture federalnykh organov ispolnitelnoy vlasti*, 24 September 1998.
21 Sevrybvod in Arkhangelsk and Karelrybvod in Karelia are to a very limited extent involved in the enforcement of the Barents Sea fisheries. Murmanrybvod was, until the recent transfer of responsibility to the Border Guard, alone responsible for enforcement at sea. 'Sevrybvod' and 'Karelrybvod' are responsible for control in the ports in their respective federal subjects, but it should be kept in mind that only very small amounts of fish are landed there.
22 There were reports of a massive catch of undersized fish in the Russian part of the Barents Sea throughout the winter 1998-99. Moreover, the Russian enforcement bodies have traditionally given priority to a passive control of documents, instead of an active, physical check of the fish (Jørgensen, 1999).
23 The Northwest Russian collective fleet – itself a remnant of the Soviet system – has at its disposal less than 10 per cent of the Russian Barents Sea quota.
24 Until the mid-1990s, representatives of the Sevryba administration used to complain in interviews with the author that the member enterprises did not comply with their orders and inform them about their activities. Since then, they seem to have accepted this change as a *fait accompli* and concentrated on retaining their influence in the management process, and subsequently on their new-found role as a 'small ship owner' (see below).

[25] In late 1997, representatives of the Sevryba' leadership acknowledged in interviews with the author that the management responsibility had been handed over to the governor's apparatus.

[26] Whether this is legally possible is a question of interpretation. According to the Russian Constitution, management of natural resources in the Russian Exclusive Economic Zone is a federal responsibility. Nevertheless, the agreement on distribution of power between the federal authorities and Murmansk Oblast of 30 October 1997 states that the federal authorities and the regional administration in Murmansk Oblast are jointly responsible for the 'rational exploitation of the natural resources in the Russian Exclusive Economic Zone in the Barents Sea'. Thus, it may be debated whether the traditional management tasks can be defined as 'rational exploitation'. At least on the federal side, one should have a good case for maintaining that this is not so. Further, the agreement states that Murmansk Oblast is entitled to enter into its own agreements with 'other states' administrative-territorial units, the subjects of foreign federations and other foreign partners based on federal legislation'. At issue here is whether the fisheries agreements with Norway can be defined as 'other foreign partners based on federal legislation'. Again, it should not be difficult for federal authorities to argue that these agreements cannot be concluded at the regional level. See also Chapter 2 by Brynjulf Risnes.

7 The Military Sector: Federal Responsibility – Regional Concern

ANNE-KRISTIN JØRGENSEN

In the Russian fisheries and oil and gas sectors – as demonstrated in Chapters 5 and 6 – the question of control over and ownership of resources is the core issue around which centre-periphery relations converge. In contrast, the military sector is itself a consumer of resources, designed to 'produce' a collective good – security – rather than economic revenue. Thus, where the military sector is concerned, the main question shaping centre-periphery relations is not 'who benefits?' but rather 'who pays?'.

In principle, of course, the defence is a federal responsibility. However, the various units and formations of the armed forces, as well as the numerous enterprises that constitute the military-industrial complex (MIC) are dispersed throughout the 89 subjects of the Federation. As vertical and sectoral ties have been relaxed over the last decade, the sharp segregation of the military from the civilian sphere has gradually weakened in the regions. The economic decline of Russia has been a crucial factor in this development. The strained federal budget has not allowed for proper financing of the armed forces and the defence industry, and thus regional authorities have been forced to play a greater part in supporting impoverished military units and defence enterprises.

Some observers have even claimed that Russia is faced with a 'regionalisation' of the armed forces, where military commanders may transfer their loyalties to the authorities in the region where their units are based – ultimately resulting in a fragmentation of the armed forces into a multitude of regional armies.[1] While such forecasts seem somewhat extreme, the growing dependency of military units on regional authorities has probably allowed the latter to strengthen their position in relation to both the military and the federal authorities. In the case of the defence industry, 'regionalisation' may not be such a sinister prospect seen from the point of view of the federal authorities. Defence enterprises that are more independent from Moscow and more integrated into regional economies constitute less of a burden – but no threat – to the centre.

The aim of this chapter is to describe the development within the military sector of Northwestern Russia in the post-Soviet period, and to discuss how it has affected the northwestern regions in general and their relations with the centre in particular.[2] I have chosen to focus on Murmansk Oblast – one of the most militarised regions in the world and home to the Northern Fleet – and on the defence industry complex in Severodvinsk (Arkhangelsk Oblast).[3] First, however, the development at the federal level will be examined in somewhat greater detail.

The Armed Forces and Defence Industry in a Period of Transition

It is generally acknowledged that the development of a military sector out of proportion to the country's economic capabilities was an important contributing factor to the decline of the Soviet Union.[4] In the years preceding the collapse, the introduction of *glasnost* led to a growing public awareness about the militarisation of the economy, and the military sector gradually came to be depicted as a black hole swallowing up national resources and impeding economic growth. Mikhail Gorbachev realised that substantial cuts in military spending were a precondition for achieving the main goal of his *perestroika* policy: economic growth.

In Russia under Yeltsin, the economic situation made further radical cuts a matter of necessity rather than political will. However, real demilitarisation of the economy requires more than just mechanical reductions in the financing of the armed forces and MIC – which is more or less what has ensued in the 1990s. In the case of Russia, it would imply a thorough restructuring of both the armed forces and the defence industry. This has proved extremely difficult to achieve, given the enormity of the task, the strained economic circumstances, and the resistance to reform from the military and MIC establishments and their political supporters. Fearing both the social and the political cost of radical reform, policy makers have chosen to spread resources thinly throughout the military sector.

The Armed Forces

After the break-up of the Soviet Union, Russia inherited a disproportionately large part of its armed forces. In 1992, when the Armed Forces of the Russian Federation were officially established, the total force levels of the Ministry of Defence were around 2.7 million.[5] In addition to this came numerous other armed formations – interior troops, the border guard service etc – whose combined strength was comparable to that of the armed forces proper. As had been the case with the Soviet Union, Russia was equipped with a military machine that outsized its economy. Thus, the country was faced with the task of streamlining the military to match the current economic capabilities and perception of threats. The idea at the time was that a gradual quantitative reduction of the armed forces would be accompanied by a process of military reform, eventually resulting in a substantially smaller, but more combat-effective military. In practice, events took a different turn.

In the course of the 1990s, force levels in the armed forces proper were more than halved, leaving some 1.2 million men per 1999.[6] However, the aim of substituting quantity for quality was not achieved. The reform process was fraught with problems linked to poor financing and lack of agreement on an overarching strategy. The Chechen wars also served to shift attention and resources away from reform. Numerous plans for reorganisation, including the shift from the army/division to a corps/brigade structure and an increase in the number of mobile and high readiness forces, were either carried out painfully slowly or 'left to gather dust in the archives' (Baev, 1996, p. 134). The number of personnel was reduced at a quicker rate than the number of units and formations, leaving Russia with a 'hollow army' (Dick, 1998, p. 61). Budgets for research and development and procurement were slashed to the core.[7] Thus, the vision of a modernised military equipped with state-of-the-art weapons – one of the planned outcomes of reform – was crushed by a stark reality where four fifths of all weapons and equipment would soon be past their intended service life.[8] Likewise, the part of the defence budget set aside for training and technical maintenance was cut, resulting in higher accident rates and lower combat readiness.

A growing part of the defence budget had to be allocated for so-called 'defended items' – salaries, food and other social costs (Arbatov,

1998). Despite this redirection of funding, it was not possible to prevent a sharp decline in social conditions for servicemen. Throughout the 1990s, military officers who used to enjoy a fairly privileged position in Soviet society found it increasingly difficult to ensure the day-to-day survival of themselves and their families. The tendency was for the younger and most resourceful officers to opt out of the military altogether, resulting in a less balanced, and, presumably, less professional officer corps. A liberalisation of the legislation on draft exemption,[9] compounded by a new phenomenon – large scale draft evasion among young men – seriously upset the ratio of officers to soldiers. Plans to switch to a system of contract service were only partly implemented due to opposition from military leaders arguing that a 100 per cent volunteer service would be far too costly. An additional headache for the Ministry of Defence was the increasingly low quality of both drafted personnel and contract soldiers. The problems most frequently pointed out were poor health, poor education, criminal tendencies and abuse of alcohol and drugs. Meanwhile, numerous newspaper articles on cases of crime and corruption in the military went to show that morale was declining among officers as well.[10]

At the same time, the internal cohesion of the officer corps grew gradually weaker. Officers left to fend for themselves felt alienated from the military top-brass, which was leading a protected life in the Ministry of Defence or the General Staff – ironically referred to as the 'Arbat Military District'[11] – while ordering those in the impoverished field units to fish, hunt and pick berries to supplement their rations.[12] Thus, servicemen in the regions could no longer expect to rely on the Ministry of Defence to cover even their most basic needs, and in this situation, many commanders chose to turn to regional civilian authorities for support.

The Military-Industrial Complex

In the Soviet Union, the production of military hardware was concentrated in a group of powerful ministries whose activity was supervised and co-ordinated by the government agency *Voyenno-promyshlennaya kommissiya* (VPK) – the Military-Industrial Commission. The enterprises subordinate to these ministries were referred to collectively as the military-industrial complex. Since these enterprises also manufactured a wide range of civilian goods, and since many of the nominally civilian ministries were also engaged in production for defence purposes, the precise scale of the defence sector has been difficult to calculate. According to Gaddy (1996), the best result is obtained by looking at the sector's share of the work force, which he estimates at around ten per cent, if only those directly engaged in arms production are counted. The defence enterprises routinely received the best raw materials; the most brilliant scientists worked in the industry's research and development organisations; and the work force received higher than average wages and often enjoyed various other privileges (Cooper, 1991; Gaddy, 1996).

The first changes in the defence industry happened in 1988. New legislation was introduced whereby industrial enterprises in general were granted a greater degree of financial autonomy, and this strongly affected the defence industry, which to some extent was forced to compete for resources it could formerly simply command.[13] The same year domestic arms procurement started to drop. As was the case with the armed forces, the real blow came with the collapse of the Soviet Union: From 1991 to 1992, the number of defence contracts were cut by 65 per cent (Arbatov, 1998), and this only marked the beginning of a downward trend.

Given these circumstances, it might be argued that the Russian authorities ought to have let all the enterprises unable to compete for orders redirect their production to civilian purposes or go bankrupt. In this way, they could have improved conditions in the remaining core of the industry, and such a strategy was indeed advocated by liberal politicians. However, a major share of the Russian defence industry is made up of monolithic enterprises with several thousand employees each. Often they constitute the backbone of the city or town where they are located, providing not only work, but also the entire social infrastructure: housing, schools, hospitals, leisure activities and the like (see Chapter 4 by Per Botolf Maurseth). Thus, the social cost of closing down an enterprise could be overwhelming. Moreover, even if the whole 'dispensable' part of the MIC was closed down, the size and structure of remaining enterprises would still not fit current economic needs very well, and the necessary restructuring would be a difficult task.

In his time, Mikhail Gorbachev decided that the key to solving the problem of the inflated defence industry would be conversion to civilian purposes. Impressed with the high performance of the defence enterprises compared to civilian ones, he thought that this move could simultaneously save the workplaces and meet the population's demand for high quality consumer goods. What he failed to see, however, was that the reason for the sector's apparent efficiency lay in the fact that it never had to compete for resources (Gaddy, 1996). In reality, most of the defence enterprises were unsuited for conversion. The manufacture of civilian consumer goods requires different production modes, facilities and technology than that of military hardware. Even with new equipment installed, the cost of maintaining unnecessary large buildings, not to mention heat and electricity, would in many cases be prohibitive.

Under Yeltsin, the chosen strategy – or non-strategy – towards the MIC was similar to that applied to the armed forces, i.e. spreading resources thinly. The military and defence industry establishments strongly argued for the necessity of keeping capabilities intact, and under the 'Law on Mobilisation Capacity', enterprises were forced to spend a large part of their resources on preserving dead assets (Arbatov, 1998). A multitude of conversion programmes were worked out, but hardly any of them were financed properly, and the funding which was actually awarded was distributed too widely to have much effect. Rather than full conversion, many enterprises opted for diversification, i.e. increasing the output of civilian goods while maintaining capabilities for arms production.[14] However, the most widespread tactic for the many enterprises receiving few or no defence orders has simply been to muddle through, stretching their meagre budgets by leasing floor-space and equipment, and shifting their employees to a partial work-week or prolonging their holidays (Arbatov, 1998). Assuming that at some point procurement will have to increase again, they try to keep their heads above water while waiting for that to happen.

The majority of the defence enterprises are still owned by the state, but the autonomy and responsibilities of the managers have increased. Under the command economy, the enterprises would receive orders from their respective ministries on what to produce, as well as the necessary resources for carrying out these orders. The director's job was to ensure that the orders were completed on time and within the limits set by the appointed resources. Today, a successful manager often equals someone skilled in lobbying for contracts at the Ministry of Defence.

Usually, however, defence orders will not be sufficient to pay for all expenses, and this has rendered the enterprises' relations with regional and local authorities more important. Regional and local administrations usually engage in broad co-operation with cornerstone enterprises, not least since the latter have frequently chosen to maintain social services, which formally are not their responsibility anymore. In return, the administration may postpone or refrain from the collection of local taxes, and provide heating, electricity and other communal services at reduced rates or for free. In regions with a very high concentration of defence industry, the economy of the enterprises and that of the region become more or less inseparable, and the managers are often deeply involved in regional politics.

The Military Sector in Murmansk Oblast

The Kola Peninsula is still an extremely militarised area, despite severe cutbacks in the military sector in recent years. It was military considerations that prompted the lengthening of the railway from Petrozavodsk to the shores of the Arctic Ocean in 1916, thus paving the way for large-scale migration from the south (see Chapter 1 by Helge Blakkisrud and Geir Hønneland). For more than half a century, the military and civilian sectors in Murmansk Oblast developed and expanded side by side, yet functionally and spatially divided.

Rise and Decline of the Military Complex

The strategic value of the Kola Peninsula was first proved during World War I, when Western supplies were imported and Russian goods exported via the Barents Sea thanks to the newly constructed Murman Railway and the port facilities in the Kola Bay. Since German submarines tried to disrupt this traffic, it became necessary to dispatch warships to the area and construct bases for them. The naval presence was to become permanent, and in 1933 the Northern Fleet was officially established. Its first base was in Polyarnyy (formerly Aleksandrovsk) on the Western shore of Kola Bay, but the headquarters were later moved across the bay to Severomorsk. The Northern Fleet played an important role during World War II, when allied convoys once more needed protection from submarine attacks. However, it remained the smallest of the four Soviet Fleets until the 1950s, when a period of expansion began that lasted well into the 1980s. Already by the late 1960s, the Northern Fleet had passed the other fleets in size and significance (Skogan, 1986).

The Soviet Union's first nuclear submarine entered service in the Northern Fleet in 1958, and during the following years, six new naval bases were constructed along the northern shores of the Kola Peninsula (Nilsen et al., 1996). The strategic submarines, equipped with ballistic missiles, which could reach the American continent from positions in the Arctic Ocean, became the most important element in the Northern Fleet.

The Kola Peninsula is also strategically important as an intermediary landing base for Long Range (Strategic) Aviation, which, together with strategic submarines and land-based inter-continental missiles, makes up the Russian strategic nuclear forces. A large number of airbases and airports allow for the transfer of aircraft to the region if need be (Ries, 1991). In addition, both the Northern Fleet and the Air Force have conventional aircraft units stationed in Murmansk Oblast.[15]

The most important Ground Force formation on the Kola Peninsula is a motorised infantry brigade stationed in the Pechenga Valley not far from the Norwegian border. The Pechenga area is also home to the Northern Fleet's naval infantry brigade and its Spetsnaz brigade.[16] Of military formations outside the Ministry of Defence structure, the most important are an Interior Troops battalion and the Border Service, which has a large number of detachments along the borders with Norway and Finland and also along the northern shores of the peninsula.

The militarisation of the area reached its peak in the 1980s. Towards the end of the decade, a gradual reduction of force levels began, and in the early 1990s the process gained momentum.[17] Since 1991, the number of vessels in the Northern Fleet has been more than halved, and one of its two naval infantry brigades has been disbanded. Likewise, one of two motorised infantry divisions has been turned into an armament and equipment storage base, while the other has been reorganised into a brigade (the one stationed in the Pechenga Valley). Over the same period of time, the training activity in the various military formations has been kept at a low level, even to the point where Western observers have questioned the ability of the troops to carry out normal military operations. The vessels of the Northern Fleet and the Border Service have been confined to port for long periods of time, partly due to fuel shortages. Thus, much of the training activities on board the naval ships as well as the Border Service's inspections of fishing vessels have had to be carried out in port.[18] The unsatisfactory maintenance of vessels has been an important factor contributing to the low sailing frequency. Lack of maintenance also results in many vessels being phased out of service ahead of time (Litovkin, 2000). Decommissioned nuclear submarines, which are stored afloat with spent fuel still in the reactors, represent a problem with ramifications way beyond the internal problems of the Russian military. The responsibility for removing the reactors and disposing of the fuel was transferred from the Ministry of Defence to the Ministry of Nuclear Energy in 1998,[19] but in practice the Northern Fleet to a large extent continues to carry out this work (*ibid.*).

The military formations in Murmansk Oblast also seem to have their share of problems with morale. In an interview with the Defence Ministry daily, *Krasnaya zvezda*, in March 1998, Defence Minister Igor Sergeyev mentioned the Northern Fleet among the units and districts where discipline problems and suicides were most widespread.[20] Former commander of the Northern Fleet Oleg Yerofeyev stated in an interview with a Severomorsk newspaper that alcohol abuse was a major reason for deaths and accidents among his personnel (Simonsen, 1996). In recent years, several serious incidents have occurred which have caused headlines even in the foreign press. In autumn 1998, a soldier barricaded himself on board a nuclear submarine and shot dead eight of his colleagues.[21] In two other incidents – one in a Northern Fleet unit, the other in one of the units in Pechenga – soldiers broke out of prison, killed the guards and put up armed resistance when hunted down – in both cases with further loss of lives as the result.[22]

It is reasonable to assume that the decline in morale has much to do with living and service conditions. Despite the redirection of funding from items such as procurement and maintenance to social welfare, the daily life of soldiers and officers on the Kola Peninsula has become more difficult over the past decade. Wage arrears of several months have not been uncommon, and child benefits, meal allowances and other extras which officers are legally entitled to are often not paid out at all (Hønneland and Jørgensen, 1999b). Cut-offs in gas and heating (usually due to non-payment) have occurred frequently (*ibid.*), and such problems are particularly serious in a region where winter temperatures of minus 30°C are common. Moreover, when people are more or less isolated in remote military garrisons, it becomes doubly important to have a meaningful job, which again requires reasonable funding for training, equipment etc.

Military-Regional Relations

Throughout the Soviet period, there was little interaction between the military and civilian spheres in Murmansk Oblast. Organisationally, both were subordinate to Moscow – the military complex to the Ministry of Defence and the civilian sphere to various civilian ministries.[23] The two structures to a large degree relied on two separate communication infrastructures, with the military one being superior. There was also a geographic separation, insofar as the majority of the servicemen and their families lived either in military towns or settlements built to serve the naval and air bases, or on the territory of the garrison where they served. Living in the region, they still were *gosudarevye lyudi* – 'the state's people'. The shops they did their shopping in, the schools they sent their children to, the hospitals they visited when they were ill, were all provided by the Ministry of Defence.

It has been claimed that in the early 1990s approximately one third of the adult citizens of Murmansk Oblast – that is, some 300,000 people – were directly or indirectly dependent on the military complex (Castberg, 1992; Sekarev, 1993). Excluding officers and their families,[24] this still leaves a large residue of civilians carrying out support functions for the Northern Fleet and other military formations. The military was not only equipped with its own social infrastructure – the Northern Fleet, at least, had a number of industrial enterprises of its own. The most important of these were the naval shipyards responsible for the repair and maintenance of submarines and surface vessels. Most of these enterprises were located in military towns. Thus, despite their civilian status, many of those working in the support industry formed an integral part of the military complex.[25]

The relations between the military and civilian sectors of Murmansk Oblast were not only marked by a relatively low level of interaction in general, but also, apparently, by a relative absence of conflict. People took the heavy military presence in their region for granted rather than questioning or problematising it. People were brought up to respect and honour the armed forces as the protectors of their country against outside aggression. The important role of the Murmansk region in World War II was kept alive in the public consciousness. People's awareness of the military's role as a major employer may also have influenced feelings towards it, although not to the degree it might have done if employment had not been guaranteed to all Soviet citizens.

Towards the end of the 1980s, the perceived threat from NATO began to wane, and at the same time the traditional secrecy surrounding the military sphere was gradually lifted. During the following years, people became increasingly aware of the negative aspects of military activities – in Murmansk Oblast notably the Northern Fleet's contribution to the rapidly growing stockpiles of radioactive waste. During this period, political activism for democratisation often centred on green issues, and in Murmansk Oblast the question of nuclear safety became a main focus for demonstrations and protest actions.[26] The military may also have been conceived of as a potential barrier to a broader development of relations with neighbouring countries. Moreover, the development of hydrocarbon resources on the continental shelf, which might become a source of regional economic activity and revenues (see Chapter 5 by Arild Moe), could easily come into conflict with military interests (Moe, 1994). The right of the Northern Fleet and Border Guards to keep large coastal areas off-limits to civilians, hereunder fishing vessels, were also questioned.

However, as Russia's economic problems deepened throughout the 1990s and the warm relations with the West gave way to what is often referred to as a 'cold peace', people's attitude towards the military underwent a change. The prestige of the armed forces may not have been restored to former levels, but the general tendency seems to be for people to feel that the military is to be pitied rather than blamed. In Murmansk Oblast, as in Russia as a whole, people are more worried about economic issues than about the environment. Thus, to the extent that people view the armed forces as a problem, this is now linked more to the fact that the increasingly impoverished military complex has gone from being one of the cornerstones of the regional economy to becoming an economic burden.

The MIC has gone from crisis to crisis throughout the second half of the 1990s. Orders from the Northern Fleet to the naval shipyards have plummeted, and the Fleet has largely been unable to pay for the work that is still carried out. As a result, strikes and social unrest have been frequent. On a number of occasions, shipyard workers have blocked the road from Murmansk to Severomorsk to protest wage arrears. At another Fleet enterprise, workers went on a hunger strike to call attention to their misfortune (Hønneland and Jørgensen, 1999b). In recent years, the Ministry of

Defence has been trying to shed some of its supporting structures, switching to a system where the military buys goods and services from independent suppliers. Thus, it has been suggested that the shipyards of the Navy, including those of the Northern Fleet, should be reorganised into a holding company.[27] In any case, the fleet's various enterprises are faced with a situation where they will either have to find new niches in the civilian market or adapt to the current situation by reducing staff and technical capabilities. However, attempts at conversion to, for example, civilian shipbuilding have so far had little success (*ibid.*).

The military not only has problems meeting its obligations towards its own support structures. Many units and garrisons are also dependent upon local or regional authorities or civilian enterprises for heating and electricity, and they are often unable to pay for these services on time and in full. In the Murmansk region, as in many other regions where military formations are stationed, there have been cases where the supply of electricity has simply been cut off in order to induce payment. However, this practice has been rendered illegal by federal legislation, so regional enterprises are in practice forced to subsidise the military sector whether they want to or not. Moreover, even if the social welfare of military personnel and their families is a federal responsibility, regional authorities are closer to the problem and often feel compelled to interfere in crisis situations. In Murmansk Oblast, a separate department has been created under the regional administration to co-ordinate efforts to alleviate social problems in the military.[28] This department is also involved in brokering deals whereby the military can raise funds – for instance by hiring out troops as labourers – which can then be transferred to food, power etc. Even more in need of support than the active duty personnel are the many officers who have been made redundant over the last decade.[29] These people have to compete with civilians for jobs, and they often lose out because their skills do not fit employers' needs.

A rather conspicuous illustration of the military's new dependence on the civilian sphere is the practice whereby civilian institutions and enterprises literally sponsor military units. The institution or enterprise in question 'adopts' the unit and agrees to render it material support, which may be anything from TV sets and books to wagonloads of cabbage or potatoes. Even items such as grease and spare parts for vessels may be supplied by adopting organisations. The practice of adoption took on new proportions in 1997, when Governor Yuriy Yevdokimov invited all the regions of Russia to sponsor the Northern Fleet's submarines. The ties between region and vessel are strengthened by renaming the vessel after the sponsoring region and manning it with draftees from that particular part of Russia. The campaign apparently has been a great success. In a TV interview in October 1999, when asked what had been his most important achievement as a politician, Yevdokimov referred to the submarine adoption campaign, which he said most of Russia's regions were now taking part in. For the military, the sponsoring clearly plays a role beyond that of moral support. Thus, an officer in one of the units stationed in Pechenga pointed to problems with attracting sponsors when called on to explain why social conditions in his unit were so much worse than in the Northern Fleet.[30]

The picture presented thus far gives the impression that regional authorities have gradually taken over much of the responsibility for the welfare of the armed forces in Murmansk Oblast. However, the burden on the region would have been significantly heavier if it had not been for one very important factor: A large share of the military population lives in closed towns – or, to use the official term, closed administrative-territorial formations (CATFs) – which are directly subordinate to the federal authorities. In the Soviet Union, there were a number of closed cities and towns, the most well-known of which were associated with research on and production of nuclear weapons (Rowland, 1996). After the collapse of the Soviet Union and the founding of the Russian Federation, the status of many of these closed cities was formalised through the 'Law on Closed Administrative-Territorial Formations', which entered into force on 14 July 1992 and was amended in 1995.[31] According to the 1995 amendments, a CATF is defined as:

> a territorial formation with bodies for local government, which contains within its boundaries industrial companies engaged in development, production, storage and use of weapons of mass destruction, preparation of radioactive materials or other material, military and other objects [...] for which a particular regime is established. This shall help secure the functioning of the city, to preserve state secrets and to maintain special conditions for the inhabitants.[32]

A vital element of the law is that it establishes the financing of activities in the CATFs as a federal responsibility. All taxes and other duties from a CATF territory go directly to its own budget and funds; other needs shall be met through subsidies and allocations from the federal government.[33] Moreover, the inhabitants are entitled to special advantages such as higher wages, particular social protection, guaranteed employment and grants for moving and settling elsewhere.

The six CATFs in Murmansk Oblast mainly serve as residence towns for the naval bases and workers in the shipyards. Four of them, Zaozyorsk, Skalistyy, Ostrovnoy and Snezhnogorsk were included in the CATF regime from the beginning. The two largest, however – Severomorsk and Polyarnyy – were given this status only in 1995 and 1996 respectively, and the decision to add them to the list seems to have been made on the basis of economic, rather than security considerations. Not surprisingly, the regional authorities actively promoted this move (Hønneland and Jørgensen, 1998; 1999b).

The law on CATFs has become costly to the federal budget, and recently there has been some discussion of introducing new legislation whereby some of the advantages granted to these entities will be abolished.[34] It has also been suggested that CATF status be removed from some of the towns that currently enjoy it.[35]

The Severodvinsk Military-Industrial Complex

The city of Severodvinsk is the second largest in Arkhangelsk Oblast, with a total of approximately 230,000 inhabitants, and it is totally dependent on the defence industry. To rephrase a formulation frequently used to describe the Soviet Union, Severodvinsk, rather than having a military-industrial complex, *is* a military-industrial complex. The development of the defence industry in the city was directly related to the growth of the Northern Fleet in the post-war period. The production of submarines and service and repair of naval vessels have traditionally been the main activities. The core of the industry is constituted by two large shipyards: *Severnoye mashinostroitelnoye predpriyatiye* (*Sevmash*), which at its peak in the 1980s had some 40,000 employees (Fattakhov, 1995) and *Zvyozdochka*, which has around 8,000 employees (Kuznetsov and Velikhov, 1997). The Soviet

Figure 7.1 The Kola CATFs

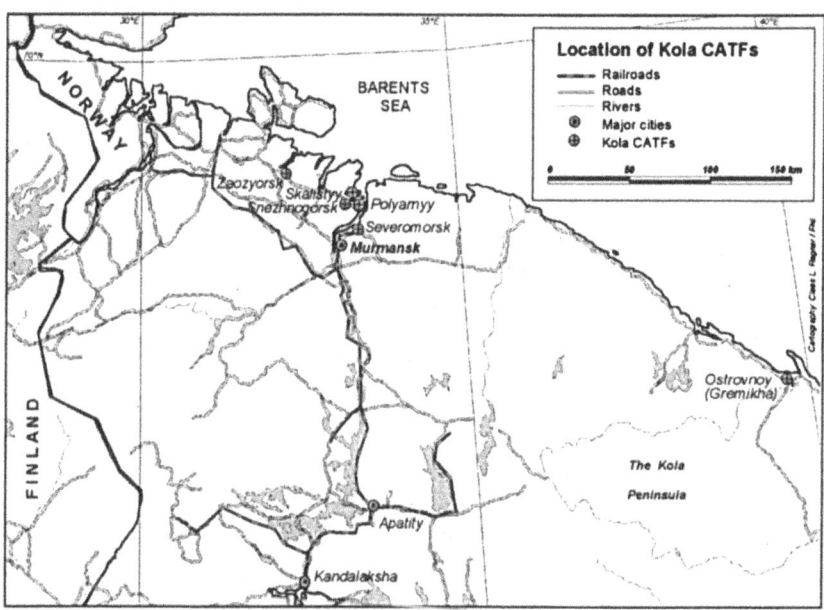

Union's first nuclear submarine was built at Sevmash, and the enterprise became the most important contractor of nuclear submarines for the Soviet Navy. At Zvyozdochka, repair works predominated.

Throughout the 1990s, the economic situation at the naval shipyards steadily declined. When the activity of the Northern Fleet was reduced, so did the need for the shipyards' services. As an illustration, the production of submarines in Russia as a whole declined from twelve in 1990 to only two in 1996 (*The Military Balance*, 1997/98). Hence, the same trend has been observed here as at the Kola shipyards, albeit on a larger scale: social conditions have deteriorated, and in 1996 shipyard workers embarked on the first major strike in the history of Severodvinsk (Bobretsov, 1998). Several large strikes and protests have followed since then. Wages – when paid at all – are reported to be far below subsistence minimum.[36] In February 1999, an open letter from the shipyard workers' trade union to the mayor of Severodvinsk was published, where the union protested increasing food prices, claiming that:

[...] the living standard of the overwhelming majority of Severodvinsk residents has declined to a catastrophic [level] [...] many workers and their families are surviving solely on bread and lunches from the company's canteens [...]. Living on the verge of hunger, some workers are unable to pay for municipal services.[37]

Similarly, in a Labour Day speech in 1999, the secretary of the local Communist Party described the city as 'poor, hungry and dying'.[38]

Attempts at Conversion

Diminishing state orders to the naval shipyards brought the question of conversion to civilian production onto the agenda already in the late 1980s. Construction of offshore equipment was singled out as the most promising direction. However, full conversion of the yards was never an option. As in so many other cases, the aim has been diversification, with defence production remaining the core activity, and on the condition that existing capabilities for this are kept intact. Thus, conversion has been capacity-driven, and with a clear bias towards high-tech solutions. As an example, even civilian shipbuilding has been referred to as beneath the skills of the work force at the yards, or, to quote a Sevmash engineer, as 'using ultra-modern computers to drive in nails' (Fattakhov, 1995, p. 2).

Financial restraints have been a major obstacle to conversion at the shipyards. In an article printed in *Novyye izvestiya* in August 1998, commenting on production of offshore equipment in Severodvinsk, it was reported that the Russian state has done very little to help finance the necessary reconstruction of the yards.[39] *The sheer size* of the shipyards, both physically and in terms of personnel, has been another barrier to effective conversion, particularly seen in conjunction with the wish to retain capabilities. It will be very difficult to offer e.g. offshore equipment at market prices if this production is to subsidise the maintenance of idle space and the salaries of idle workers. However, in addition to the perceived need to protect the 'unique technology' of the yards, social considerations may have made managers reluctant to outsource activities that have the potential of becoming profitable. They may not even be allowed to do so by the owner of the enterprises – the Russian state.

Due to the preconditions and restraints mentioned above, the partial switch to civilian production which has taken place at the shipyards seems to have come about in a haphazard fashion, and in part independently of whether actual conversion has been carried out or not. Despite the wish to concentrate on high-tech projects, the yards do produce consumer goods and other items that have little or nothing to do with their core activities. Examples include manufacturing of medical equipment, agricultural machinery, nuts and bolts and even furniture (Fattakhov, 1995). There is no information available on the precise extent or range of this production. Some of it seems to be of a small-scale and *ad-hoc* character, based on the tools and equipment available at the yards – in fact, a temporary survival strategy. Thus, the quality of the goods often leaves a lot to be desired. However, some larger projects, requiring considerable investments in new equipment, have also been initiated. For instance, Sevmash is reported to have launched a conversion project involving production of equipment for making peat briquettes.[40]

The most successful civilian projects initiated thus far have been those requiring the least technological adaptation. In many cases, it has been difficult to make projects economically viable when they are *less* technologically demanding than the average defence production project. As an example, the production at Zvyozdochka of advanced ship propellers for superliners has been a commercial success. This does not seem to apply to the construction at the same enterprise of hulls for Russian fishing vessels. In the former case, the technical skills of the work force is the very quality which makes Zvyozdochka's products competitive. The same quality has almost become a drawback where the latter project is concerned. This illustrates the problem of 'technological overkill' that is apt to occur when unnecessarily sophisticated equipment and production modes are applied to the construction of relatively simple items.

Production of offshore equipment seemed such an attractive option precisely because its design and construction is regarded as sufficiently advanced to be suitable for highly qualified specialists. Moreover, the presence of large hydrocarbon resources on the Russian Arctic shelf indicated a potential for very large orders. However, having no experience in this particular field, the yards needed government backing to be able to achieve their goals. What they got was the government's support in founding the enterprise Rosshelf – in which Gazprom got a controlling interest – which was subsequently awarded the licence for development of the Prirazlomnoye oil field (see Chapter 5 by Arild Moe). Rosshelf can hardly be described as an offshore enterprise, since it has no capabilities for such operations, though it is frequently presented as one. Essentially, it was Gazprom that got the licence, on the condition that the shipyards would be the main contractors for equipment. A comprehensive plan for the development of the shelf was produced by Rosshelf, presupposing large-scale construction activities at the yards (Kuznetsov and Velikhov, 1997). In reality, the output of offshore equipment has been fairly limited. The first large project, the construction at Sevmash of a production platform for Prirazlomnoye, has been carried out very slowly and still remains to be finished. The foundation for a small drilling rig – the 'Arkticheskaya' – has been completed, and some orders from foreign companies have been taken on, e.g. the delivery of steel constructions for a platform to be used on the Norwegian shelf.[41]

The civilian production has only kept a fraction of the workforce at Sevmash occupied, while Zvyozdochka has done rather better. Defence-related activities – including export-oriented ones, such as the recent modernisation of an Indian submarine[42] – continue to dominate, but are still too few and far between to make much of a difference.

Severodvinsk in a Regional Context

Despite the fact that the defence industry in Severodvinsk is sometimes portrayed by regional authorities as an asset to Arkhangelsk Oblast, it unquestionably stands forth as a sore point in the regional economy. As expressed by Professor Yuriy Lukin of the Arkhangelsk Lomonosov University:

> The decrease or cut in the financing from the federal budget of the enterprises of the military-industrial complex [...] has become a permanent source of non-stability: non-payment for electroenergy, non-payment to pension funds and other funds, delayed payment of wages, invisible and visible unemployment etc (Lukin, 1999, p. 15).

How does the region cope with this situation? On the one hand, the regional authorities are trying to integrate the defence enterprises into the civilian economy, e.g. by way of development and conversion programmes.[43] The main focus has been on the defence industry's possible contribution to the development of the offshore sector. Other potential areas of co-operation include the production of energy – constantly in short supply in the region – and diamonds.

On the other hand, authorities at all levels as well as industrial leaders seem to agree that defence production must remain the core activity of the Severodvinsk enterprises, which implies that the federal budget must remain the city's main source of income. However, despite a recent increase in orders from the Ministry of Defence (see next section), production capacity still exceeds demand by a wide margin. Moreover, the reduction in force levels – not least in the Northern Fleet – indicates that the production activity will finally have to stabilise at a level well below that of the Soviet period. Thus, the period of restructuring and adaptation to the new circumstances is far from over, and Severodvinsk is likely to be dependent on various forms of outside support for many years to come. The question is where that support will come from.

The local authorities in Severodvinsk clearly want federal authorities to take on the responsibility for the city's future. In early 1999, they initiated the process of application for CATF status. Mayor Aleksandr Belyayev claimed that there is no other way out of the crisis.[44] In the spring of 1999, the local newspaper repeatedly reported that the issue was near its solution, and that a positive outcome was to be expected. However, the process seems to have dragged on, possibly as a result of a more restrictive attitude towards the CATF regime at the federal level (see next section). As could be expected, the regional authorities support Severodvinsk's aspirations to become a CATF.[45] The taxes thus lost to the regional budget would be more than compensated for, since Severodvinsk is now a net receiver of funds from the budget. Moreover, an improvement in the city's financial situation would equal a decrease in the spill-over of economic and social problems to other parts of the oblast.

Implications for Centre-Periphery Relations

The Russian military sector has shrunk considerably in the course of the last decade, but so have the country's economic capabilities. Consequently, the sector remains a great burden on the national economy. State control over the economic sphere has become a thing of the past, and the federal budget is gravely affected by problems with tax collection. Thus, regional authorities are forced to yield part of their support to the military directly rather than via taxes – which places a disproportionate part of the cost on the most heavily militarised regions.

The regions are not formally obliged to support the military sector financially, but regional authorities and/or companies are more or less forced to offer municipal services for free or at reduced prices, and to come to the rescue when social problems get acute.

In Northwestern Russia, the political machinations related to the CATF regime illustrate the economic tug-of-war which is going on between regional and federal authorities, both trying to make the other take on a larger share of the financial responsibility for the military sector. In Murmansk Oblast, regional military and civilian authorities joined forces and succeeded in persuading the federal authorities to grant CATF status to Severomorsk and Polyarnyy. Another military town, Vidyayevo, is currently struggling to be included in the regime.[46] Meanwhile, federal authorities have signalled that this status may be removed from one of the smaller CATFs – Ostrovnoy (also referred to as Gremikha).[47] They also seem reluctant to grant such status to Severodvinsk in Arkhangelsk Oblast.

A rather ingenious move from an economic point of view is Murmansk Governor Yevdokimov's campaign for adoption of military vessels. By inviting all regions of Russia to take part, he has lessened the burden on his region, while at the same time earning himself and Murmansk Oblast credit points for their concern for the armed forces.

This brings us to another question of interest: how do the regional contributions to the military affect relations with the federal authorities? As mentioned previously, one possible outcome may be an increasing 'regionalisation' of the military, where regional leaders and armed formations stationed on their territory form alliances against the centre. A case in point may be Primore Governor Yevgeniy Nazdratenko's actions in the summer of 1997, when he joined forces with local Cossack army units to protest an agreement between Russia and China, whereby a piece of land would be handed over to the Chinese to secure access to the Sea of Japan.[48] Likewise, the well-known General Lebed, currently Governor of Krasnoyarsk Kray, threatened to take control over strategic rocket force units stationed in the region, arguing that federal authorities were not sufficiently committed to military reform (Nunn and Stulberg, 2000). Such scenarios do not seem likely in Northwestern Russia. The region is known to be among the most politically stable in Russia, and among the most 'obedient' to the centre. Nevertheless, it cannot be excluded that support to the military may be used as a card in negotiations on specific issues. It is also possible that their supporting role could help regional authorities achieve some concessions from their military counterparts in areas where their interests are at odds. There is no evidence to support such speculations, but then again, the negotiation processes in question would most likely not be open to public scrutiny. I am prone to believe that the military still has the upper hand in issues directly affecting it, at least when it comes to blocking civilian initiatives it does not approve of. When, for instance, Governor Yevdokimov in 1998 promised Norwegian inspectors access to a storage facility for nuclear waste in the Andreyeva Bay, the military authorities resolutely put their foot down – and that was the end of the discussion.[49]

Where the defence industry is concerned, the regional authorities hardly have anything to win by pointing out their support – except, of course, in pleas for more money from the federal budget. Although the industry is arguably a matter of national interest, it does not fall so unequivocally into the federal realm of responsibility as do the armed forces. Defence enterprises – at least those of lesser importance – may eventually be privatised. Currently, the number of enterprises is much too high considering the state's demand for their products, and the regions will have to carry a large share of the burden as the process of restructuring continues.

However, President Putin has signalled that the military sector will receive higher priority in the future than it has until now. In early summer 2000, Deputy Prime Minister Ilya Klebanov said Russia's strengthening economy would make it possible to modernise the military and reduce the number of defence enterprises considerably, which may mean that more money will be directed towards restructuring and conversion.[50] The defence budget was increased substantially in 2000, and both in the Northern Fleet and at the enterprises in Severodvinsk the situation reportedly started to change for the better already in early 1999.[51] At the same time, Putin is committed to strengthening central control over the regions. Taken together, these factors would seem to indicate that regional influence over the military sector is likely to diminish.

Notes

1. This has already happened in Chechnya, although it seems reasonable to treat this republic as a special case. However, even in other southern republics, attempts have been made at gaining greater control over local security issues by setting up regional armies and adopting military legislation in conflict with federal laws etc (Nunn and Stulberg, 2000).
2. In the context of this chapter, the term *military sector* refers to the armed forces and the defence industry. The major part of the chapter is based on Hønneland and Jørgensen (1999b). The sections *The Severodvinsk Defence Complex* and *Attempts at Conversion* are taken from Moe and Jørgensen (2000).
3. Murmansk Oblast is by far the region in Northwestern Russia with the heaviest military presence. However, the defence *industry* plays a very minor role in Murmansk Oblast and the Republic of Karelia. Gaddy (1996) divides the Russian regions into three categories, depending on the share of the work force employed in the defence industry. Murmansk Oblast and the Karelian Republic are both defined as 'non-militarised', Arkhangelsk Oblast as 'militarised', while none is characterised as 'hyper-militarised'.
4. See, for instance, Gaddy (1996).
5. *The Military Balance 1992-1993*.
6. *The Military Balance 1999-2000*.
7. According to Arbatov (1998), the ratio of maintenance to investment as a percentage of the defence budget was reversed from 30:70 in the Soviet Union in the 1970s and 1980s to 70:30 in Russia after 1994.
8. In 1998, Defence Minister Sergeyev said in an interview with the Ministry of Defence daily *Krasnaya zvezda* that 80 per cent of all weapons and equipment would be outdated by the year 2001.
9. Deferment or exemption can be obtained by many categories of young men, including students and fathers of two or more children. Dick (1998) claims that 80 per cent of all draft-age males are eligible for deferment.
10. In an interview with *Krasnaya zvezda* in 1998, Defence Minister Sergeyev said criminal activity was on the rise among officers. More than 18,000 breaches of the law by officers were registered in 1997 (*Krasnaya zvezda*, 11 March 1998).
11. Stephen Foye, 'Warning Signs: Anticipating Russia's Debacle', *Transition*, 15 July 1996, p. 11, cited in Epperson (1997).
12. In August 1998, the Ministry of Defence publicy encouraged officers to stretch funds for food by organising hunting, fishing and similar activities in their units ('Ministry of Defence Advises Servicemen to Hunt for Food', *Russia Today*, European Internet Network Inc., 20 August 1998).
13. Gaddy (1996) points out that the 'Law on State Enterprises' and the 'Law on Co-operatives' made it possible for enterprises to decide to whom they would sell their products, and for individuals to decide where they would work.
14. This usually implies that the principle of dual technology is applied, whereby equipment originally designed for production of military hardware is used to make civilian items in between defence orders. Naturally, this greatly limits the range of items which may be manufactured, and more often than not the results are low-quality, unduly expensive and generally unmarketable products.
15. *The Military Balance 1999-2000*.
16. *ibid.*

17 The following description of reductions in force levels is based on comparison of data in *The Military Balance 1992-1993* and *The Military Balance 1999-2000*.
18 *Nordisk Sikkerhet. Militærbalansen 1998-1999*; author's interview with representatives of the Border Service in Murmansk 14 January 1999.
19 Government Resolution No. 518 of 28 May 1998.
20 *Krasnaya zvezda*, 11 March 1998.
21 *Washington Post*, 12 September 1998.
22 *Polyarnaya pravda*, 30 March 2000.
23 In addition, of course, both were subordinate to the Communist Party.
24 Officers are not included as a separate group in official employment statistics. Castberg (1992) has attempted to infer the number of officers in Murmansk Oblast on the basis of residuals in official statistics. He puts their number (as of 1991) at approximately 60,000.
25 See Hønneland and Jørgensen (1999b).
26 During this period, protests took the form of bold and visible actions, like attempting to stop nuclear ice-breakers from leaving port (author's interview with Lyubov Nikiforova and Sergey Filippov of Bellona Murmansk, Murmansk 14 June 2000).
27 *Polyarnaya pravda*, 3 July 1998.
28 The full title of the department is: Department for the Problems of Military Garrisons and for the Social Protection of Military Servicemen.
29 In early 1998, around 10,000 officers in the closed towns were reported to have been retired ahead of time on the Kola Peninsula alone.
30 *Polyarnaya pravda*, 10 February 2000.
31 *O zakrytom administrativno-territorialnom obrazovanii*, 14 July 1992. A discussion of the act and the grouping of the various types of closed cities regulated by it is found in Rowland (1996). See Hønneland and Jørgensen (1998) for a discussion of the CATFs of Murmansk Oblast.
32 *O zakrytom administrativno-territorialnom obrazovanii*, 14 July 1992, Article 1; *O vnesenii izmeneniy i dopolneniy v Zakon Rossiyskoy Federatsii 'O zakrytom administrativno-territorialnom obrazovanii'*, 9 November 1995, Article 1. The original wording of the 1992 act is as follows '...or other objects [...] that *require* a particular regime...' (emphasis added).
33 *ibid.*, Article 5.
34 The main problem is linked to yet another advantage granted to CATFs – the right to introduce local tax reliefs in order to stimulate the development of new businesses. Thus, many CATFs have turned into on-land 'offshore zones' – which reportedly resulted in a 60 billion rouble loss to the federal budget in 1999 alone (*Polyarnaya pravda*, 18 April 2000).
35 *ibid.*
36 *Severnyy rabochiy*, 11 January 1999.
37 *Severnyy rabochiy*, 3 February 1999.
38 *Severnyy rabochiy*, 2 May 1999.
39 *Novyye izvestiya*, 5 August 1998.
40 ITAR TASS, 3 January 1999.
41 *Severnyy rabochiy*, 30 March 1999.
42 www.milparade.com.
43 *Severnyy rabochiy*, 16 March 1999.

[44] *Pravda severa*, 26 May 1999.
[45] *http://www.bellona.no/imaker?id=15200&sub=1#16921*.
[46] *Polyarnaya pravda*, 18 April 2000.
[47] *ibid.*
[48] *http://www.fas.harvard.edu/~ponars/POLICYMEMOS/busza44.html.*
[49] *Dagbladet*, 26 August 1998.
[50] *RFE/RL Newsline*, 3 July 2000.
[51] *http://www.bellona.no/imaker?id=9524&sub=1.*

PART IV
CONCLUSIONS

8 Conclusions

HELGE BLAKKISRUD AND GEIR HØNNELAND

As is established in the preceding discussion, Russian centre-region relations are still in the making. In this chapter, we will summarise the main findings of the previous chapters, before addressing the various hypotheses put forth in Chapter 1 about the influence of various common traits of Northwestern Russia (i.e. dependence on natural resources, a heavy military presence, general peripheral traits and the status as a gateway region) on the development of centre-region relations. Finally, we will offer some tentative conclusions on the nature and further development of the relationship between the Northwest Russian federal subjects and the federal centre.

The Legal Framework

In Chapter 2, Brynjulf Risnes presented the legal framework for the development of relations between Moscow and Northwestern Russia. Risnes described a constitutionally entrenched federal framework with clearly defined jurisdictions of federal, regional and joint competence. The fact that federal relations are now regulated by law and have a legal character, i.e. that both the federal centre and the regions have an obligation to comply with the enacted legal framework and that alleged non-compliance can be challenged in an independent court of law, represents a major step towards a more meaningful Russian federalism. The declaratory Soviet legislative basis with its pseudo-federal trappings has been replaced with a principally new approach to the regulation of centre-region relations. Moreover, the constitutional basis and the integral procedures for constitutional amendments virtually give the federal subjects veto right over attempts at re-centralisation.

Although the Russian Constitution of 1993 is universally acknowledged as the legal basis of the new Russian federalism, the nature of

Russian federal relations is not undisputed. An analysis of the basic laws of the northwestern federal subjects reveals that there are fundamentally different understandings of where power emanates and how it is distributed between the subjects and the centre. While the Charters of Murmansk and Arkhangelsk posit power as delegated top-down within the federal structure, the Karelian Constitution emphasises a bottom-up perspective in which the republic is the supreme source of state authority. Moreover, the Russian Constitution provides only a framework which in turn has to be filled in with supplementary legislation. Throughout the 1990s, the legislative process at the federal level has been slow. Several important issues, such as the question of how to regulate landownership, have repeatedly been postponed. In the ensuing legislative vacuum, the federal subjects have often had to adopt regional legislation that precedes federal regulation in areas of joint jurisdiction.

Risnes identified this trend towards regional legal separatism as the most significant trend in the development of legal ties between the regions and the federal centre, and warned about the potentially destabilising effect this might have on centre-region relations. So far, the federal authorities have been unable to stem this process, and although as of late they have increased their pressure on the regions for bringing regional laws into compliance with federal legislation, Risnes questioned whether the federal subjects are ready to give up their attempts at creating a comprehensive regional legal framework.

In addition to working through the above-mentioned regional legal initiative, some federal subjects have tried to reduce the impact of the legislative vacuum by concluding bilateral agreements with the federal centre. Although initially conceived as a way to bring a reluctant Tatarstan back into the Federation, the bilateral treaties soon developed into a dynamic tool for regulating centre-region relations (by now more than half of the federal subjects have adopted such agreements). Risnes pointed to the adoption of bilateral agreements as an effective way for regions to reach agreements with Moscow in matters of urgency to the regions. Even though such agreements strengthen the legal basis of centre-region relations, they nevertheless simultaneously increase the diversity and inconsistency of the legal system as a whole. The preservation of the Russian Federation as a single legal space therefore requires that the federal authorities stop resorting to *ad hoc* and individualised legal solutions, and adopt relevant federal legislation.

The Political Framework

In Chapter 3, Helge Blakkisrud followed up with an analysis of the political dynamics of the centre-region relationship. A key characteristic of the Soviet system was the inconsistency between formal legal rights and political realities. What are the relations between formal rights (as outlined in Chapter 2) and political practices in post-Soviet Russia? More specifically, Blakkisrud asked whether the devolution of power has reflected the legal stipulations (i.e. decentralisation by design) or whether centre-region relations primarily have been formed in a more *ad hoc* manner (i.e. devolution by default).

The analysis revealed elements of both approaches. By the mid-1990s, the basic legislative framework had been adopted, and President Yeltsin's second term in office saw attempts at strengthening the political-administrative basis for Russian centre-region relations. Most importantly, control over the regional executive was transferred from the president to the regional electorate. Whereas three out of four federal subjects in Northwestern Russia had been governed by presidential appointees up to 1996, since the onset of Yeltsin's second term all subjects have had popularly elected executives. The legal framework has thus been strengthened through its actual implementation along the executive vertical.

Nevertheless, the institutional basis for regional autonomy continued to be weak due to the persistence of the habit of conducting politics outside the formal political-administrative structures. Centre-region relations tended to develop through lobbying, compromise and horse trading, all through informal channels. This trend was further stimulated by Yeltsin's inclination to rely on *ad hoc* and personalised relations, and it clearly undermined the element of federal design in the devolution process. Instead, informal patron-client relationships came to dominate Russian politics. Power and resources were distributed within these networks with little respect for legal norms and formal procedures.

In addition, the element of design was undermined by the federal centre's increasing difficulties with fulfilling its obligations towards the regions. The element of default, that is, the centre's reluctance to act, or even neglect of regional problems, led to a situation in which federal subjects, wanting or not, had to take upon themselves increased responsibilities. In contrast to the formal top-down model for the devolution of power, decentralisation thus often took place in a haphazard and *ad hoc* manner.

The Northwest Russian federal subjects have not been among those which set the agenda for centre-region relations in Russia in the 1990s. With the exception of the limited mobilisation during the 'Parade of Sovereignties', even the ethnic autonomies have been more reactive than proactive. There are several reasons for this. First, the ethnic argument pushed by Karelia and Nenets did not turn out to be a particularly effective lever for obtaining concessions from the federal centre. Second, and more importantly, decentralisation did not stem economic decline in Northwestern Russia. Instead, the federal subjects continued to depend on economic support from Moscow. Although the new governors were able to effectively consolidate power within their respective federal subjects, they thus nevertheless continued to actively court the centre in order to tap into the informal networks that could provide financial and political support.

The change of president at the turn of the millennium seems, however, to have brought about a shift in the way the federal centre prefers to conduct centre-region relations. Yeltsin's *laissez faire* approach has been supplanted by a new emphasis on formality and procedure (cf. 'the dictatorship of law'). Where Yeltsin struck individual deals to accommodate unruly regional leaders, Putin has demanded that regional legislation is brought into line with federal norms. With the new emphasis on a strong state, the Putin administration appears to seek a stronger executive vertical and a certain re-centralisation. After a decade of mainly devolution by default, Russia thus seems set to embark upon a path where centre-region relations are to be developed by design.

The Economic Framework

For the devolution of power to be more than a judicial and/or political exercise of good intentions, it has to be accompanied by the setting up of sufficient and independent sources of revenue at the regional level. In Chapter 4, Per Botolf Maurseth examined the regional dimension of Russia's post-Soviet economic transition.

Maurseth found that the Soviet heritage to a large extent was detrimental to the prospects for regional economic development in a post-Soviet environment. Under the Soviet central planning system, political priorities, not market mechanisms, determined which resources should be developed and where production should take place. The extremely centralised decision-making process, low perceived transportation costs and remote sources of raw materials contributed to a decentralised economic geography. A by-product of Soviet resource exploitation and industrial policy was the construction of a large number of mono-industrial towns in the resource rich, formerly largely unpopulated northern peripheries of the Soviet Union. A typical example of this is Murmansk Oblast with its large industrial towns centred on mining facilities.

During the Soviet period, the centripetal forces that have depopulated western peripheral regions were not in operation in Russia. Paradoxically, the introduction of decentralised economic decision making may reactivate these centripetal forces. Exposed to new demands for profitability and competitiveness, the transport intensive Soviet-style economy faces severe structural problems. For a purely Soviet-type region like Murmansk, this development might entail the closure of former key industries and partial depopulation.

A prime example of a mono-industrial society at risk is the nickel-based cluster of towns Nikel, Zapolarnyy and Monchegorsk. Marketisation raises the question whether the nickel production in Murmansk Oblast is sustainable. A downscaling (which seems to be in the offing) will threaten more than 8,000 workplaces. Since the production of nickel is the economic backbone of these towns, however, all inhabitants in Nikel, Zapolyarnyy and Monchegorsk will be affected. In the worst case scenario, the end of nickel production will affect more than 100,000 people.

For a region like Arkhangelsk, while poorer than Murmansk, the challenges of transition may be less severe. Arkhangelsk has a more diversified industrial structure. As such, its development may run in tandem with the general Russian economic development.

Murmansk and Arkhangelsk have both been hard hit by the crisis in the Russian economy. The development in the two oblasts seems to reflect the typical post-Soviet Russian trend with a dramatic overall decline in industrial production, but with raw material extraction and export-oriented production generally doing better than industrial production for the home market. Nevertheless, both oblasts have done better than the Russian average, stabilising in the late 1990s at 60 per cent of the 1991 volume of industrial production.

Although as a rule Maurseth found that population decline has been greater in poor regions than in wealthier, relatively rich Murmansk has experienced a higher fall in population in the 1990s than the somewhat poorer Arkhangelsk (12.6 per cent and 5.8 per cent, respectively). Maurseth explains the deviant behaviour of Murmansk by the harsh climate and the relative rootlessness of the population. Large-scale migration may also continue from mono-industrial towns where the key industry has had difficulties in adapting to the new economic circumstances. The picture is not clear-cut, however. Other mono-industrial towns, such as relatively successful Apatity, may prove industrially competitive on international markets. The highly specialised industrial towns in Russia will therefore experience very uneven developments according to their inherited industrial specialisation.

The depopulation may spark a negative spiral at the regional level: Less people means a decreasing home market for the local industry. This has two implications for a region's industrial potential. First, it reduces the market for the local supply industries. Second, it reduces the incentives for the location of other industries to the region. For Murmansk Oblast in particular, population decline therefore represents a major threat to future industrial development. Paradoxically, economic decentralisation in a post-Soviet Russian context thus might lead to depopulation and centralisation.

Offshore Hydrocarbon Resources

After examining the framework for centre-region relations in the Russian Federation, we turned to case studies of various sectors of particular importance to Northwestern Russia to see how the above-mentioned framework has affected operations within these sectors.

In Chapter 5, examining the exploitation and management of the offshore hydrocarbon resources of the Barents and Kara Seas, Arild Moe pointed out that Murmansk and Arkhangelsk Oblasts and Nenets Autonomous Okrug do not have uniform interests and priorities, which probably has weakened their power in relation to the federal centre. In recent years, the policy of the federal authorities has primarily acted as a constraint on the development of the Arctic shelf. The attitude of Moscow seems to be that it is in Russia's long-term interest to minimise foreign involvement in the process of developing the shelf, even if this means that the benefits will be postponed.

Decision makers in the federal subjects bordering on the Barents Sea consider the benefits that would accrue to the region from increased activity on the shelf to be great. The regional authorities in Murmansk Oblast would like to see an increase in activity on the shelf as soon as possible.

The development of the Shtokmanovskoye field is probably a top priority, since all spin-off effects from this project would benefit the Murmansk region exclusively, and since this field is perceived as important for increasing the supply of gas to the oblast itself. It also seems that the oblast is highly interested in developing the Prirazlomnoye field, since Murmansk appears to be the most likely location for bases, as well as for a reloading port.

The position of Arkhangelsk Oblast is less clear. It appears that the development of the shelf is viewed as important in Arkhangelsk too, but that the presence of onshore resources in the region can make it acceptable to proceed more slowly offshore. It may also be in the interest of Arkhangelsk for foreign companies to play a lesser role in the development of the shelf if Russian control over projects implies more contracts for the naval shipyards. All in all, Arkhangelsk Oblast seems to have less to lose and more to gain by a 'wait-and-see' strategy than does Murmansk Oblast.

Despite the interest of the three involved Russian regions in increased activity on the shelf, it seems likely that the development of offshore hydrocarbons in the Barents Sea will be slow, at least in the near future. This clearly demonstrates the power of the current opponents of such development. Over the longer term, the outlook for development in the Barents and Kara Seas will be shaped mainly by changes in the strength of various forces outside the region. If the three federal subjects were able to overcome their current differences and formulate and present a coordinated vision of offshore development, their prospective influence on central decision makers would undoubtedly be enhanced. Currently, however, the influence that the regional level can exert over offshore development is more of a negative than a positive kind. The regional level will have to be consulted on major decisions regarding offshore development, such as the development of bases and landing sites. The federal level will have difficulty forcing through decisions against the will of the adjacent regions, but the regions have very few possibilities of accelerating developments offshore on their own.

By allying themselves with forces at the federal level that support speeding up developments, the northwestern federal subjects may exert greater influence. If a situation arises where the federal level supports an accelerated Arctic exploration and development programme, the regions can be expected to negotiate solutions with the federal authorities that will give them reasonable benefits from offshore developments. Such developments are also likely to enhance the general position of the affected regions versus the centre.

Fisheries Management

In the fisheries management system of Northwestern Russia, there has – as observed by Geir Hønneland in Chapter 6 – in recent years been a constant power struggle between various governmental bodies at the federal and regional levels, and between the two levels. There has also been a more or less continuous change in the 'power balance' between various structures, leaving a considerable amount of insecurity as to who is at any given time actually in charge.

The general trend towards regionalisation in the first years after the break-up of the Soviet Union spurred the administration of Murmansk Oblast to claim influence in the fisheries management, which had hitherto been the responsibility of the Moscow authorities and their executive body in the region, Sevryba. The oblast administration gained such influence on paper, but this did not imply a *de facto* transfer of decision-making power. The result was first a period when both Sevryba and the Murmansk Oblast administration claimed they were in charge of the distribution of quotas, then a compromise which left the actual delimitation of responsibility somewhat blurred.

A similar state of flux appeared at the federal level – as well as in the enforcement sector at the regional level – when various 'power structures' started to demand increased influence over fisheries management in 1997. The old system continued to function for a long time after the reorganisation decrees were issued. When the changes were actually implemented, a compromise evolved which secured the continued existence also of the old systems.

The discussion of management authority in current Northwest Russian fisheries cannot be limited to a straightforward argument of centre-periphery tensions. Fisheries management is also influenced by other general tensions in Russian politics and society, such as the ones between the presidential administration and the government, the power structures and other parts of the executive branch, and perhaps most important in this case, the one between the old industrial complexes (here the fisheries complex) and the political-administrative branches of government.

Northwest Russian fisheries are not regionalised in the sense that management authority has been transferred from the federal to the regional level. Nevertheless, a greater role for the regional authorities can be witnessed compared to the Soviet period. This change has primarily taken place at the expense of the old fishery conglomerate in the region. Hence, it can be argued that management tasks have been transferred from one regional actor to another. On the other hand, the administration of Murmansk Oblast is more independent from federal fisheries management authorities than Sevryba is. It should also be observed that the new quota distribution system proposed by the federal authorities in 1997 was halted by joint opposition from the regional level. More than anything, however, it should be noted that the current Northwest Russian fisheries management system is fragile in the sense that the power balance between the various actors may easily change according to the overall political development in Russia.

The Military Sector

As shown by Anne-Kristin Jørgensen in Chapter 7, in contrast to the hydrocarbon and fisheries sectors, the military is in itself a consumer of resources, designed to 'produce' a collective good – security – rather than economic revenue. Thus, where the military sector is concerned, the main question shaping centre-periphery relations is not 'who benefits?' but rather 'who pays?'

The federal subjects are not formally obliged to support the military sector financially, but the regional authorities and companies are more or less forced to offer municipal services for free or at reduced prices, and to come to the rescue when social problems get acute. In Northwestern Russia, the political machinations related to the CATF regime illustrate the economic tug-of-war which is going on between the regional and federal authorities, both of which are trying to make the other take on a larger share of the financial responsibility for the military sector. In Murmansk Oblast, the regional military and civilian authorities joined forces and succeeded in persuading the federal authorities to grant CATF status to Severomorsk and Polyarnyy. Another military town, Vidyayevo, is currently struggling to be included in the regime. Meanwhile, federal authorities have signalled that this status may be removed from Ostrovnoy. They also seem reluctant to grant such status to Severodvinsk in Arkhangelsk Oblast.

A conspicuous effort from an economic point of view is Murmansk Governor Yevdokimov's campaign for the adoption of military vessels. By inviting all federal subjects to take part, he has lessened the burden on his region, while at the same time earning himself and Murmansk Oblast credit points for their concern for the armed forces.

As far as the defence industry is concerned, the regional authorities hardly have anything to win by pointing out their support – except in pleas for more money from the federal budget. Although the industry is arguably a matter of national interest, it does not fall so unequivocally into the federal realm of responsibility as do the armed forces. Defence enterprises – at least those of lesser importance – may eventually be privatised. Currently, the number of enterprises is far too high considering the state's demand for their products, and the regions will have to carry a large share of the burden as the process of restructuring continues.

President Putin has signalled that the military sector will receive higher priority in the future than it has until now. The defence budget was increased substantially in 2000, and both in the Northern Fleet and at the enterprises in Severodvinsk the situation reportedly started to change for the better already in early 1999. At the same time, Putin is committed to strengthening central control over the regions. Taken together, these factors would seem to indicate that regional influence over the military sector is likely to diminish.

Centre-Periphery Relations Revisited

In Chapter 1, we noted that the geographical area of Northwestern Russia, despite obvious differences between the rural areas of Arkhangelsk, Nenets and Karelia and the Soviet-type, highly industrialised and urbanised territory of Murmansk Oblast, shares some common traits. It is to a large extent dependent on the extraction of various natural resources; it has a relatively heavy military presence on its territory; it is a typical peripheral region; and, located on the fringe of the Russian Federation, it is a so-called gateway region, enjoying geographical proximity to foreign states. The different chapters of this book did not aim at covering all relevant issues related to the discussion of how these features influence relations between Northwestern Russia and the federal centre. Throughout the book, however, many of the most important factors have been touched upon in one or several of the chapters. A brief review of some of the main arguments presented throughout the discussion is rendered below.

Dependence on Natural Resources

The abundance of natural resources in Northwestern Russia is striking. The forests of Arkhangelsk and Karelia have for centuries constituted one of the main foundations for settlement in these areas. Oil and gas in Arkhangelsk and Nenets, as well as offshore hydrocarbon resources in the Barents and Kara Seas, are promising for the future economy of Murmansk, Arkhangelsk and Nenets. On the Kola Peninsula, the extraction of natural resources, such as minerals and fish, spurred the establishment of several mono-industrial towns and still forms the basis for economic activity in these settlements (see Chapter 4 by Per Botolf Maurseth).

How does the existence of these resources affect centre-periphery relations? On the basis of the discussions in the chapters of the book, it seems fair to conclude that each sector influences relations with the federal centre in more general terms. For instance, in Chapter 3 Helge Blakkisrud reported how an integral part of the sovereignisation process of the republics and okrugs in the early 1990s was to seek control over natural resources located on their territories. The Republic of Karelia, among others, used the ethnic argument to pursue more general political and economic interests. Moreover, in Chapter 2 Brynjulf Risnes demonstrated how the existence of natural resources in various federal subjects has influenced their relations with Moscow in general, and the bilateral power-sharing agreements between region and centre in particular.

Despite attempts at increased influence, the control of the federal subjects over the management and exploitation of natural resources in the exclusive economic zone is still limited. The Northwest Russian federal subjects, and in particular Murmansk Oblast, have worked consciously to increase regional influence upon decisions related to the management of the hydrocarbon resources of the Barents and Kara Seas, and the Barents Sea fish stocks (see Chapters 5 and 6 by Arild Moe and Geir Hønneland). Related to the extraction of offshore hydrocarbon resources, the federal subjects of Northwestern Russia seem to be in a position to hamper projects they strongly oppose, but have literally no influence of a positive character. In the fisheries sector, the regional administrations have achieved a role as participants in the management process, but all important decisions have to be sanctioned by the federal State Committee on Fisheries.

In sum, the natural resources seem to be an asset to the region not only in economic but also in political terms. While regional influence on decisions related to the management and exploitation of resources in the exclusive economic zone is clearly limited, it is not as absent as one might expect on the basis the Russian Constitution (see Chapter 2 by Brynjulf Risnes). Moreover, post-Soviet Russian experience shows that the location of natural resources on its territory can be utilised by a federal subject as a bargaining tool in relations with Moscow (see Chapter 3 by Helge Blakkisrud). This potential strength has so far been used by the Northwest Russian federal subjects only to a very limited extent. It might be further utilised in a crisis situation, particularly in the fisheries sector where regional involvement in the management process is already quite considerable (although actual *power* is so far not).

A Heavy Military Presence

The heavy military presence in Northwestern Russia is most notable in the stationing of the Northern Fleet of the Russian Federation in Murmansk Oblast, and the considerable military-industrial complex of Arkhangelsk Oblast. Being one of the most heavily militarised areas of the world, is it at all realistic to expect any degree of regional autonomy for Northwestern Russia? Or, taking the economic development over the last years into consideration, are the federal authorities interested in handing over the economic, social and environmental burden of military activities to the regions?

As shown by Anne-Kristin Jørgensen in Chapter 7, the military sector of Northwestern Russia has indeed become a burden to regional authorities during the latter part of the 1990s. This is particularly true of the shipyard towns in both Murmansk and Arkhangelsk Oblasts, but also of the Northern Fleet naval bases. This has strengthened ties between the civil and military sector of the region and, interestingly, also between the regions of Northwestern Russia and the rest of Russia. The 'adoption campaign' initiated by Murmansk Governor Yuriy Yevdokimov in 1997 is characteristic of this development.

Some observers have indicated that regional leaders may take advantage of federal poverty by 'buying' military support for their own purposes. Such scenarios do not seem likely in Northwestern Russia. Notwithstanding the current problems related to the military sector, the location of military installations on the territory of the Northwest Russian federal subjects might under certain circumstances nevertheless become a bargaining point similar to the existence of natural resources on their territory. It is, for instance, possible that their supporting role could help regional authorities achieve some concessions from their military counterparts in areas where their interests are at odds. Interestingly, this does not seem to have occurred so far, which further strengthens the picture of the Northwest Russian federal subjects as 'obedient' in a centre-periphery context. The military still seems to have the upper hand in issues directly affecting it, at least when it comes to blocking civilian initiatives it does not approve of. The increased budget for the military sector announced by President Putin, as well as his commitment to strengthening federal control over the regions, indicate a reduced possibility for the regions to influence the military sector.

General Peripheral Traits

On top of the general dynamics of contemporary Russian federalism, relations between the federal centre and the northwestern federal subjects have no doubt also been influenced by the fact that this region constitutes an absolute periphery. Murmansk, Arkhangelsk, Karelia and Nenets all hold general features characteristic of peripheral regions, such as an underdeveloped transport infrastructure, the concentration of production in mono-industrial towns, dependence on federal transfers and threats of depopulation.

As the initial euphoria over the administrative and economic decentralisation subsided, the leaders of Northwestern Russia woke up to the grim realities of transition. As pointed out by Per Botolf Maurseth in Chapter 4, the heavily centralised Soviet planned economy contained an element of decentralisation in geographic terms. The resource rich northern periphery had therefore been developed industrially with scant consideration of cost and economic viability. As long as the Soviet economy was largely insulated from the world economy and market principles, the centripetal forces operating in market economies could also more or less be ignored. With the transition towards a more market-oriented economy, however, former key factories, around which entire towns had been built up in Soviet times, now risked being shut down as former markets disappeared and obsolete technology and inhibitive transport costs often prevented the creation of new ones.

Simultaneously, the negative economic development put heavy strains on the federal budget which, among other things, led to a partial breakdown in the social security system, and more specifically, in the former system of compensation for living and working in the harsh climatic conditions of the Russian Far North. The combination of these developments consequently led to a shift in the migration balance, a trend that can be observed throughout the northern periphery from Murmansk in the West to the Bering Strait in the East. As is typical for peripheral regions in times of crisis, it has generally been the most resourceful people who have left for more central areas, whereas the old and uneducated remain, thus further undermining the potential for economic revival in the periphery.

Consequently, decentralisation meant not only greater room for regional initiative and issue adaptation, but also an end to the preferential treatment and state sponsored development of the northwestern regions. The peripheral dimension therefore became particularly acute in centre-region relations.

How did the new leaders of the northwestern regions respond? As pointed out in Chapter 3 by Helge Blakkisrud, Northwestern Russia continued to be dominated by 'survivors' from the old nomenklatura, and it should thus not come as a surprise that the tradition of looking to Moscow for solutions to regional problems persisted. In general, the new leaders chose a non-confrontational approach. When Governor Yefremov in Arkhagelsk underlined the need to look for 'non-traditional approaches' to resolve the problem of non-payment (as quoted in Chapter 3 by Helge Blakkisrud) or Governor Yevdokimov in Murmansk threatened to develop offshore resources without consulting the federal authorities if certain 'errors' committed by the latter were not corrected (as quoted in Chapter 5 by Arild Moe), this represents exceptions to the rule.

On the whole, the leaders of the northwestern federal subjects have avoided confrontation. One indication of this is the apparent needlessness of bilateral agreements to further regulate relations with the federal centre. As pointed out by Helge Blakkisrud in Chapter 3, only one of the Northwest Russian federal subjects has entered into a bilateral agreement with the federal centre, whereas the national average is one out of two. Neither have they, as revealed by Brynjulf Risnes in Chapter 2, challenged the supremacy of the federal Constitution or federal legislation. Instead they have, as is typical of peripheral regions, favoured close connections and friendly relations with the centre. For fear of losing indispensable financial support, the leaders of the northwestern federal subjects have sought to lobby the centre and court potential patrons.

A rather extreme example of how the regional authorities try to re-transfer responsibility for local development to the federal centre was given by Anne-Kristin Jørgensen in Chapter 7 when she described how the regional authorities in both Murmansk and Arkhangelsk have tried to introduce CATF status for formerly closed towns. Basically, this implies that the regional authorities give up all further responsibility for parts of their former constituency.

Most efforts at overcoming the periphery-related problems and potential marginalisation has been directed at the centre, calling for a federal intervention to alleviate regional problems. Less emphasis has been put on cross-regional co-operation between the federal subjects. As such, Governor Yevdokimov's innovative scheme of inviting Russian regions to adopt naval vessels, described by Jørgensen in Chapter 7, shows a rare example of bypassing the centre when attempting to lessen regional problems.

In general, decentralisation within the post-Soviet Russian context has led to a rise in the importance of the peripheral traits in centre-region relations. Whereas these have always been present, the transition has increased their importance as a central element in the Northwest Russian regions' relations with the federal centre. As pointed out by Per Botolf Maurseth in Chapter 4, the imbalance between present industrial location and market forces may result in greater regional economic differences in Russia, as well as considerable migration in the future. We are thus left with the paradox that in a post-Soviet Russian peripheral region, decentralisation could lead to increased centralisation.

Gateway Regions

The disadvantages associated with the peripheral status of Northwestern Russia could potentially be offset against the region's location at the intersection of a western prosperity zone. Bordering on the Nordic countries (Murmansk borders with Norway and Finland and Karelia with Finland), the region's location could be turned into an advantage. As pointed out in Chapter 1, the main focus in this book has been on *internal* Russian developments. Nevertheless, several of the contributors have touched upon the inherit potential in the geographic location of the northwestern federal subjects.

As the Russian authorities started to integrate the economy into the world economy, the proximity to Western countries seemed to put Northwestern Russia in a favourable position in relation to foreign investment and co-operation. Indeed, the gateway perspective was an underlying principle for the establishment of the Barents Euro-Arctic Region in 1993, a programme set up to spur cross-regional co-operation and economic development. This programme has later been incorporated in the European Union's Northern Dimension and is thus now part of a more far-reaching attempt to stimulate cross-regional development in the Nordic/Northwest Russian/Baltic region. Under the latter, a programme to develop a Karelian Euroregion consisting of Karelia and a number of Finnish regions is currently being developed.

Nevertheless, when discussing the relations between Northwestern Russia and the federal centre, the effect of its location as a potential gateway for Russian export to the West and a bridge to the EU appears to have had quite limited influence. The gateway perspective seems to have had its heyday in the early 1990s. However, due to a combination of unreasonably high expectations and the apparent lack of tangible economic results, politicians and entrepreneurs on both sides of the border seem to have got increasingly disillusioned with respect to the possibility of short-time gains. As a result, the regional authorities in Northwestern Russia have chosen to play the periphery, rather than gateway card in order to cater for regional needs.

The need for access to foreign markets and greater co-operation with foreign investors is undoubtedly present. As Arild Moe pointed out in Chapter 5, the development of offshore resources such as Shtokmanovskoye will depend on export outlook and the key to accelerating developments on the continental shelf is the creation of greater possibilities for foreign involvement. All the same, playing the peripheral rather than the gateway card has implied calls for the protection of Russian state interests and local industries against competition from the outside. As Moe indicated in Chapter 5, the naval shipyards' bid to supply the offshore industry currently serves as a constraint on the development of the shelf. Nevertheless, as the short-term interests of Arkhangelsk will be better served by keeping up employment at the shipyards, the regional authorities have lobbied for construction contracts to Russian shipyards.

It should also be mentioned that location as a gateway region may have unexpected, and not only positive, consequences for the development of the regional economy. In Chapter 6, Hønneland showed how the opening of the borders between Russia and Norway has resulted in Russian fishermen delivering the bulk of their catches in Norway. This has had catastrophic consequences for the local fishing industry in Murmansk and Arkhangelsk, and spurred further demands for protection of Russian resources.

On the whole, the Northwest Russian regions thus seem not to have been able to fully exploit their gateway position in order to attract foreign investment. In data on regional foreign investment for the first six months of year 2000, Arkhangelsk scored highest of the four, with USD 9,916,000, but this only gave the oblast the 25th place in the national ranking. Karelia followed on the 27th place (USD 9,056,000), Murmansk on 28th (USD 8,617,000) and Nenets shared the last place, with no direct foreign investment at all.[1] Although local industry, as demonstrated by Per Botolf Maurseth in Chapter 4, has fared somewhat better than the Russian average, it seems that this cannot be explained in terms of the gateway location. Raw material extraction and export-oriented production have done better than industrial production for the home market in both Murmansk and Arkhangelsk, but this reflects a general trend throughout the Russian Federation and is thus not a gateway-specific feature.

Concluding Remarks

A federal structure will always be some sort of a compromise between centripetal and centrifugal forces within a given state. As such, the equilibrium between these opposing forces is not given once and for all, but is open to renegotiation as the strength and/or perceived needs of the federal subjects and the centre change over time.

Although the establishment of a Russian federal structure formally took place in the 1920s, attempts at filling this structure with a meaningful division of power and responsibilities were not undertaken until after the demise of the Soviet Union. The current federal organisation has therefore had less than a decade to work out the balance of power between the federal subjects and the centre. Russian centre-region relations are thus still in an early, formative stage where the pendulum might be expected to swing both more frequently and further between decentralisation and recentralisation than in more well-established federations. Moreover, the extremely centralised nature of the Soviet predecessor has undoubtedly made it difficult to work out a viable compromise. The last decade has seen both attempts at gaining far-reaching autonomy for the regions and at reasserting federal power. The changes introduced by President Putin after he took up office at the turn of the millennium appears to herald yet another attempt at re-institutionalising the centre's control.

As has been pointed out above, the Northwest Russian federal subjects have not been among the most active participants in the debate on the delimitation of power and responsibilities within the new federal structure. Despite their potential as a gateway region, they have generally rather emphasised their peripheral location when defining their policies towards the federal centre. While this approach might seem rational in a short-term perspective, taking into account the severe constraints that the transition has put on the regional economy, it does not, as have been demonstrated by several of the authors of this book, necessarily serve the long-term interest of Northwestern Russia. In order to achieve stable economic growth, Northwestern Russia would need to attract foreign investment and develop exports to its western neighbours. In the current political situation, however, such a redefinition of orientation does not seem imminent.

Note

[1] *RFE/RL Russian Federation Report*, 13 September 2000.

Bibliography

Aghion, P. and Howitt, P. (1998), *Endogenous Growth Theory*, The MIT Press, Cambridge, Massachusetts.

Alexseev, M.A. (ed) (1999), *Center-Periphery Conflict in Post-Soviet Russia*, St Martin's Press, New York.

Arbatov, A.G. (1998), 'Military Reform in Russia: Dilemmas, Obstacles and Prospects', *International Security*, Vol. 22, pp. 83-134.

Arkhangelsk Regional Committee of State Statistics (1998), *Towns of the Arkhangelsk Oblast*, Arkhangelsk.

Arkhangelsk Regional Committee of State Statistics (1999), *Short Run Economical Indicators of Arkhangelsk Oblast*, Arkhangelsk.

Baev, P.K. (1996), *The Russian Army in a Time of Troubles*, SAGE Publications, London.

Barro, R.J. and Sala-I-Martin, X. (1995), *Economic Growth*, MacGraw-Hill, NewYork.

Belonin, M.D., and Podolski, Y.V. (1995), *Geological and Economic Estimates of the Potential in the Timan-Pechora Province, the Barents and Pechora Seas: Possible Dynamics of their Development*, Conference Proceedings, VNIGRI and IKU, Trondheim.

Bergesen, H.O., Moe, A. and Østreng, W. (1987), *Soviet Oil and Security Interests in the Barents Sea*, Frances Pinter and St Martin's Press, London and New York.

Bjorvatn, T. and Castberg, R. (1994), *Næringsliv og utenrikshandel i Arkhangelsk fylke*, R:002-1994, The Fridtjof Nansen Institute, Lysaker.

Bjørkvoll, T. and Sandvik, C.O. (1997), *Energy Production and Transportation in the Barents Region*, Report No. STF38A97613, SINTEF, Trondheim.

Blakkisrud, H. (1997), *Den russiske føderasjonen i støpeskjeen. Etniske og territorielle utfordringer*, Spartacus, Oslo.

Blakkisrud, H. (forthcoming), 'Federal Reform and Intraperipheral Conflict: The Case of Nenets Autonomous Okrug', in T.D. Clark and D.R. Kempton (eds), *Unity or Separation: Center-Periphery Relations in the Former Soviet Union*, Praeger, New York.

Bobretsov, A. (1998), 'Stroki Biografii', in *Severodvinsk. Ispytaniye na prochnost*, Pravda Severa, Severodvinsk.

Boone, P. and Fedorov, B. (1997), 'The Ups and Downs of Russian Economic Reforms', in W.T. Woo, S. Parker and J.D. Sachs (eds), *Economies in Transition*, The MIT Press, Cambridge, Massachusetts, pp. 161-188.

Busygina, I.M. (1996), 'Das Institut der Vertreter des Präsidenten in Rußland. Probleme des Werdegangs und Entwicklungperspektiven', *Osteuropa*, Vol. 46, pp. 664-675.

Busygina, I.M. (1997), 'Die Gouverneure im föderativen System Rußlands', *Osteuropa*, Vol. 47, pp. 544-556.

Bylov, G.V. (1998), *The Wealth of Russian Regions*, Discussion Paper C3, Turku School of Economics and Business Administration, Turku.

Castberg, R. (1992), *Næringsstruktur og utenriksøkonomi i Murmansk fylke*, The Fridtjof Nansen Institute, Lysaker.

Centre of Economic Analysis (1995a), *Russia – 1995 Economic Situation 2*, Moscow.

Centre of Economic Analysis (1995b), *Russia – 1995 Economic Situation 3*, Moscow.

Chand, S.K. and Moene K.O. (1999), *Rent Grabbing and Russia's Economic Collapse*, Memorandum No 25/99, Department of Economics, University of Oslo, Oslo.

Connor, W. (1984), *The National Question in Marxist-Leninist Theory and Strategy*, Princeton University Press, Princeton.

Cooper, J. (1991), *The Soviet Defence Industry. Conversion and Reform*, The Royal Institute of International Affairs/Pinter Publishers, London.

Dahlström, M., Eskelinen, H. and Wiberg, U. (eds) (1995), *The East-West Interface in the European North*, Nordisk Samhällsgeografisk Tidskrift, Uppsala.

Dellenbrant, J.Å. and Olsson, M.O. (eds) (1994), *The Barents Region. Security and Economic Development in the European North*, CERUM, Umeå.

Dellenbrant, J.Å. and Wiberg, U. (eds) (1997), *Euro-Arctic Curtains*, CERUM, Umeå.

Dick, C. (1998), 'Russian Military Reform: Status and Prospects', in A. Toivonen (ed), *Russia's Security Political Prospects*, National Defence College, Helsinki, pp. 59-72.

Duchacek, I.D. (1987), *Comparative Federalism: The Territorial Dimension of Politics*, University Press of America, Lanham.

EcoWin (1999), *The Economic Window*, Gothenburg.

Epperson, R.H. (1997), 'Russian Military Intervention in Politics 1991-96', *The Journal of Slavic Military Studies*, Vol. 10, pp. 90-108.

Fattakhov, A. (1995), 'Shelf prokormit vsekh', *Chyornoye zoloto*, September 1995.

Flikke, G. (ed) (1998), *The Barents Region Revisited*, NUPI Conference Proceedings, NUPI, Oslo.

Fujita, M., Krugman, P. and Venables, A.J. (1999), *The Spatial Economy – Cities, Regions, and International Trade*, The MIT Press, Cambridge, Massachusetts.

Gaddy, C.G. (1996), *The Price of the Past. Russia's Struggle with the Legacy of a Militarized Economy*, Brookings Institution Press, Washington D.C.

Gaddy, C. and Ickes, B.W. (1998), *To Restructure or Not to Restructure: Informal Activities and Enterprise Behavior in Transition*, unpublished manuscript.

Garipov, V.Z. (1998), 'Plan osvoyeniya uglevodorodnykh resursov Barentseva i Pechorskogo morey, provedeniye litsenzionnykh konkursov na period 1998-2005', *Razvedka i okhrana nedr*, pp. 4-5.

Glukhova, N., Niktin, B. and Pakhomova, N. (1999), 'Gazovye perspektivy arkticheskogo shelfa', *Neftegazovaya Vertikal*, p. 12.

Gorter-Grønvik, W.T. (1998) 'History, Identities and the Barents Euro-Arctic Region: The Case of Arkhangelsk', in G. Flikke (ed), *The Barents Region Revisited*, NUPI Conference Proceedings, NUPI, Oslo, pp. 97-110.

Goskomstat (1999), http://www.gks.ru.

Hansen, E. and Tønnessen A. (1998), *Environment and Living Conditions on the Kola Peninsula*, FAFO-Report 260, FAFO, Oslo.

Hanson, P. (1999), 'The Russian Economic Crisis and the Future of Russian Economic Reform', *Europe-Asia Studies*, Vol. 51, pp. 1141-1166.

Hanson, P. (2000), *How is the Russian Economy Different? Size and Regional Diversity*, unpublished manuscript.

Hanson, P., Artobolevskiy, S., Kouznetsova, O. and Sutherland, D. (2000), 'Federal Government Responses to Regional Economic Change' in P. Hanson and M. Bradshaw (eds), *Regional Economic Change in Russia*, Edvard Elgar, Cheltenham, pp. 97-132.

Härdle, W. (1990), *Applied Nonparametric Regression*, Cambridge University Press, Cambridge.

Hoel, A.H. (1994), 'The Barents Sea: Fisheries Resources for Europe and Russia', in O.S. Stokke and O. Tunander (eds), *The Barents Region. Co-operation in Arctic Europe*, SAGE Publications, London, pp. 115-130.

Holt, J. (1993), *Transport Strategies for the Russian Federation*, Studies of Economies in Transformation, The World Bank, Washington, D. C.

Hønneland, G. (1998), 'Autonomy and Regionalisation in the Fisheries Management of Northwestern Russia', *Marine Policy*, Vol. 22, pp. 57-65.

Hønneland, G. (1999), 'Regional Self-Government in North-West Russia' in B. Risnes and H. Blakkisrud (eds), *Perspectives on the Development of Russia as a Federation*, NUPI Report No. 243, NUPI, Oslo, pp. 49-66.

Hønneland, G. (2000a), *Coercive and Discursive Compliance Mechanisms in the Management of Natural Resources. A Case Study from the Barents Sea Fisheries*, Kluwer Academic Publishers, Dordrecht.

Hønneland, G. (2000b), 'Enforcement Co-operation between Norway and Russia in the Barents Sea Fisheries', *Ocean Development and International Law*, Vol. 31, pp. 249-267.

Hønneland, G. and Jørgensen, A.K. (1998), 'Closed Cities on the Kola Peninsula: From Autonomy to Integration?', *Polar Geography*, Vol. 22, pp. 231-248.

Hønneland, G. and Jørgensen, A.K. (1999a), 'A Cross-Border Perspective on a North Russian Gateway', *Post-Soviet Geography and Economics*, Vol. 40, pp. 44-61.

Hønneland, G. and Jørgensen, A.K. (1999b), *Integration vs. Autonomy: Civil-Military Relations on the Kola Peninsula*, Ashgate, Aldershot.

Hønneland, G. and Nilssen, F. (2000), 'Co-management in Northwest Russian Fisheries', *Society and Natural Resources*, Vol. 13, pp. 635-648.

Ickes, B.W. (forthcoming), 'Dimensions of Transition in Russia', in B. Granville and P. Oppenheimer (eds), *The Russian Economy in the 1990's*, Oxford University Press, Oxford.

IMF, World Bank, OECD and EBRD (1991), *A Study of the Soviet Economy*, Paris.

Ivanova, N. and Wyplosz, C. (1999), 'Arrears: The Tide that is Drowning Russia', *Russian Economic Trends*, Vol. 8, pp. 24-35.

Jones, P.E. (1988), *Oil*, Woodhead-Faulkner, Cambridge, UK.

Jørgensen, A.K. (1999), *Norsk og russisk fiskerikontroll i Barentshavet – en sammenligning med hensyn til effektivitet*, MA Thesis, Department of Political Science, University of Oslo, Oslo.

Kirkow, P. (1997a), 'Transition in Russia's Principal Coastal Gateways', *Post-Soviet Geography and Economics*, Vol. 38, pp. 296-314.

Kirkow, P. (1997b), 'Russia's Regional Puzzle: Institutional Change and Economic Adaption', *Communist Economies and Economic Transformation*, Vol. 9, pp. 261-287.

Kirkow, P. and Hanson, P. (1994), 'The Potential for Autonomous Regional Development in Russia: The Case of Primorskiy Kray', *Post-Soviet Geography*, Vol. 35, pp. 63-88.

Kotilaine, J.T. (1999), 'Quantifying Russian Exports via Arkhangelsk in the XVIIth Century', *Journal of European Economic History*, Vol. 28, pp. 249-300.

Krugman, P. (1991), *Geography and Trade*, The MIT Press, Cambridge, Massachusetts.

Krugman, P. and Obstfeld, M. (1988), *International Economics – Theory and Policy*, Scott, Foresman and Company, Glenview, Illionois.

Krylov, B.S. (1997), 'Kak razrushayetsya osnova federalizma', *Nezavisimaya gazeta*, 3 September 1997.

Kryukov, V. and Moe, A. (1998), 'Joint Management of Oil and Gas Resources in Russia', *Post-Soviet Geography and Economics*, Vol. 39, pp. 588-605.

Kundryatsev, Yu. (ed.) (1996), *Kommentarii k Konstitutsii Rossiyskoy Federatsii*, Fond, Moscow.

Kuznetsov, P. and Velikhov, E. (1997), *Russia's Marine Oil and Gas Industry Approaches the Arctic Shelf. A History of Rosshelf*, Europa-programmet, Oslo.

Lenin, V.I. ([1914] 1975), 'The Right of Nations to Self-Determination', in R.C. Tucker (ed), *The Lenin Anthology*, Norton, New York, pp. 153-180.

Litovkin, D. (2000), 'CTR and Nuclear-powered Submarines Dismantlement in the North Fleet', in I. Safranchuk (ed), *Cooperative Threat Reduction Program: How Efficient?*, PIR Centre, Moscow, pp. 34-40.

Lukin, Y. (1999), 'Iz 90-kh godov v XXI vek: regionalnaya strategiya na blago severyan', in Y. Lukin (ed), *Arkhangelskaya oblast: sotsialno-ekonomicheskoe razvitiye, istoriya, kultura, obrazovaniye*, The Pomor State University (imeni) M.V. Lomonosov, Arkhangelsk.

Makfol, M. and Petrov, N. (eds) (1998), *Politicheskiy almanakh Rossii 1997*, Tsentr Karnegi, Moscow.

Makhlina, M. (1996), 'Rossiyskiy federalnyy zakon 'O soglasheniyakh o razdele produktsii'', *Neft, gaz i pravo*, No. 5, pp. 35-41.

Malovitskiy, Ya.P., Martirosyan, V.N. and Federovskiy, Yu.F. (1998), 'Geologo-geofizicheskaya izuchennost i neftegazonosnost dna Barentseva i Pechorskogo morey', *Razvedka i okhrana nedr*, No. 4-5, pp. 8-12.

Maurseth, P.B. (1996), *Investeringer og handel i overgang mellom plan og marked – norske bedrifters erfaringer i Russland*, NUPI Report No. 207, Oslo.

Maurseth, P.B. (1997), *Fra kald krig til økonomisk samarbeid – Perspektiver for handel og integrasjon mellom Norge og Russland i nord*, NUPI Report No. 216, Oslo.

Maurseth, P.B. (1999), *Convergence, Geography and Technology*, NUPI Working Paper No. 601, Oslo.

McAuley A. (1997), 'The Determinants of Russian Federal-Regional Fiscal Relations: Equity or Political Influence?' *Europe-Asia Studies*, Vol. 49, pp. 431-444.

McAuley, M. (1997), *Russia's Politics of Uncertainty*, Cambridge University Press, Cambridge.

Mikheeva, N. (1999), *Differentiation of Social and Economic Situation in the Russian Regions and Problems of Regional Policy*, EREC Working Paper No. 99/09, Moscow.

Moe, A. (1994), 'Oil and Gas: Future Role of the Barents Region,' in O.S. Stokke and O. Tunander (eds), *The Barents Region: Cooperation in Arctic Europe*, Sage Publications, London, pp. 131-144.

Moe, A. and Jørgensen, A.K. (2000), 'Offshore Mineral Development in the Russian Barents Sea', *Post-Soviet Geography and Economics*, Vol. 41, pp. 98-133.

Moltz, J.C. (1992), 'Transborder Economic Ties (in Panel on Patterns of Disintegration in the Former USSR)', *Post-Soviet Geography*, Vol. 33, pp. 368-371.

Moltz, J.C. (1996), 'Core and Periphery in the Evolving Russian Economy: Integration or Isolation of the Far East', *Post-Soviet Geography and Economics*, Vol. 37, pp. 175-194.

Murmansk Regional Committee of State Statistics (1996), *Murmansk Region in Figures*, Murmansk.

Murmansk Regional Committee of State Statistics (1999a), *Murmansk Region in Figures*, Murmansk.

Murmansk Regional Committee of State Statistics (1999b), *Social Economic Relations in Murmansk Oblast, January – May*, Murmansk.

Nemkovic, Y., Druzinin, P. and Baibusinov, S. (1994), 'Economic Reforms and Scenarios', in H. Eskelinen, J. Oksa and D. Austin (eds), *Russian Karelia in Search of a New Role*, Karelian Institute, Jonesuu, pp. 78-86.

Nikitin, B.A. (1999), 'Arktika zhdyot,' *Gazovaya promyshlennost*, No. 1, pp. 20-23.

Nikitin, B.A., Vovk, V.S. et al. (1999a), 'Podgotovka syrevoy bazy na arkticheskom shelfe', *Gazovaya promyshlennost*, No. 7, pp. 6-10.

Nikitin, B.A., Vovk, V.S. et al. (1999b), 'Strategiya osvoyeniya uglevodorodnykh resursov shelfa Arktiki', *Gazovaya promyshlennost*, No. 7, pp. 11-14.

Nilsen, T., Kudrik, I. and Nikitin, A. (1996), *The Russian Northern Fleet: Sources of Radioactive Contamination*, Bellona Report No. 2, Bellona, Oslo.

Nordisk Sikkerhet. Militærbalansen 1998-1999, Den norske Atlanterhavskomité, Oslo.

Nunn, S. and Stulberg, A.N. (2000), 'The Many Faces of Modern Russia', *Foreign Affairs*, Vol. 79, pp. 45-62.

Oates, W.E. (1999), 'An Essay on Fiscal Federalism', *Journal of Economic Literature*, Vol. 37, pp. 1120-1149.

OECD (1995), *The Russian Federation*, OECD Economic Surveys, Paris.

OECD (1997), *The Russian Federation*, OECD Economic Surveys, Paris.

OECD (2000), *The Russian Federation*, OECD Economic Surveys, Paris.

Orlov, V.P. (1998), 'Osvoyeniye uglevodorodnykh resursov Barentsevo morya – blizhayshchaya perspektiva', *Razvedka i okhrana nedr*, No. 4-5, pp. 3-4.

Ostistyy, B.K. (1999), 'Chyornoye zoloto Kolskogo kraya trebuyet obychnykh zelyonykh', *Komsomolskaya pravda* (Murmansk supplement) 24 March.

Paliy, V.V., Lakhov, A.G. and Loboda, V.G. (1999), 'Pyat let vo ldakh', *Gazovaya promyshlennost*, No. 7, pp. 4-5.

Petrov, N. (1999), 'The 1996 Gubernatorial Elections in Russia', in B. Risnes and H. Blakkisrud (eds), *Perspectives on the Development of Russia as a Federation*, NUPI Report No. 243, NUPI, Oslo, pp. 23-49.

Piskotin, M.I. (1997), 'Federatsiya – eto yedinoye gosudarstvo', *Nezavisimaya gazeta*, 27 November.
Ponte Ferreira, M. (1995), *Transition in the Russian Economy – Success or Failure?* NUPI Working Paper No. 529, NUPI, Oslo.
Quah, D. (1996), 'Regional Convergence Clusters in Europe', *European Economic Review*, Vol. 40, pp. 951-958.
Regiony Rossii (1998), Goskomstat Rossii, Moscow.
Ries, T. (1991), 'Sovjetiska strategiska intressen i nordväst', in T. Huitfeldt, T. Ries and J.K. Skogan, *Sovjet i nord etter CFE*, Institutt for Forsvarsstudier, Report No. 5, Oslo, pp. 10-26.
Ries, T. (1994), *The Republic of Karelia. The First Years After the USSR: Some Basic Data*, The Norwegian Ministry of Foreign Affairs, Oslo.
Ross, C. (1999), 'Respublikanizatsiya Rossii: Federalizm i demokratizatsiya v perekhodnyy period', *Konstitutsionnoye pravo: Vostochnoye obozreniye*, Vol. 4, unpaginated.
Rowland, R.H. (1996), 'Russia's Secret Cities', *Post-Soviet Geography and Economics*, Vol. 37, pp. 426-462.
Sachs, J.D. (1997), *Geography and Economic Transition*, unpublished manuscript.
Sakwa, R. (1993), *Russian Politics and Society*, Routledge, London.
Sakwa, R. (2000), 'Putin's New Federalism', *EWI Russian Regional Report*, 31 May.
Sekarev, A.V. (1993), 'Russian Military Presence at Kola: Strategic Significance and Burdens on the Transitory Society (An Abstract)', in J.K. Skogan (ed), *Civil-Military Relations in the Post-Communist States in Eastern and Central Europe. A Conference Report*, NUPI, Oslo, pp. 76-78.
Semenyaka, A.N. (1999), 'Finansirovaniye proyektov po transportirovke gaza', *Gazovaya promyshlennost*, August 1999.
Senik-Leygonie, C. and Hughes, G. (1992), 'Industrial Profitability and Trade among the Former Soviet Republics', *Economic Policy* No. 15, pp. 353-377.
Shlapentokh, V., Levita, R. and Loiberg, M. (1997), *From Submission to Rebellion. The Province versus the Center in Russia*, Westview Press, Boulder.
Shpak, V. (1998), 'Federalizma v Rossii poka ne sushchestvuyet', *Kommersant-Daily*, 20 January 1998.
Simonsen, S.G. (1996), *Den russiske Nordflåten i tung sjø*, Den norske Atlanterhavskomité, Oslo.
Skogan, J.K., *Sovjetunionens Nordflåte 1968-85*, NUPI Report No. 105, NUPI, Oslo.
Slider, D. (1994), 'Federalism, Discord, and Administration', in T.H. Friedgut and J.W. Hahn (eds), *Local Power and Post-Soviet Politics*, M.E. Sharpe, London, pp. 239-269.
Smirnyagin, L. (2000), 'The Great Seven', *EWI Russian Regional Report*, 24 May.

Smith, G. (ed) (1995), *Federalism: The Multiethnic Challenge*, Longman, London.

Stoner-Weiss, K. (1997), *Local Heroes: The Political Economy of Russian Regional Governance*, Princeton University Press, Princeton.

Statisticheskiy yezhegodnik: Murmanskaya oblast v 1997 godu, Murmansk Regional Committee on State Statistics, Murmansk, 1998.

Stavrakis, P.J., DeBardeleben, J. and Black, L. (eds) (1997), *Beyond the Monolith: The Emergence of Regionalism in Post-Soviet Russia*, Johns Hopkins University Press, Washington, D.C.

Stokke, O.S. (1995), *Fisheries Management under Pressure. A Changing Russia and the Effectiveness of the Barents Sea Regime*, R:001-1995, The Fridtjof Nansen Institute, Lysaker.

Stokke, O.S. (1998), *The Loophole of the Barents Sea Regime*, POLOS Report, No. 8/1998, The Fridtjof Nansen Institute, Lysaker.

Stokke, O.S. and Hoel, A.H. (1991), 'Splitting the Gains: Political Economy of the Barents Sea Fisheries', *Co-operation and Conflict*, Vol. 26, pp. 49-65.

Stokke, O.S., Anderson, L.G. and Mirovitskaya, N. (1999), 'The Barents Sea Fisheries', in M.A. Levy and O.R. Young (eds), *The Effectiveness of International Regimes*, MIT Press, Cambridge, MA, pp. 91-154.

Stokke, O.S. and Tunander, O. (eds) (1994), *The Barents Region. Cooperation in Arctic Europe*, SAGE Publications, London.

Sutherland, D. and Hanson, P. (1996), 'Structural Change in the Economies of Russia's Regions,' *Europe-Asia Studies*, Vol. 48, pp. 367-392.

Sutherland, D. and Hanson, P. (2000), 'Demographic Responses to Regional Economic Change' in P. Hanson and M. Bradshaw (eds), *Regional Economic Change in Russia*, Edvard Elgar, Cheltenham, pp. 76-96.

Taagepera, R. (1999), *The Finno-Ugric Republics and the Russian State*, Hurst, London.

Tabata, S. (1998), 'Transfers from Federal to Regional Budgets in Russia: A Statistical Analysis', *Post-Soviet Geography and Economics*, Vol. 39, pp. 447-460.

The Military Balance 1992-1993 (1992), International Institute for Strategic Studies, London.

The Military Balance 1999-2000 (2000), International Institute for Strategic Studies, London.

United Nations (1999), *Economic Survey of Europe*, Economic Commission for Europe, New York.

Van Selm, B. (1998), 'Economic Performance in Russia's Regions', *Europe-Asia Studies*, Vol. 50, pp. 603-618.

Vitebsky, P. (1996), 'The Northern Minorities', in G. Smith (ed), *The Nationalities Question in the Post-Soviet States*, Longman, London, pp. 94-112.

Yuffe, A.I. (1999), *Politicheskiy almankh Rossii 1997*, Moskovskiy tsentr Karnegi, Moscow.

Zhuravskaya, K. (1999), 'Inter-Governmental Relations in Russia', *Russian Economic Trends*, Vol. 8, pp. 44-47.

Zorin, L.Z. (1997), 'Na poroge kladovykh arkticheskogo shelfa', *Gazovaya promyshlennost*, No. 11, pp. 51-52.

Åslund, A. (1995), *How Russia Became a Market Economy*, The Brookings Institute, Washington, D.C.

Index

Adygeya, Republic of, 6, 87
Aleksandrovsk, 22, 193
Amderma, 17
Amur Oblast, 84
Apatity, 23-24, 118, 125, 218
Arctic Marine Engineering and
 Geological Expedition (AMIGE), 139
Arkhangelsk Collective Fishing Fleet,
 171
Arkhangelsk Oblast
 industrial production, 119
 industrial structure, 118
 population, 116
 Sobraniye, 74
Arkhangelsk Trawl Fleet, 171, 176
Arkhangelskgeoldobycha, 141
Arkhangelskgeologiya, 140
Arktikmorneftegazrazvedka (Arctic
 Marine Oil and Gas Exploration
 Company), 139-141, 151, 153, 162,
 164
asymmetric federation, 39
August 1998 crisis, 97, 99-100, 124,
 202, 208-209
August Coup, 72, 87
Azerbaijan, 96

Baglay, Marat, 51
Balakshin, Pavel, 72-73
Barents Euro-Arctic Region, 3, 9, 28, 32,
 89, 228, 233
Barents Sea, ix, 26, 119, 133-135, 137,
 140, 143, 146, 151, 153, 154-155,
 157, 159-160, 162-169, 171, 173,
 175-176, 179-180, 184-186, 193,
 218-219, 223, 231, 233-234, 236, 238
 exploration drilling, 134, 146, 154
 loophole, 169, 184, 238
 overfishing, 167

Bashkortostan, Republic of, 6, 67, 84,
 87-88, 106
Baydaratskaya Bay, 155
Belgorod Oblast, 87
Belogubova, Marina, 59, 88
Belomorsk, 148
Belyayev, Aleksandr, 205
Border Guard, 178-180, 183, 185, 197
Bryansk Oblast, 87
Buryatia, Republic of, 45

Chancellor, Richard, 18
Checheno-Ingushetia, ASSR, 31
Chechnya, Republic of, 31, 45-46, 60,
 67, 75, 81, 87, 107, 126, 207
Chernomyrdin, Viktor, 76
Chernychenko, Igor, 59, 88
Chilingarov, Artur, 77
Chubais, Anatoliy, 79
Chukchi Autonomous Okrug, 87
Chuvashia, Republic of, 87-88
Civil War (Russia 1918-20), 11, 19, 22
closed administrative-territorial
 formations, 199-200, 205-206, 209,
 221, 227
Committee for Constitutional Control,
 50
Congress of Russian Communities, 77
Constitution of the Russian Federation,
 5, 36-47, 50-56, 58-60, 69-71, 73, 76,
 78-79, 84, 86, 88-89, 107, 138, 186,
 213, 224, 226
Constitutional Commission, 69
Constitutional Court, 50-54, 60, 79
conversion (to civilian production), 141,
 158, 191-192, 198, 202-204, 207-208,
 232
Czech Republic, 128

Dagestan, Republic of, 87
Dolgan-Nenets Autonomous Okrug, 32

Estonia, 96
Evenk Autonomous Okrug, 6

federal administration in the regions, 49
Federal Fund for Financial Support of the Regions, 108
federal security service (FSB), 178
Federal Treaty, 4-6, 12, 37, 39, 45, 66-71, 78, 87, 107
Federation Council, 38, 47-48, 59, 69, 73, 76, 82, 84, 88
fields
    Kolokolmorskiy, 152
    Ledovoye (gas and condensate), 135, 137, 148, 163
    Leningradskoye (gas), 137
    Ludlovskoye (gas), 135, 137, 148, 163
    Medynskoye-More (oil), 135, 137
    Murmanskoye (gas), 135, 152, 158
    Pomorskoye (gas and condensate), 135, 152, 163
    Prirazlomnoye (oil), 134-135, 137-138, 141-142, 144, 147-148, 150-151, 157-158, 162, 203, 219
    Rusanovskoye (gas), 137
    Severo-Dolginskaya, 136
    Severo-Gulyayevskoye (oil and condensate), 135
    Severo-Kildinskoye (gas), 135
    Shtokmanovskoye (gas and condensate), 134-135, 137-138, 141-143, 145, 148, 151-152, 155-158, 164, 219, 228
    Varandey-More (oil), 135, 137, 152-153
    Yuzhno-Dolginskaya, 136
Franz Josef Land, 20, 165

Gazprom, viii, 140, 142-143, 147-148, 151, 153, 156, 158-160, 162-164, 203
Gelendzhik, 139, 152, 163

Gorbachev, Mikhail, 8, 188, 191
Gremikha, 206
Gromov, Boris, 89
Guskov, Yuriy, 77

Ingushetia, Republic of, 31, 84, 126
International Council for the Exploration of the Sea, 166
Iskateley, 17

Jewish Autonomous Oblast, 31
joint jurisdiction (Russian Constitution), 41-44, 48, 56-59, 145, 214
Joint Russian-Norwegian Fisheries Commission, 166, 168

Kaliningrad Oblast, 9, 45, 89, 185
Kalmykia, Republic of, 79
Kaluga Oblast, 87
Kandalaksha, 24, 32
Kara Sea, 136-138, 140, 148, 218-219, 223
Karachayevo-Cherkessia, Republic of, 76, 87
Karelia, Republic of
    Chamber of Representatives, 74
    Chamber of the Republic, 74
Karelian Collective Fishing Fleet, 171
Karelian Culture Society, 65
Karelian Isthmus, 10-12, 31
Karelian Workers' Commune, 11
Karelo-Finnish Soviet Socialist Republic, 12
Karelrybflot, 171, 176
Katanandov, Sergey, 81-82
Khabarov, Vladimir, 77
Khakassia, Republic of, 87
Khanty-Mansi Autonomous Okrug, 52
Kholmogory, 18, 21
Khrushchev, Nikita, 170
Kirov Oblast, 9, 32, 89
Kirovsk, 23
Klebanov, Ilya, 207
Kolguyev Island, 14, 136, 138, 140
Kolokolmorskiy, *see* fields, 152

Kolskiy monklinal, 146
Komarov, Yevgeniy, 72, 76
Komarovskiy, Yuriy, 72-73
Komi, Republic of, 9, 15, 17, 20, 87, 89, 119, 137
Kondopoga, 12
Koryazhma, 20
Kostomuksha, 12
Kotlas, 20
Kovdor, 118
Krasnodar Kray, 45, 139
Kursk Oblast, 87

land code, 46, 59
Law on Closed Administrative-Territorial Formations, 199
Law on Subsurface Resources, 149-150
Law on the Continental Shelf, 142, 145
Lebedev, Igor, 59, 88
Ledovoye, *see* fields, 135, 137, 148, 163
legislative initiative (State Duma), 47-48
Leningrad Oblast, 8, 10, 22, 31, 64, 89, 185
Leningradskoye, *see* fields, 137
Liinakhamari, 32, 143
Lipetsk Oblast, 87
Lovozero, 24, 118
Ludlovskoye, *see* fields, 135, 137, 148, 163
Lukin, Yuriy, 204
Lukoil, 140, 144, 160, 162
Luzhkov, Yuriy, 7, 82

Marine Arctic Geological Expedition (MAGE), 139-140, 162
Medynskoye-More, *see* fields, 135, 137
Mezenskaya sinekliza, 146
Military-Industrial Commission, 190
military-industrial complex, 20, 110, 187-188, 190-192, 197, 200, 204, 224
Ministry of Agriculture, 177-178
Ministry of Defence, 189-190, 192, 194-196, 198, 205, 208
Ministry of Economics, 178
Ministry of Finance, 178
Ministry of Foreign Economic Relations and Trade, 178
Ministry of Fuel and Energy, 139, 151-152, 159
Ministry of Internal Affairs, 178
Ministry of Natural Resources, 138, 151-152, 154, 159, 162, 185, 223, 234
Monchegorsk, 23-24, 118, 123, 217
mono-industrial towns, 91, 113-114, 117, 123, 125, 217-218, 223, 225
Mordovia, Republic of, 87-88
Moscow Oblast, 89
Murmanrybprom (Murmansk Fish Production Association), 171, 176
Murmanrybvod, 168, 176, 179-180, 183, 185
Murmansk Collective Fishing Fleet, 171, 176
Murmansk Fishing Combinate, 169
Murmansk Oblast
    Duma, 59, 74, 88
    employment, 117
    industrial production, 117
    output of industrial products, 121
    population, 116
Murmansk Trawl Fleet, 169, 171-172, 176
Murmanskoye, *see* fields, 135, 152, 158

Narva, 18
Naryan Mar, 16-17
National Congress of the Karelian, Finnish and Veps Peoples, 65
Nazdratenko, Yevgeniy, 82
Nenets Autonomous Okrug
    National Okrug, 15, 32
    Sobraniye, 74
NIIMorgeofizika, 139-140
Nikel, 23, 118, 123, 217
Nikitin, Boris, 147, 163-164
Nizhniy Novgorod Oblast, 106, 111
Norilsk, 123
Norilsk Nikel, 123
North Ossetia, Republic of, 87

Northeast Atlantic Fisheries
　Commission, 166
Northern economic region, 9
Northern Fleet, 22, 26, 88, 159, 162,
　188, 193-197, 199-201, 205, 207,
　222, 224, 236
Northern Kray, 15, 19
Northern Sea Route, 123
Northwestern Association, 9, 83, 89
Northwestern economic region, 8
Novaya Zemlya, 14, 20, 134, 165
Novgorod Oblast, 8, 11, 15, 18, 21
Novodvinsk, 20
nuclear cities, 209

Olenegorsk, 118
Oryol Oblast, 87
Ostrovnoy, 200, 206, 221
Otechestvo, 82, 83
Our Home is Russia, 83

Parade of Sovereignties, 12, 63, 65-66,
　68-69, 74-75, 85, 216
Pechenga, 22, 32, 118, 123, 143, 148,
　163, 194-195, 199
Pechora Sea, 134-138, 142-144, 146,
　151, 160, 162, 231
　exploration drilling, 134, 146, 154
Pechormorneft, 139, 151, 163
People's Congress, 87
Petrozavodsk, 12, 148, 193
Petsamo, 32
PINRO, 166, 169, 176
Poland, 128
Polyarnye Zori, 118
Polyarnyy, 22, 193, 200, 206, 221
Pomorskoye, *see* fields, 135
power-sharing agreements, 45-47, 50-51,
　53, 55, 59, 78, 85, 107, 214, 226
presidential representatives, 73, 75, 82-
　83, 88
price liberalisation, 98
Primakov, Yevgeniy, 7, 81

Prirazlomnoye, *see* fields, 134-135, 137-
　138, 141-142, 144, 147-148, 150-151,
　157-158, 162, 203, 219
privatisation, 98
production-sharing agreements
　(exploitation of hydrocarbon
　resources), 149, 150, 153, 163
Pskov Oblast, 8, 89
Putin, Vladimir, 43, 49, 53, 59, 82, 83-
　86, 106, 207, 216, 222, 225, 230, 237

Rakhimov, Murtaza, 6
referendum on Constitution, 45, 59, 70
Regional Fishery Council, 175-177
Rodin, Aleksandr, 179
Rosshelf, 141, 147, 153-154, 158-160,
　162-163, 203, 235
RSFSR (The Russian Soviet Federative
　Socialist Republic), 4, 11, 30, 36-37,
　58-59, 62-64, 66, 104
Rusanovskoye, *see* fields, 137

Sablin, Leonid, 64
Sakha, Republic of, 6, 67, 88, 106
Segezha, 12
Seleznyov, Gennadiy, 89
Sergeyev, Igor, 195
Severo-Dolginskaya, *see* fields, 136
Severodvinsk, 15, 20-21, 27, 80, 119,
　141-142, 147, 158-159, 188, 200-202,
　204-208, 221-222, 232
Severo-Gulyayevskoye, *see* fields, 135
Severo-Kildinskoye, *see* fields, 135
Severomorsk, 24, 26, 193, 195, 197, 200,
　206, 221
Sevmash, 21, 147, 162, 200-204
Sevryba, 169-171, 173-177, 180-186,
　220-221
Sevrybkholodflot, 171
Sevrybpromrazvedka (Northern Fishery
　Survey/Research Fleet), 171
Shaymiyev, Mintimer, 6
Shtokmanovskoye, *see* fields, 134-135,
　137-138, 141-143, 145, 148, 151-152,
　155-158, 164, 219, 228

Siberian Accord, 31
Skalistyy, 200
Skuratov, Yuriy, 53
Smolensk Oblast, 87
Snezhnogorsk, 200
Sortavala, 12
Soyuzmorgeo (Scientific Production Association for Offshore Geology and Geophysics, 139, 163
Special Economic Zones, 107
St Petersburg, 9, 14, 19, 89, 110, 148, 155
State Committee on Ecology, 185
State Committee on Fisheries, 166, 173-174, 176-181, 183, 185, 223
State Duma, 38, 42-43, 45, 47-48, 77, 81-82, 84, 149-150, 153
Stepanov, Viktor, 69, 73, 88, 89
Stepashin, Sergey, 53
Supreme Soviet, 31, 51, 63, 65, 68-73, 87-88
Svalbard, 165
Sverdlovsk Oblast, 87, 106

Tambov Oblast, 60, 87
Tatarstan, Republic of, 6, 45-46, 63, 66-67, 75, 87-88, 106, 214
tax reform, 99, 107
Taymyr, *see* Dolgan-Nenets Autonomous Okrug
Technical-Scientific Catch Council, 173, 175-176
Teriberka, 143, 148
trade liberalisation, 98
transfers from federal authorities, 108
Trest Sevmorneftegeofizika (Northern Marine Oil and Geophysics Trust), 139

Tumanov, Vladimir, 51
Tyumen Oblast, 52, 54, 102, 109
Tyva, Republic of, 87

Udmurtia, Republic of, 87
Union of Private Fishery Enterprises in the North, 170-171
Union of the Karelian People, 65

Varandey-More, *see* fields, 135, 137, 152-153
Volgograd Oblast, 87
Vologda Oblast, 9, 15, 19, 89
Voronezh Oblast, 87

Winter War (Russo-Finnish), 12

Yamal-Nenets Autonomous Okrug, 32, 52, 54
Yasavey, 65
Yedinstvo, 82
Yefremov, Anatoliy, 77, 80-81, 83
Yeltsin, Boris, 63-64, 66, 68-76, 78-79, 81-83, 85-88, 142, 177-178, 188, 192, 215, 216
Yerofeyev, Oleg, 195
Yevdokimov, Yuriy, 76, 81-83, 152, 199, 206-207, 222, 224, 226-227
Yuzhno-Dolginskaya, *see* fields, 136

Zaozyorsk, 200
Zapolyarnyy, 118, 123, 217
Zavolochya, 18
Zhirinovskiy, Vladimir, 7
Zlobin, Vladimir, 88
Zvyozdochka, 21, 200-201, 203-204